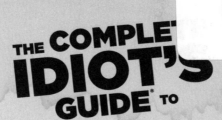

THE COMPLETE
IDIOT'S
GUIDE® TO

The New World Order

THE COMPLETE IDIOT'S GUIDE TO

The New World Order

by Alan Axelrod, Ph.D.

ALPHA

A member of Penguin Group (USA) Inc.

ALPHA BOOKS

Published by the Penguin Group

Penguin Group (USA) Inc., 375 Hudson Street, New York, New York 10014, USA

Penguin Group (Canada), 90 Eglinton Avenue East, Suite 700, Toronto, Ontario M4P 2Y3, Canada (a division of Pearson Penguin Canada Inc.)

Penguin Books Ltd., 80 Strand, London WC2R 0RL, England

Penguin Ireland, 25 St. Stephen's Green, Dublin 2, Ireland (a division of Penguin Books Ltd.)

Penguin Group (Australia), 250 Camberwell Road, Camberwell, Victoria 3124, Australia (a division of Pearson Australia Group Pty. Ltd.)

Penguin Books India Pvt. Ltd., 11 Community Centre, Panchsheel Park, New Delhi—110 017, India

Penguin Group (NZ), 67 Apollo Drive, Rosedale, North Shore, Auckland 1311, New Zealand (a division of Pearson New Zealand Ltd.)

Penguin Books (South Africa) (Pty.) Ltd., 24 Sturdee Avenue, Rosebank, Johannesburg 2196, South Africa

Penguin Books Ltd., Registered Offices: 80 Strand, London WC2R 0RL, England

Copyright © 2010 by Alan Axelrod, Ph.D.

THE COMPLETE IDIOT'S GUIDE TO and Design are registered trademarks of Penguin Group (USA) Inc.

International Standard Book Number: 978-1-61564-039-3
Library of Congress Catalog Card Number: 20109202234

12 11 10   8 7 6 5 4 3 2 1

Interpretation of the printing code: The rightmost number of the first series of numbers is the year of the book's printing; the rightmost number of the second series of numbers is the number of the book's printing. For example, a printing code of 10–1 shows that the first printing occurred in 2010.

Printed in the United States of America

Note: This publication contains the opinions and ideas of its author. It is intended to provide helpful and informative material on the subject matter covered. It is sold with the understanding that the author and publisher are not engaged in rendering professional services in the book. If the reader requires personal assistance or advice, a competent professional should be consulted.

The author and publisher specifically disclaim any responsibility for any liability, loss, or risk, personal or otherwise, which is incurred as a consequence, directly or indirectly, of the use and application of any of the contents of this book.

Most Alpha books are available at special quantity discounts for bulk purchases for sales promotions, premiums, fundraising, or educational use. Special books, or book excerpts, can also be created to fit specific needs.

For details, write: Special Markets, Alpha Books, 375 Hudson Street, New York, NY 10014.

Publisher: *Marie Butler-Knight*
Associate Publisher: *Mike Sanders*
Senior Managing Editor: *Billy Fields*
Executive Editor: *Randy Ladenheim-Gil*
Senior Development Editor: *Phil Kitchel*
Production Editor: *Kayla Dugger*

Copy Editor: *Tricia Liebig*
Cover Designer: *Kurt Owens*
Book Designers: *William Thomas, Rebecca Batchelor*
Indexer: *Heather McNeill*
Layout: *Ayanna Lacey*
Proofreader: *Laura Caddell*

For Anita, My Secret Sharer.

Contents

Part 1: Our Secret Society 1

1   Conspiracy Theory 3

The Shadows of Socrates 4

Nationality 5

Government 5

War 6

The Substance 7

Official Conspiracies 7

Secret Societies in Plain Sight 9

The Usual Suspects 9

An Ancestry of Secrecy 12

Furtive Fallacy or Conspiratorial Reality? 13

2   The Council on Foreign Relations 17

The Inquiry and Beyond 18

The "Colonel" and the Conspiracy 19

The Birth of the CFR 20

Open and Shut 21

Notable Members 22

Connections 23

Peace and War 23

World War II and After 24

Korea and Vietnam 26

Normalization with Communist China 27

CFR and NWO 27

From Means to Motive 28

3   The Bilderberg Group 31

"To Plan Events That Later Appear Just to Happen" 32

Founding Fathers 32

U.S. Involvement 35

The Organization Is Born 36

An Unofficial CFR 36

Bilderbergers and the Trilateral Commission 36

The Rockefeller Connection *36*

The Roster Includes *38*

What the Bilderbergers Want (Maybe) 38

Measuring the Motive *40*

The Secrecy Syndrome *40*

4   The Trilateral Commission 43

Birth of a Commission...44

Zbigniew Brzezinski *44*

More on the Bilderberg-TC Connection *45*

All Aboard *46*

The Public Record 47

1975 Full Meeting, Kyoto *47*

1976 Plenary Meeting of Regional Groups, Kyoto *48*

Present Day *48*

The TC Conspiracy Theory 50

Four Goals *51*

Criticism from the Right *51*

... and from the Left *52*

... as Well as the Center *52*

The Reagan Revolution?..53

5   Around the Round Table.........................57

The Philosopher Magnate 58

Colossus with Asthma *58*

Formative Influences *58*

A Diamond Empire *59*

Rhodes's Round Tables 60

Origin *60*

Early Growth *61*

After Rhodes: The Round Table Movement 62

The Movement Spreads *62*

Curtis and Lippmann *63*

Chatham House...65

Chatham House Rule *66*

Influence of Chatham House *66*

Place in NWO Conspiracy Theory *67*

6 The United Nations **69**

At the Heart: War 70

The United Nations' Genesis 71

   Dumbarton Oaks.. 72

   Yalta—and the Korean Connection 73

   San Francisco Launch 74

The United Nations System 75

   The General Assembly 75

   The Security Council 76

   The United Nations Secretariat 77

   The Economic and Social Council............................... 77

   The International Court of Justice............................... 77

   The "World Moderator" 78

End or Means? 78

7 Bonesmen **81**

Alma Mater 82

   Frat Boys 83

   The Next Level 83

Conspiracy Theories 84

   Memento Mori 84

   Mumbo Jumbo, Metaphor, or Conspiracy? 86

History of the Mystery 87

   Version 1: The Standard Story.................................... 87

   Version 2: The Conspiratorial Story............................ 88

Roll Dem Bones.. 89

   Criteria 90

   The Cement of Secrecy 90

8 The Oligarchs.. **93**

Military-Industrial-Congressional Complex............... 94

   The Real Status Quo... 95

   Report from Iron Mountain 97

Family Affairs 99

   The House of Rothschild 99

   The House of Morgan 101

   The House of Rockefeller 102

Ultimate Stewardship or Rule of the Many by the Few?......... 104

9   Secrets of the Federal Reserve 107

Secret Planners, Secret Plans 108

  Reform Agenda... *109*

  Engineered Panic *109*

A History Lesson... 110

  The Function of a Central Bank *110*

  A Revolutionary Cause *111*

  A Counterrevolutionary Response.............................. *111*

  The Monster *113*

  From National Bank to National Banks *113*

  The Power of One *113*

The Federal Reserve Act of 1913....................................114

  Official Function of the Fed *115*

  Proof of the Pudding... *115*

"Invisible Government" 116

The Money Cult...118

10   New Age and End Time 121

From Global Federation to Synarchy................................ 121

  The Open Conspiracy *122*

  The New World Order *123*

  The Failed Promise of the Socialist World State *123*

  Enter Alice Bailey... *123*

New Age Beliefs as New World Order Conspiracy 125

The New World Order Conspiracy as an Imperial Cult........ 126

Part 2:   Roots... 129

11   Ancient Secrets 131

Litmus Test... 132

The New World Order Conspiracy, Old School 132

  Who Has the Power? *133*

  Suppressing Alternate Realities.............................. *134*

Esoteric Knowledge 135

  The Gnostics *135*

  The Essenes *136*

Coded Revelation 137

  Back to Sumer *138*

  Cabala *138*

Ultimate Secret? Ultimate Truth 140

12   The Templars and Others 143

Out of the Crusades 144

The World Order, Eleventh Century 145

The Subversive Truth 145

The Magdalene Theory 146

The "Poor" Knights 147

Sacred Ancestry? 147

The Templars Rise 148

Templars as Global Bankers 149

The Templars Fall 150

Strange Bedfellows 151

The Assassins as a Secret Society 152

Outside Religion and Beyond Loyalty 153

Templar Diaspora 154

Coming to America? 154

Heritage of the Hospitallers 155

13   Illumination..159

The SCP Theory.. 160

The Revival Begins 161

Secret Life: Matvei Vasilyevich Golovinski 162

Three World Wars and SOS.................................. 162

The Role of "Lucifer"... 163

Trouble in Bavaria 164

The Founding 164

Historical Connection to the Freemasons 165

Membership 166

Opposition.. 167

Proud to Be the Founder of the Illuminati............... 167

The Illuminist Lens 168

14   The Rose Cross..171

Rosicrucians: The Historical View 172

Origin 172

Symbolism 173

Seventeenth and Eighteenth Centuries 173

Decline and Rebirth 174

AMORC and Others 174

    Golden Dawn 175

    Societas Rosicruciana 176

    The One-World Conspiracy Connection 177

The Gladio Affair... 178

    The Solar Temple Deaths.................................... 178

    Dr. Abgrall's Accusations 179

    What Does It All Mean? 180

    Guilt by Association?.. 180

15   **Men in Aprons** **183**

Conspiracy Theories.. 184

    The Anti-Masonic Background 184

    A Catalog of Conspiracy.................................... 187

The Craft.. 188

    Scope.. 188

    Origins 188

    Operative and Speculative Masons........................ 189

    Eighteenth-Century Evolution.............................. 190

    In Revolutionary America.................................. 190

    Revolution Elsewhere 191

    Twentieth Century.. 191

Freemasonry and the New World Order.......................... 191

    Some Basic Assumptions 192

    More on the Illuminati Connection 193

    Operation Gladio—Again................................... 193

Once Feared, Still Dangerous 194

Part 3: **History as Conspiracy**................................**197**

16   **Revolution: America and France** **199**

Francis Bacon, Founder of America........................... 199

    The New Atlantis.. 200

    A Freemason? A Rosicrucian?.................................. 201

    American Ventures 202

The Masons Come to America 202

    The Revolutionary Masons.................................. 203

    A Masonic War 203

Revolutionary Goals *205*

The Great Seal and the Masons *205*

Behind Another Revolution 207

17   Conspiracy, Italian Style 211

The Charcoal Burners 212

Organization and Ritual *213*

History *214*

Professed Values *214*

Actual Aims *215*

Ferdinand *216*

The Soul of Italy 217

From Italian Unification to One-World Government *217*

3WW 218

The Pike Connection *218*

The Pike-Mazzini Letter *219*

The Conspiracy Paradox 221

Flimsy Evidence … *221*

… and Solid History *222*

18   Internationale 225

Communism: The Ultimate One-World Conspiracy 226

The Rise of Communism: A Tale of Two Histories 227

Communist History: The Mainstream Version *227*

Communist History: The Alternative Version *230*

Outsiders Get Inside *232*

Deeper Background 233

The Proto-Bolsheviks *233*

Who Is Arkon Daraul? *233*

A Bridge to Bolshevism *234*

19   Roosevelt's Revolutions 237

New Deal or New World Order? 238

Crash! *238*

"Prosperity Is Just Around the Corner" *238*

The 1932 Election *239*

A Hundred Days and Beyond *239*

Open to Criticism *240*

In the Age of Great Dictators.. 241
    The Court-Packing Scheme.. *241*
    Over the Line *242*
Slouching Toward War 242
    CFR.. *243*
    Armed Neutrality... *243*
    The Churchill-Roosevelt Courtship............................... *243*
    Gearing Up *244*
    The Atlantic Charter *245*
Day of Infamy.. 245
    Sticking It to Japan.. *246*
    The Pearl Harbor Conspiracy Theory *247*
Roosevelt the Warmonger 248

20   From Third Reich to Fourth **251**
Behind the Buzz 252
    Jewish Fascism.. *252*
    Fascism as a Definition of the NWO........................... *253*
    Fascism as the Source of the NWO............................... *254*
The Fall of the Third Reich 254
    The Alternative History *256*
    Hitler's Legacy.. *257*
Safe Haven 257
    ODESSA *257*
    The Spider.. *258*
    Operation Paperclip *258*
Nazi Nexus 258
    Made in the USA *259*
    The Neo-Nazi Misnomer... *260*

21   Wars Cold and Hot.. **263**
The Korean "Conflict" 263
    Korea: The Mainstream Story...................................... *264*
    Korea: The NWO Version *269*
Why Are We in Vietnam? 269

22   New World Order: Bush 41 and After................. **273**
"It Is Iraq Against the World ..." 274
    The Globalist *274*
    Tough Act to Follow... *276*

The First New World Order Speech *276*

The Second New World Order Speech *277*

New World Order Breakthrough (Not!) *278*

The False Flag of 9/11 279

Conspiracy Views *280*

Why? *280*

The Leading Theories *281*

Oil Wars 282

The "Join or Die" Fraud 284

The Open Question 284

Appendixes

A   Who's Who in the New World Order **287**

B   The New World Order in Pop Culture **295**

C   Recommended Books and Websites **299**

D   A New World Order Address Book **307**

Index **313**

Introduction

The Holy Grail of modern physics is the formulation of a successful "unified field theory"—in short, a single theory that explains everything. Albert Einstein spent much of his creative life on the hunt for it, but even he came up short.

Conspiracy theorists are students of "alternative history" who believe that historical truth is a chain of cause and effect hidden beneath the surface events that are studied by mainstream historians. For them, the equivalent of the physicist's unified field theory, the theory that explains everything, is the idea of the New World Order.

Expressed at its most basic, the New World Order (NWO) is one-world government, in which a central global bureaucracy controlled by an unseen, unelected power elite wields (or seeks to wield) absolute authority over the planet's population. The NWO conspiracy is the movement toward this one-world government. It is the covert work of financiers, industrialists, and media moguls in league with certain government and military officials to rule the world through an unelected global government. It would be entirely autonomous from all national governments and would replace those governments, absorbing sovereign nation-states into a single worldwide collective.

Some idealists and utopianists publicly favor such a one-world government because they believe it will forever put an end to the international power struggles that historically have brought the catastrophe of war. NWO conspiracy theorists counter that such an argument is just a cover for the real motive of those who aspire toward one-world government, which is, simply put, to acquire the practically boundless power and virtually infinite wealth that come with being one of the few who rule the many.

NWO conspiracy theorists identify specific individuals and organizations they believe are dedicated to bringing about one-world government. Some of these already enjoy so much power that, even now, they may be said to constitute a shadow government, the power behind the throne—or behind the president, Congress, and the courts.

But most versions of the NWO conspiracy do not end with identification and discussion of the recent and current agents of the conspiracy. For many writers on the subject, the NWO is a lens through which they view all history, politics, religion, and mythology. For them, the NWO is (to shift our metaphor) the Rosetta Stone by which the meaning of virtually all human behavior may be fully and truly translated and understood. They point out that although the NWO unfolds in the present and looks toward the future, it is rooted in the past—perhaps as far back as the origin of civilization in Sumer. Maybe even to a more distant past, some 450,000 years back, when the people of the earth had a brush with beings from another world.

The purpose of this book is to offer a guide to a remarkable body of conspiracy literature and theory. It is neither an argument intended to prompt belief in the theory or any part of it, nor to debunk or disprove any or all of it. Instead, the reader is invited to draw his or her own conclusions. Some will find the material they encounter here to be a revelation. Others will dismiss some, much, or all of it as improbable or even impossible.

Fair warning: Unlike physics, conspiracy theory is far from emotionally neutral. It can be exhilarating. It can be outrageous. It can also be ugly, partaking of the kind of intolerance that has been used to justify everything from blackballing a fraternity membership to committing genocide. In these pages, I have acknowledged the outrageous and the ugly when I have encountered them, but I have attempted to avoid delivering my own judgment upon these opinions and their authors. You judge them.

How to Use This Book

This book is divided into three parts:

Part 1, Our Secret Society, begins with a chapter that defines and describes the New World Order (NWO) as today's most important and most widely discussed conspiracy theory. Chapters 2 through 10 identify and discuss the modern organizations, institutions, and individuals most often identified with the NWO conspiracy.

Part 2, Roots, delivers the history of the NWO from what some believe are its ancient origins through its development by such key secret societies as the Knights Templar, the Assassins, Illuminati, Rosicrucians, and Freemasons as movements bent on creating one-world rule.

Part 3, History as Conspiracy, explores the conspiracy theory alternative to so-called mainstream history. In the chapters of this part, you see the American and French revolutions, the Italian struggle for independence, the Bolshevik Revolution, World War I, Franklin Roosevelt's New Deal and his involvement in World War II, the evolution and survival of the Nazi Party, the Korean War, the Vietnam War, Persian Gulf War, and the Iraq War as aspects of—and in some cases, products of—the NWO conspiracy.

Extras

Throughout the book, you'll find the following types of sidebars:

PASSWORDS

Here are revealing quotations relating to the New World Order.

SECRET LIVES

These present biographical sketches of key figures in the New World Order.

DEFINITION

This feature is your guide to terms important to understanding the New World Order.

INTEL

Look here for interesting facts as well as major events related to or allegedly caused by the New World Order conspiracy.

Acknowledgments

As always, my gratitude goes to the copy editor, Tricia Liebig, and Alpha editorial staff, especially Randy Ladenheim-Gil, Phil Kitchel, and Kayla Dugger, who not only made this book better in the end, but made it possible in the first place.

Trademarks

All terms mentioned in this book that are known to be or are suspected of being trademarks or service marks have been appropriately capitalized. Alpha Books and Penguin Group (USA) Inc. cannot attest to the accuracy of this information. Use of a term in this book should not be regarded as affecting the validity of any trademark or service mark.

Our Secret Society

The New World Order is the most ambitious, most popular, and most pervasive conspiracy theory in circulation today. Those who believe in it are confident that they have discovered the key not only to recent history, but to the history of civilization—perhaps even the history of all human behavior.

The chapters of Part 1 introduce you to the theory and present the major secret societies, organizations, institutions, and individuals that conspiracy theorists believe are responsible for creating a shadow American government. It is one you did not elect and that is committed to building a global government that will swallow up the United States and every other country on the planet.

Conspiracy Theory

In This Chapter

- The New World Order as one-world government
- The role of the New World Order in nationhood, government, and war
- Major institutions, groups, and secret societies promoting the New World Order
- The historical background of the modern New World Order
- Real history or "furtive fallacy"?

Ask a savvy college professor, and you will be told that the New World Order (NWO) is a conspiracy theory describing the evolution, emergence, or existence of a one-world government. It is administered by a powerful elite who seek to establish themselves as an autonomous governing body independent of, superior to, and transcending all national governments. You might also be told that the government under the NWO takes the form of what the renegade Soviet revolutionary Leon Trotsky called *bureaucratic collectivism*, a system in which the state owns the means of production: everything used to create all goods and products. The profit produced by these means is enjoyed by the ruling elite (in the Soviet Union, the Communist Party inner circle). The masses, the workers who actually produce the goods and products, get nothing but subsistence doled out by the state.

Thus, the professor would likely conclude, the NWO is government by global oligarchy, a cabal of people distinguished and united by a combination of wealth, family connection, royal status, or military or religious authority.

Two things a college professor probably won't tell you are 1) whether the NWO is a theory or a reality, and 2) whether the concept is a good thing or a bad thing. But ask a nonacademic believer in the conspiracy, and you will be told straight-up that the

NWO is real and it is evil. You will be told that it is a plot by a handful of "globalists" conspiring to rule the world absolutely, to end national governments and patriotic loyalties, and to reduce government by the people to rule by the few.

And there is one more type of person to ask about the NWO. Suppose you could talk to one of the elite—an international financier or a leader of a multinational think tank, perhaps. This man or woman would tell you that the NWO describes nothing more or less than uniting the planet's states, especially its superpowers, to secure global peace and prosperity. What could be wrong with that?

The Shadows of Socrates

Picture a group of people who have lived their entire lives chained in a cave, facing away from the opening and looking at a blank wall. Actually, they're looking at the shadows that move across the wall—shadows cast by objects that pass before a fire that burns just outside the cave. It is these shadows that the chained people call "reality."

DEFINITION

Bureaucratic collectivism is a term coined by Leon Trotsky (1879–1940) to describe a political and economic system. In this system, the state owns the means of production (everything used to create products) and reserves for the state's ruling elite all profit from this production, doling out to the workers (most of the population) who produce the products subsistence only.

About 380 B.C.E., the Greek philosopher Plato presented this allegory as the work of his teacher, Socrates, who was endeavoring to explain to Glaucon, Plato's brother, the way the mass of humanity thinks and lives. In contrast to this mass, a few exceptional people—called philosophers, Socrates explained—think and live like former prisoners liberated from the cave. They see that the shadows are not truth, but an illusion of truth: weak, distorted images of the reality that exists outside the cave.

Those who believe they understand the NWO conspiracy are similar to Socrates's philosophers. They see beyond the cave in which the mass of humanity has been chained by the powerful few who pull the world's strings. Whereas the prisoners see the shadows created by the conspirators and take them for reality, the conspiracy theorists see the reality itself. They choose to persuade the cave dwellers to at least imagine what lies outside the cave—to separate the shadows from the substance.

Persuading the cave dwellers isn't easy because, having been born into the world of shadows, shadows are all they know. The truths Socrates offered presented such a threat to those around him that he was tried and executed for "corrupting the minds of youth." Those who claim to see the conspiracies beyond society's shadows face resistance from the masses. They must also overcome the powerful few who manipulate the shadows and hide the light.

Most people reject conspiracy theories because of the combination of mass habits of thought and the coercive influence of the powerful few.

Plato and Socrates tried to explain that what almost all of us call reality is actually a collection of shadows and that the reality lies elsewhere. Similarly, those who believe in an NWO conspiracy try to explain that much of what we take for granted as real are the projected shadows a few powerful people want us to see. For conspiracy theorists, the shadows are many, but they can be classified into three broad categories: nationality, government, and war.

Nationality

We call ourselves Americans, Italians, and Chinese, and we think of ourselves as citizens of the United States, Italy, and China. The powerful few behind the NWO not only want to transcend, supersede, and eliminate all national allegiance and nations themselves, but they have already done so to a very significant degree. The global economy has created a level of planetary interdependence that is making nationhood virtually irrelevant.

Consider this fictional illustration: an American living in Oshkosh, Wisconsin, may feel a bit queasy because the local company he works for is owned by a Franco-German conglomerate financed in large part by a holding company based in Dubai and dedicated to designing widgets that are made in China. The American living in Oshkosh may suffer heartburn when he thinks that anonymous Frenchmen, Germans, Arabs, and Chinese have a hand in his livelihood, but anyone with insight into the NWO understands that the nationality of those pulling the strings is meaningless to those who pocket the profits. Finance has trumped geopolitics and has rendered nationality, to say nothing of patriotism, obsolete.

Government

We pay taxes, we vote, we go to the post office. The government, obviously, is all around us. Maybe we don't know the name of our representative in Congress, but we can look him up, and we certainly know who the president is. That's knowledge so basic that if you get hit on the head and taken to the hospital, one of the first things they ask you is "Who is the president?" just to make sure you're all there. Even more important, your vote helped put him into office—or if you wanted someone else to win, the guy who is there now got the most votes, so he's the president. You may not be happy, but that's our government. It's called democracy, and at least there's some comfort in that.

Conspiracy theorists argue that democracy—all government including democracy, monarchy, and dictatorship—is a shadow. The real power rests with an unseen few who may share certain cultural or religious values, or may be bound by family ties. They are most strongly united by massive financial interest. These few are the puppeteers. The congressmen, the senators, the presidents, the kings, the generalissimos, the dictators—all are mere shadows. The true power is *always* behind the throne.

SECRET LIVES

Jim Marrs (b. 1943) is the most widely published and best-known NWO researcher. Beginning in 1976, Marrs taught a course on the JFK assassination at the University of Texas at Arlington. *Crossfire: The Plot That Killed Kennedy,* published in 1989, became a bestseller and served as the basis for Oliver Stone's 1991 film *JFK*. Marrs went on to write about UFOs (*Alien Agenda,* 1998). He then published *Rule by Secrecy* in 2000, his most complete exposition of the NWO conspiracy.

Marrs has also written about alleged 9/11 conspiracies, and in 2008 published *The Rise of the Fourth Reich: The Secret Societies That Threaten to Take Over America,* a book that focuses on the alleged role of neo-Nazis in creating an NWO.

War

Swiss historian Jean-Jacques Babel estimated that during the 5,500 or so years that represent recorded history, there have been a scant 292 years of peace. The evidence seems lamentably clear: humans do not need to be spurred to war by secret conspiracies. War, it would seem, comes naturally to them. Yet, as a rule, people don't simply go to war instinctively. They find or make reasons to fight, and you can find those reasons in any number of history books.

Conspiracy theorists may or may not agree that war comes easily to humanity, but either way, many of them argue that every major war since the American and French revolutions of the late eighteenth century has been at least in part the product of conspiracy. This is by a relatively few powerful people who have all tended toward the creation of an NWO—a world ruled by the few, the same few who have incited any number of wars. Motown soul singer Edwin Starr had a big hit in 1970 with a Vietnam-era single titled "War," which asked the question, "War, what is it good for?" and answered, "Absolutely nothing." NWO conspiracy theorists have a different answer: *War, what is it good for?* Profit—on a scale big enough to rule the world.

PASSWORDS

"It is evident that, to whatever degree, individuals connected by blood, titles, marriage, or membership in secret societies have manipulated and controlled the destinies of entire nations through the fomentation and funding of war. These people consider themselves above the morality and ethics of the average man. They obviously look to some higher purpose—whether that be sheer wealth and power or perhaps some hidden agenda concerning mankind's origin, destiny, and spirituality."

—Jim Marrs, *Rule by Secrecy,* 2000

The Substance

Nationality and government are the shadows behind which moneyed interests get populations to do what they want. War is less about self-defense or aggressive national conquest than it is a means of generating profit (spiritual, ego-gratifying, monetary, or some combination thereof) for the few. Thus the shadows of nationality, government, and war hide the substance, which is power and profit held by the fewest possible conspirators.

As most NWO investigators see it, the nature of the NWO is not mystical or even mysterious. Its motives are, in fact, so mundane that we can all easily understand them. At bottom, the NWO is about power and money—and insofar as money is a product of power as well as a means of acquiring power, you can safely reduce the leading motives to one: money.

Official Conspiracies

In his classic 1844 detective story, *The Purloined Letter,* Edgar Allan Poe puts into the mind of his detective-hero, C. Auguste Dupin, the insight that a long sought-after blackmailer's letter has repeatedly eluded the most thorough of police searches precisely because it has been *hidden in plain sight*. Much the same can be said about the evolution of the NWO.

Throughout the twentieth century, a number of prominent political leaders and diplomats have openly used the phrase "new world order" to describe the bright, even utopian, prospects for global politics after World War I, after World War II, and, again, after the Cold War. Leaders as diverse as Woodrow Wilson and Adolf Hitler used the phrase in the aftermath of World War I to label their very different visions of world government and their nation's role in such government. Whereas Wilson used the phrase to frame the League of Nations as a global deliberative and adjudicative body, Hitler used it to suggest that Germany would come to occupy the center of power in Europe and the world during the twentieth century. Otto Von Bismarck, similarly, elevated Prussia to control over a unified Germany, and Germany, in turn, to dominance over much of Europe in the nineteenth century.

After World War II, the "new world order" label was applied to the United Nations, the General Agreement on Tariffs and Trade (GATT), and even the North Atlantic Treaty Organization (NATO). It described proposals and institutions aimed at solving global problems beyond the capacity of individual nations or even lesser alliances to address. In this sense, there was no suggestion of world government per se, simply a formalized system of cooperation and collaboration among nations. However, utopian writers such as H. G. Wells suggested that such ideas as the United Nations be escalated into democratic world government.

Most recently, as the Soviet Union collapsed and the 50-year Cold War ended, President George H. W. Bush titled his September 11, 1990, address to a joint session of Congress "Toward a New World Order." It presented a vision of a "world of barbed wire and concrete block, conflict and cold war" transformed into a "world in which there is the very real prospect of a new world order. In the words of Winston Churchill, a 'world order' in which 'the principles of justice and fair play … protect the weak against the strong …'" The president went on to speak of a "world where the United Nations, freed from cold war stalemate, is poised to fulfill the historic vision of its founders."

To some, this seemed the frank statement of a proposal for genuine world government, with the United Nations at its center, ultimately superseding the national governments of its constituents. President Bush's use of the phrase alarmed both those on the far left and the far right. The former saw it as implying a new era of U.S. imperialism—as if the United States intended to use the United Nations to impose the will of its leaders on the rest of the world. The latter believed it signaled an abrogation of U.S. sovereignty, and its absorption with other nations, into a collectivist United Nations.

Even more recently, during the global economic crisis that began in 2008, leaders ranging from British Prime Minister Gordon Brown to U.S. President Barack Obama have applied the phrase "new world order" in advocating a return to *Keynesian economic* reform—where free-market capitalism is supplemented (some would say supplanted) by government regulation and government spending.

> **DEFINITION**
>
> **Keynesian economics** describes a macroeconomic theory developed by British economist John Maynard Keynes (1883–1946) during the Great Depression of the 1930s. It holds that strongly centralized (government, or "public sector") economic regulation and spending are required to stabilize the economy, especially during economic crises. The NWO is said to employ such Keynesian centralization of monetary and economic policy, as well as massive government spending, to concentrate control of global commerce and the global economy in the hands of a few leaders who dictate economic policy.

Secret Societies in Plain Sight

Popularly elected leaders have been remarkably open in their use of the phrase "new world order" and have used it in connection with the United Nations and other official policies or proposals that at the very least flirt with one-world government. A number of smaller, more exclusive organizations associated with elected as well as unelected leaders of government, society, industry, and finance have pushed the concept of what conspiracy theorists call "rule by the few" much further.

Yet although these groups and institutions are elite in their membership, conducting much of their business behind closed doors, they are hardly secret. As with Dupin's "purloined letter," they hide in plain sight.

The Usual Suspects

The rest of the chapters in Part 1 discuss what most students of the NWO believe to be the secret societies by which the NWO is being formed and promoted.

The Council on Foreign Relations (CFR), founded in 1921, is officially a privately funded and administered foreign-policy *think tank* said to exert inordinate influence on the leaders of many nations with the ultimate goal of creating (or even secretly conducting) a one-world government (see Chapter 2). Some see it as the equivalent of a shadow global government.

The "Bilderberg Group" (see Chapter 3) has no official name, but has long been known by the name of the first place its members convened in 1954, the Hotel de Bilderberg near Arnhem, Netherlands. Entirely without official standing, this invitation-only, annual international conference brings together 130 highly influential persons active in world politics, commerce, and banking to discuss world issues. NWO theorists see the Bilderbergers as an evolutionary outgrowth of the CFR, a cabal of the world's nonelected, unofficial, yet real power brokers (the men and women who actually pull the strings of one-world government).

DEFINITION

A **think tank** is an organization (either a nonprofit institute or a for-profit corporation or other group) that conducts research in and makes recommendations concerning social, political, economic, military, legal, or foreign policy. Although nongovernmental, think tanks are often retained by governments as consultants. Most NWO writers believe certain think tanks exert undue influence on elected leaders and may even constitute a shadow government.

Although both the CFR and Bilderberg Group are still active—with many members in common—NWO theorists regard the Trilateral Commission (TC; see Chapter 4) as a more recent incarnation of both bodies. Founded in 1973 by CFR chairman David Rockefeller, the stated purpose of the TC was to foster cooperation among three centers of world power: the United States, Japan, and Europe. Those who believe in an NWO conspiracy see the Trilateralists as going far beyond the stated purpose of international cooperation and believe the group is a high-level secret society dedicated to overthrowing national governments and creating a one-world rule.

The English imperialist and diamond magnate Cecil Rhodes bequeathed a large trust used to fund the creation of the Round Table movement in 1909 (see Chapter 5). Ostensibly, the movement was intended to promote a closer union between Great Britain and its self-governing colonies. NWO writers point to connections between the Round Tables and the Society of the Elect, a secret society founded by Rhodes, to suggest that the declared purpose of the movement was really a cover under which the power of the British Empire could be extended to create a one-world government. When most of the constituents of the empire achieved full independence or progressed unmistakably toward it, the Round Table groups gave rise in 1919 to the Royal

Institute of International Affairs. After having officially adopted its informal name, Chatham House, it continues to function today as a London-based nongovernmental organization (NGO) putatively dedicated to promoting understanding of international issues. As with the Round Table movement, conspiracy theorists see it as a secret society dedicated to promoting one-world government.

What conspiracy theorists refer to as "mainstream history" depicts the United Nations (see Chapter 6) as the world's attempt to reinvent the defunct League of Nations, created after World War I. Established by charter in 1945 during the waning days of World War II, the United Nations is officially a forum for promoting and enabling international cooperation in many fields; for peacefully adjudicating disputes among nations (thereby creating an alternative to war); for protecting human rights; and for making and keeping world peace. Those who believe in the stealthy encroachment of an NWO conspiracy reject the official definition, and instead see the United Nations as the biggest and boldest of all organizations ever created to impose transnational, one-world government on the peoples of the planet.

None of the organizations discussed in Chapters 2 through 6 would describe themselves as a secret society. Founded in 1832 at what was then Yale College (today Yale University), Skull and Bones (see Chapter 7) is frankly just that: a secret society in the guise of a university fraternity, or perhaps a university fraternity in the guise of a secret society. Its membership is highly exclusive and by invitation only. The Order (as the club is often called) has counted the scions of American wealth and power among its members, including presidents Bush 41 and 43, as well as George W. Bush's second-term Democratic opponent, John Kerry. Skull and Bones is certainly a means by which powerful people network with one another—a kind of institutionalized "old boys' club." NWO theorists take its role a step further, however, seeing in the Order an incubator of the power elite. Some also point to its having played a role in the rise and international legitimization of the Nazi Party during the 1930s, and therefore see its hand in the creation of a so-called Fourth Reich—a particularly sinister incarnation of one-world government, which is discussed in Chapter 20.

Although some writers on the NWO ascribe New Age or specific religious (including millenarian or "End Times" faiths) motives to some one-world government conspiracies (see Chapter 10), most locate the motivation of such conspiracies in an overweening lust for material gain. Chapter 8 identifies the *oligarchs* that NWO theorists typically identify with one-world government movements. These include some of the world's leading financial dynasties, among them the Rothschilds, Morgans, and Rockefellers.

> **DEFINITION**
>
> An **oligarch** is a person whose power and authority are derived from his or her elite status, including royalty, great wealth, lofty intellectual reputation, family connection, or exalted religious office. An **oligarchy** is a form of government in which all real power is exercised by the elite—the oligarchs. At the heart of NWO conspiracy theories is the belief that one-world government is an effort by the elite to create a global oligarchy.

The NWO organization most intimately tied to the current U.S. government is the Federal Reserve System (see Chapter 9), which was established by Congress in 1913. The Fed conducts the nation's monetary policy and functions as a quasi-public central bank, yet it is neither a government agency nor a private, profit-making institution. It claims to be "an independent entity within the government, having both public purposes and private aspects."

In an effort to defeat passage of the Federal Reserve Act of 1913, Congressman Charles Lindbergh Sr. (father of the aviator) characterized it as the legalization of an "invisible government of the monetary power," and others since have condemned the Fed as "a super-state controlled by international bankers." For NWO conspiracy theorists, it is the single most visible and powerful instrument of one-world shadow government, intimately yet vaguely integrated into the official structure of the U.S. government.

An Ancestry of Secrecy

The organizations, institutions, and secret societies currently identified with the NWO movement and discussed in Part 2 did not start spontaneously. Conspiracy theorists see them as the endpoints of an ancestry dating back to certain pre-Christian cults and secret societies (see Chapter 11) as well as early Christian and Islamic groups of the Middle Ages (see Chapter 12). Some may see foreshadowings of one-world government in the Cabalists, the Sumerian Anunnaki, and others in the ancient world (as discussed in Chapter 11), as well as the Knights Templar, Cathars (French Gnostics), and Hashashins (Assassins) of the Middle Ages (see Chapter 12).

But the eighteenth-century Enlightenment introduced what many NWO writers identify as the archetypal and prototypical conspiratorial movement toward universal shadow government. The Illuminati (see Chapter 13), founded in 1776 by Bavarian Adam Weishaupt, is second only to Freemasonry (see Chapter 15) as history's most famous and pervasive secret society. Some recent writers believe that modern efforts to create and promote a New World Order are direct outgrowths of the original Illuminati.

Rosicrucianism (see Chapter 14) resembles Illuminism in that its adherents believe themselves to be in possession of an esoteric knowledge unavailable to the common man, which provides secret insights that in turn confer power on the initiates. Unlike the Illuminati, the Rosicrucians—who date their beliefs to late medieval Germany—do not see themselves as members of an elite secret society but as adherents of a mystical religion guided by an elite theology. Nevertheless, according to some NWO theorists, Rosicrucianism became a vehicle of the power elite and may therefore be regarded as a precursor and contributor to the creation of rule by shadow government.

Rosicrucian doctrine is intimately related to certain strains of Freemasonry (see Chapter 15), a widespread fraternal movement that played an important part in secretly marshalling the most powerful men in the world. It was especially active in America both before and after independence; indeed, Freemasons' lodges became important meeting places for the architects of the American Revolution. George Washington was a Mason, as was Benjamin Franklin and at least eight other signers of the Declaration of Independence (an additional 11 signers are also believed, but not confirmed, to have been Masons). Some conspiracy theorists assert that U.S. history was largely written by Freemasons, and some believe that the NWO is a direct outgrowth of Freemasonry.

> **PASSWORDS**
>
> "To enlarge the sphere of social happiness is worthy the benevolent design of the Masonic Institution; and it is most fervently to be wished, that the conduct of every member of the fraternity, as well as those publications which discover the principles which actuate them may tend to convince Mankind that the grand object of Masonry is to promote the happiness of the human race."
>
> —George Washington, letter to the Massachusetts Masons Grand Lodge, December 27, 1792

Furtive Fallacy or Conspiratorial Reality?

As mentioned in the Introduction, the purpose of this book is neither to advance nor to refute the existence of a New World Order conspiracy, but to outline and explain this increasingly popular and influential theory. Nevertheless, it is important to recognize the two main opposing positions in the debate over the validity of the NWO before proceeding further.

It is possible to refute (or attempt to refute) particular assertions by various NWO writers just as any historian attempts to refute assertions by any other historian: by bringing to bear more persuasive facts and/or interpretations of facts. As stated in the Introduction, to do this is beyond both the scope and purpose of this book; however, there is one general objection that may be considered when evaluating any and all assertions of historical conspiracy.

The historian and historiographer David Hackett Fischer, author of *Historians' Fallacies* (1970), among many other works, coined the term *furtive fallacy* to describe the assumption of some historical writers that all significant facts of history are by nature sinister. Fischer argues that such a view of history does not take into account the mere possibility of ulterior motives and secretive deeds, but *insists* on them, also assuming that absolutely nothing happens by accident or error—or even for the reasons the doer of a deed or maker of a decision offers.

DEFINITION

Furtive fallacy is a term coined by historian and historiographer David Hackett Fischer to describe the tendency some historical writers have to interpret virtually all significant facts of history as sinister, thereby presenting (as Fischer explains) history as "a story of causes mostly insidious and results mostly invidious."

Historians who see history as invariably a conspiracy may well be committing the furtive fallacy; however, students of the NWO point to the fact that the CFR, the TC, and the Bilderberg Group do exist, consist of powerful individuals, and meet more or less in secret. Because of their secrecy, it is impossible to say just how much influence these secret societies have on major world events. On the other hand, these organizations bring together some of the most influential, wealthy, and powerful men and women on Earth.

DEFINITION

Globalization is a somewhat vague term that may be applied to the process by which national and regional economies, societies, and cultures are increasingly integrated through networks of communication and exchange. In business and commerce, the term is usually applied more narrowly to the integration of national economies into a global economy through international trade, investment, and other economic forces. For NWO conspiracy theorists, globalization is code for the creation of one-world government.

Also incontrovertible, conspiracy theorists point out, is the continued and growing trend toward *globalization*—of trade, technology, communication, and political integration. Put all these strands together—secrecy, demonstrated influence, and the current trend of global politics—and it is reasonable to assume (NWO advocates say) that efforts are afoot, behind the scenes and inaccessible to the masses, to bring about one-world government administered by the few and presumably for the benefit of the few.

The Least You Need to Know

- Recent conspiracy theorists describe the New World Order as a movement to create one-world government controlled by a secretive elite consisting of financiers and other oligarchs.
- Conspiracy writers disagree on the extent to which one-world government already exists, but they see the NWO as promoting its spread, to the eventual elimination of individual nations.
- As believers in the existence of the NWO see it, elected officials and other public rulers are subordinate to secretive elites, who constitute the true power behind the throne.
- War is the major means by which the power elite intend to bring about the NWO and establish themselves at the head of a one-world government.

The Council on Foreign Relations

In This Chapter

- The Council on Foreign Relations as a secret society for globalists
- The role of CFR founders in the Treaty of Versailles and creation of the League of Nations
- The CFR's relationship with government and the corporate world
- The role of the CFR in twentieth-century wars
- The recent CFR globalization initiatives

The Council on Foreign Relations (CFR) describes itself as "an independent, non-partisan membership organization, think tank, and publisher dedicated to being a resource for its members, government officials, business executives, journalists, educators and students, civic and religious leaders, and other interested citizens in order to help them better understand the world and the foreign policy choices facing the United States and other countries." Reflecting the consensus of New World Order (NWO) conspiracy theorists, author Jim Marrs calls it something very different, the "granddaddy of modern American secret societies," and sees its globalist mission as creating "a one-world community."

What is undeniable is the large number of highly placed U.S. government officials who claim membership in the group. According to the CFR's own website, two widely quoted critics of the organization, Laurence H. Shoup and William Minter, reviewed the biographies of 502 "government officials in high positions" from 1945 to 1972 and found that more than half were members. Richard Barnet, who is both a CFR member and critic of the organization, remarked that membership in the organization could be deemed "a rite of passage for an aspiring national security manager," and journalists of all political stripes have called it the nation's most influential foreign-policy think tank.

Although the public profile of the CFR is high, and its bimonthly magazine *Foreign Affairs* is the leading U.S. journal of international relations with a circulation exceeding 200,000, the organization is also characterized by a high level of secrecy in many of its proceedings and special publications intended for selective circulation.

The Inquiry and Beyond

In 1917, during World War I, President Woodrow Wilson asked his closest confidant and adviser, Edward M. House, to assemble about 150 academics in a wide variety of fields to prepare studies and other materials that might be useful in peace negotiations, assuming a U.S./Allied victory in the war. House tapped ethical philosopher Sidney Edward Mezes, the Harvard-educated president of the College of the City of New York, who had written a standard ethics textbook and a volume on the "conception of God," to supervise the study group, which was dubbed The Inquiry.

The name chosen for the group might be seen as academically neutral and objective or downright sinister, with "Inquiry" ominously echoing "Inquisition." In any case, the group was not called The Inquiry for long. In 1919, with the war ended and work on the Treaty of Versailles underway, the group was renamed the American Commission to Negotiate Peace and, in what was now a full-fledged official capacity, traveled with President Wilson to the Paris Peace Conference.

INTEL

Woodrow Wilson was elected president of the United States for the first time in 1912. He introduced a broad agenda of progressive reforms (including the graduated income tax and the Federal Reserve System), then faced a tough re-election bid in 1916. He managed to defeat Republican contender Charles Evans Hughes largely on the strength of his campaign slogan, "He Kept Us Out of War."

Yet less than six months after he was re-elected, Wilson asked Congress to declare war. U.S. financiers and industrialists were heavily invested in an Allied victory and urged Wilson to enter the war. He himself saw the war as an opportunity to shape a new world order, of which the League of Nations would be the organizing body. NWO conspiracy theorists see the League as the twentieth century's first big step toward one-world government.

The "Colonel" and the Conspiracy

If the very name The Inquiry conveys the whiff of conspiracy, the role of "Colonel" House in the Wilson White House must arouse some suspicion even in those least inclined to embrace conspiratorial theories. Born in Houston, Texas, in 1858, House was the product of East Coast prep schools and enrolled at Cornell University. When his father died he was forced to drop out and assume management of the family's cotton plantations. He eventually left the business to become a banking investor and, in 1902, moved to New York's Wall Street—but not before proving himself a Texas kingmaker. House was so powerful in his native state that he was instrumental in propelling four governors into office between 1892 and 1902. The first he launched was James S. Hogg, who appointed House to his staff, a position that carried with it the strictly honorific title of "Colonel."

Colonel House, now a powerful Wall Street financier, embraced Woodrow Wilson in 1911 and did for him what he had done for those four Texas governors. He propelled him to the Democratic presidential nomination in 1912, and then played a leading role in assembling Wilson's first cabinet. The president offered him his choice of Cabinet posts (except secretary of state, which he pledged to William Jennings Bryan in return for his support in the Democratic National Convention). House declined any official role, offering instead to serve the president "wherever and whenever possible." He became so intimate an adviser that Wilson gave him living quarters in the White House.

It is difficult *not* to see House as a power behind the throne, although this is not necessarily sinister, and would not seem so if not for the fact that, in 1912, the year of Wilson's nomination and election, House anonymously published a curious novel called *Philip Dru: Administrator, a Story of Tomorrow.* The title character gathers together and leads a conspiracy in the western United States to foment a popular democratic rebellion against the plutocratic East. Emerging triumphant, Dru becomes the nation's dictator and imposes upon it complete control of political parties, a graduated income tax, and the creation of a powerful central bank. Among the sweeping progressive reforms ushered through Congress during the Wilson administration were the graduated income tax (Sixteenth Amendment, ratified in 1913) and the establishment of the Federal Reserve System (created by the Federal Reserve Act of 1913). Conspiracy theorists believe the powerful central bank is at the very heart of the NWO concept (see Chapter 9).

The Birth of the CFR

House is one of those unelected yet inordinately powerful behind-the-scenes figures who raise red flags in the minds of conspiracy theorists. House was instrumental in advising President Wilson on his famous Fourteen Points—the terms on which the president proposed to end World War I. He was among those who actually drafted the Treaty of Versailles and the Covenant of the League of Nations (the later widely seen by conspiracy theorists as the twentieth century's first major step toward true one-world government).

Although it is true that House fell out of favor with Wilson in the course of the Paris Peace Conference, because Wilson felt he compromised too liberally with the other Allies, it is also true that House was at the height of his influence when he masterminded the creation of The Inquiry. It produced some 2,000 studies and other documents that House and Wilson used in hammering out the Fourteen Points.

Moreover, as the American Commission to Negotiate Peace, the group met in London with the British scholars, social thinkers, and policymakers who would form the Royal Institute of International Affairs (officially called Chatham House since 2004), the British counterpart of the CFR. Indeed, in 2009, the CFR's *Foreign Policy* magazine named Chatham House the top *non-U.S.* foreign-policy think tank. Some see the meetings between the American and British policy thinkers as steps toward designing one-world government.

PASSWORDS

"The world must be made safe for democracy. Its peace must be planted upon the tested foundations of political liberty."

—Woodrow Wilson, war message to Congress, April 2, 1917

Joining House and the American Commission scholars in Paris were Paul Warburg and Bernard Baruch. Born in Hamburg, Germany, in 1868, to a prominent family of bankers, Warburg in 1895 married Nina J. Loeb, daughter of Solomon Loeb, who founded the New York investment firm Kuhn, Loeb & Company. In 1902, Warburg settled permanently in New York as a partner in his father-in-law's firm, became a U.S. citizen in 1911, and, in 1914, was appointed to the newly created Federal Reserve Board. He was a powerful advocate of the creation of the Federal Reserve System.

Bernard Baruch was born in Camden, South Carolina, in 1870, but was raised from the age of 11 in New York City, where he became a wildly successful broker. He earned the sobriquet "the Lone Wolf of Wall Street" because he refused to become associated with any bank or brokerage. When the United States entered World War I, President Wilson tapped Baruch to chair the War Industries Board, which, under his guidance, established strong government control of American industry to achieve a staggering volume of war production. The president frequently sought his advice on finance and international affairs, as would the next Democratic war president, Franklin D. Roosevelt.

Wilson, House, and the others labored intensively in Paris, pointedly excluding from their deliberations the Republican caucus in the House and Senate. Alienated and therefore understandably suspicious, the Republican-dominated Senate, led by the formidable Henry Cabot Lodge, refused to ratify the Treaty of Versailles and the Covenant of the League of Nations. Nevertheless, Colonel House brought the American Commission and the British Chatham House group together at the Hotel Majestic in Paris on May 30, 1919. The group formally resolved to create an Institute of International Affairs—a nongovernmental international body that did not require the Senate's approval or even its knowledge. The British branch formally became the Royal Institute of International Affairs. The American branch, incorporated on July 21, 1921, became the Council on Foreign Relations (CFR).

INTEL

The Treaty of Versailles formally ended the Great War (World War I). It was signed on June 28, 1919. Although Germany and the other Central Powers signed the treaty, they did so under protest, having been given no voice in its creation. The treaty required that all signatories also sign the Covenant of the League of Nations (June 28, 1919), which established the League, a global deliberative and adjudicative forum, and enrolled all signatories in it. The U.S. Senate rejected the Covenant as well as membership in the League.

Open and Shut

Critics of the CFR characterize the organization as an elite gentlemen's club, a central node in the "old boy's network." This characterization is not without basis. At its inception, the names of virtually all members would have been found on the social register as well as on the membership rolls of the most exclusive clubs in New York and Washington, D.C. This is still largely true today; however, social standing alone will not get you into the CFR.

For individuals, membership is available in two tiers: term and life. Term members must be between the ages of 30 and 36 at the time of their application, and term memberships are limited to five years. A candidate must be nominated by one CFR member and supported by a minimum of two other individuals. He or she then submits a biography and a resumé. Membership is restricted to U.S. citizens and permanent residents who have applied to become citizens.

Candidacy for life membership requires a nomination by one CFR member and support from three other individuals—preferably but not necessarily current CFR members. Both term and life candidates are reviewed by a membership committee and screened by a professional staff; competition for openings is extremely intense.

Currently there are 5,000 members, most of them term members. Membership is open not only to individuals, but also to corporations. Some of the biggest corporations to have joined CFR include ABC News, American Express, AIG, Bank of America, Bloomberg L.P., Boeing, BP, Chevron, De Beers, Halliburton, Merck, Time Warner, and Visa, to name only a few.

Although individual membership is highly selective, it is—and has been from the CFR's inception—open to people of all political affiliations (Democrat, Republican, Independent), religions, and races. In the beginning, membership was exclusively male, but is now open to women as well (although they still constitute a small minority). Membership is open to individuals from all regions of the country, but the majority lives in or near Washington, D.C., or New York (and has been described even by CFR insiders as belonging to the "East Coast liberal elite"). However, in the 1970s, a number of Committees on Foreign Relations were created in various American cities, with membership drawn from local leaders.

PASSWORDS

"Full freedom of expression is encouraged at Council meetings. Participants are assured that they may speak openly, as it is the tradition of the Council that others will not attribute or characterize their statements in public media or forums or knowingly transmit them to persons who will. All participants are expected to honor that commitment."

—The Council on Foreign Relations, *By-Laws,* Article II

Notable Members

More than 12 former or serving U.S. secretaries of state (beginning with Elihu Root, secretary of state to Theodore Roosevelt) have been CFR members, as have numerous high government officers. Among them are Allen W. Dulles, who became the CIA's most dynamic and perhaps most controversial chief; W. Averill Harriman, longtime U.S. ambassador to the Soviet Union; Zbigniew Brzezinski, national security advisor to President Jimmy Carter; John McCain, U.S. senator and 2008 presidential candidate; and Dick Cheney, secretary of defense under George H. W. Bush (who is also a CFR member) and vice president under George W. Bush. Financial figures from President Kennedy's treasury secretary C. Douglas Dillon to longtime Federal Reserve chairman Alan Greenspan, and media personalities from influential post–World War I journalist Walter Lippmann to PBS newsman Bill Moyers and CNBC news anchor Erin Burnett are currently or have been members.

Financiers figured prominently in the CFR from the beginning, with John W. Davis, personal attorney to J. P. Morgan, even serving as the founding president. Morgan, John D. Rockefeller, Jacob Schiff, Otto Kahn (himself a member), and Paul Warburg (also a member), all multimillionaires, provided the start-up financing. Funding today comes chiefly from CFR's corporate members plus a number of major nonprofit foundations, including the Ford Foundation and the Rockefeller Brothers Fund, among others.

Connections

In addition to holding influential jobs ranging from vice president of the United States to CIA director to television news anchor, members are typically associated with a host of other organizations that exert influence on the government and its policies. CFR board members also hold membership in or sit on the boards of such bodies as the Institute for International Economics, the Committee for a Responsible Federal Budget, the Urban Institute, the Business Roundtable, the U.S. Chamber of Commerce, the National Alliance for Business, the Brookings Institution, the Hoover Institution, the Center for Strategic and International Studies, and the Wilderness Society.

Peace and War

Although the CFR had its origin in helping to create the ultimately tragic peace of Versailles after World War I, critics of the organization point out that it has played a role in virtually every armed conflict since then, largely by promoting American global activism.

World War II and After

During the Franklin D. Roosevelt administration, beginning in 1939 and continuing throughout the duration of World War II, the CFR served as an advisory pipeline to the U.S. Department of State, feeding it a stream of top-secret "War and Peace Studies" funded exclusively by the Rockefeller Foundation. These studies were produced by a CFR inner circle and were not available to members outside the circle. The inner circle was itself compartmentalized into four topical groups: economic and financial; security and armaments; territorial; and political.

The inner circle issued 682 study memorandums to the State Department, many of which have never been declassified. No historian has ventured to estimate the effect CFR studies actually had on U.S. foreign policy during the World War II era. It is significant, however, that the leader of the security and armaments group was Allen Dulles, who went on during World War II to become a principal in the Office of Strategic Services (OSS), precursor of the CIA, of which he later became director. It is also significant that another study group member, State Department diplomat George Kennan, transmitted from the U.S. Embassy in Moscow the so-called "Long Telegram" shortly after World War II. In it he analyzed the motives for postwar Soviet aggressive expansion. This became the basis for "The Sources of Soviet Conduct," an essay he published (under the pseudonym "X") in CFR's *Foreign Affairs* in July 1947.

Together, the "Long Telegram" and the *Foreign Affairs* essay served as the virtual playbook for U.S. foreign policy during the Cold War. The essay articulated the *containment* concept of opposing Soviet or Soviet-backed communist expansion wherever and whenever it occurred, using economic means when possible, but also applying military force if necessary—albeit short of all-out war.

DEFINITION

Containment, the foundation of U.S. foreign policy during the Cold War era, was a strategy by which the United States used economic, political, propaganda, and military means to counter Soviet and Soviet-backed communist expansion throughout the world. Containment prompted U.S. intervention on a global basis because of necessity.

The biggest economic measure promoting containment was the European Recovery Plan, better known as the Marshall Plan. The United States funded this massive program of postwar European economic recovery, in part from humanitarian motives and in part to block Soviet influence in Western Europe. The highest-profile military measure implemented in the name of containment was the North Atlantic Treaty Organization (NATO), an alliance that originally included the United States, Canada, and most of the western European states. It now encompasses a total of 28 nations. Considering its size, this alliance may be the most dramatic manifestation of one-world thinking to emerge from the Cold War period.

The Marshall Plan and NATO took shape during the administration of Harry Truman (1945–1953), but, if anything, his successor, Dwight D. Eisenhower (president from 1953 to 1961), was arguably even more directly influenced by the CFR. Before he became president of the United States, Eisenhower was president of Columbia University and chaired a CFR study group. This group became the nucleus for a larger CFR study group, "Americans for Eisenhower," which promoted Ike's candidacy and election. It is not surprising that President Eisenhower drew on the CFR for a number of his cabinet appointments, most notably Secretary of State John Foster Dulles, brother of Allen Dulles.

SECRET LIVES

The Dulles brothers, John Foster (1888–1959) and Allen Welsh (1893–1969), both CFR members, were extraordinarily influential in American government and foreign policy during the early Cold War era. John Foster Dulles was secretary of state under Eisenhower from 1953 to 1959 and was an uncompromising advocate of a hard line against communism around the world.

Younger brother Allen Dulles directed the covert OSS office in neutral Switzerland during World War II, effectively serving as the chief spymaster for the United States in the European theater. In 1953, he became the first civilian director of the CIA and served until 1961, longer than any other director.

Eisenhower not only drew on the CFR to staff his administration, his policies in turn influenced CFR activity. When, through John Foster Dulles, the president announced a shift in military policy from the local deterrents of containment to a focus on "strategic" (that is, nuclear) weapons, a young Henry Kissinger—Harvard professor and future national security adviser and secretary of state—chaired a study group devoted to nuclear weapons and foreign policy. In contrast to the World War II study groups, the fruits of this one were made public by Kissinger himself. His book *Nuclear Weapons and Foreign Policy* became a bestseller in 1957.

The CFR continued to serve as a think tank for U.S. nuclear policy, helping formulate the concept of *mutual assured destruction* (*MAD*) and the international policy of nuclear nonproliferation, encouraging and incentivizing other nations not to acquire nuclear weapons.

> **DEFINITION**
>
> **Mutual assured destruction (MAD)** is the cornerstone of the U.S. nuclear deterrent policy. It held that if both of the world's nuclear superpowers, the United States and the Soviet Union, possessed sufficient nuclear arsenals to destroy one another (and, in the process, global civilization), and both believed that a nuclear attack from one side would provoke a nuclear response from the other, neither side would start a major war with the other or its allies.

Korea and Vietnam

The Marshall Plan and the Berlin Airlift (the remarkable 1948–1949 effort to supply West Berlin with food and fuel after the Soviets imposed a blockade on the city) were unquestionably successful manifestations of the containment policy fostered by the CFR. However, the result of the Korean War, which broke out on June 25, 1950, during the Truman administration, was far more ambiguous. Faced with choosing between making no response to the communist invasion of South Korea, or making a massive response that might ignite World War III, Truman ultimately chose a military strategy to "contain" the invasion. Insofar as this resulted in the preservation of South Korea without touching off a larger war, the strategy was successful; however, to this day, the Korean peninsula is divided and North Korea remains a threat to the region. Moreover, many still see the outcome of the Korean War as a humiliating defeat for the U.S. military, possibly even a willful capitulation to communism in the name of globalism.

The CFR promoted U.S. accommodation with communist Vietnamese nationalist Ho Chi Minh in his effort to achieve independence from French colonial control after World War II. In November 1953, a CFR study group advised the U.S. Secretary of State John Foster Dulles that Ho was less a communist than he was a nationalist, whom the United States (pledged to promote national self-determination) had every reason to support. Moreover, the study group pointed out that the U.S. government could cooperate with Ho in ways that would promote his independence movement while also steering him and his nation *out* of the Soviet orbit.

Dulles rejected the study group's advice, believing it a mistake not only to compromise with a communist leader, but to intervene in Vietnam in any way. The eventual result of this uncompromising policy was a deeper involvement in Vietnam than anyone could have imagined in 1953.

Normalization with Communist China

Throughout the Cold War, relations between the communist People's Republic of China and the United States were unremittingly hostile, with many Americans dismissing China as a "mad dog" among nations. The United States refused to recognize the legitimacy of the communist government and had no official diplomatic relations with it.

From 1964 to 1968, during the administration of President Lyndon Johnson, the CFR studied Sino-American relations and concluded that a "more open" relationship was called for. Kissinger took this attitude with him when President Nixon appointed him his national security adviser in 1969. Of course, Kissinger was instrumental in paving the way for Nixon's epoch-making visit to China in 1972, which was followed by full normalization of relations during the administration of President Jimmy Carter. His secretary of state, Cyrus Vance, was also a CFR member.

CFR and NWO

Whereas most Americans point to the opening of Sino-American relations as a positive step that has made the world safer, some conspiracy theorists see it as one of the twentieth century's biggest steps down the slippery slope of globalization and into one-world government. Of course, there is no reason to believe that either President Nixon or President Carter saw normalization this way, yet it is not so easy to dismiss assumptions that the CFR regarded Sino-American rapprochement as a deliberate and desirable move toward one-world government.

In 2008, the CFR embarked on a projected five-year program titled "International Institutions and Global Governance: World Order in the 21st Century." The stated objective of the program is to design and create a variety of global institutions intended to promote "global governance" for the purpose of more effectively dealing with such transnational issues as the global environment (including global climate change), energy policy, international terrorism, epidemic and pandemic infectious disease, and the proliferation of weapons of mass destruction.

Although the goals identified in the program seem laudable, selfless, and necessary, it is impossible to overlook the choice of words. "Global *governance*" flirts with "global *government*," and "world order" is just one adjective shy of "*new* world order."

Is the CFR tweaking its critics? Is it defying them? Or is it demonstrating indifference to them?

From Means to Motive

Although "global governance" suggests "global government," and "world order" suggests "new world order," governance is not government, and world order is not necessarily new world order. As stated in the Introduction, this book's purpose is simply to present the leading theories of an NWO conspiracy, not to prove or to refute them. But let's assume, for the sake of argument, that the long-held intention of the CFR is to create one-world government. We know that the organization possesses the *means* to advance this agenda:

- It is a collection of America's best, brightest, wealthiest, most influential, and most powerful, who clearly have the ear of highly placed government officials, especially (and for a long time) in the Department of State.

- It enjoys abundant finance.

- It publishes a periodical, *Foreign Affairs*, that is widely accepted as authoritative.

- It is structured to combine a high public profile with deep secrecy.

- It enjoys a reputation among certain agencies of government as *the* go-to think tank for advice.

But does the CFR also have the *motive* to promote one-world government? Do CFR members possess shared ideological convictions sufficiently compelling to prompt them to move toward this goal? When you look at the range of CFR membership, it seems unlikely that such ideological unanimity could exist—unless you look only at the figures who, historically, have predominated on the CFR board and in its ranks. They are not the politicians, statesmen, or journalists, but the bankers, financiers, industrialists, and actual corporations.

Rear Admiral Chester Ward, a CFR member for 16 years and judge advocate general of the U.S. Navy from 1956 to 1960, declared, "The main purpose of the Council on Foreign Relations is promoting the disarmament of U.S. sovereignty and national independence and submergence into an all-powerful, one-world government." This was reported by Barry Goldwater, long-time Arizona senator and the 1964 Republican candidate for the presidency, in his 1979 political memoir, *With No*

Apologies. Goldwater continued the quotation: "Primarily, they want the world banking monopoly from whatever power ends up in the control of global government."

Behind the mystique of power, intellect, and ideology lurks the motive of profit for the powerful few. It is a motive—and a theme—that occurs over and over in every account of the NWO conspiracy.

The Least You Need to Know

- The Council on Foreign Relations was founded in 1921, having developed from a World War I think tank called The Inquiry.
- Exclusive and highly sought-after, the CFR's membership has long included high government officials, financiers, corporate directors (and actual corporations), certain journalists, and certain scholars who have been, collectively and individually, influential on U.S. government policy.
- The CFR combines a high public profile (especially through its influential bi-monthly magazine, *Foreign Affairs*) with secrecy and has produced confidential studies and white papers for the U.S. Department of State.
- CFR critics believe the organization has had a hand in every American war since World War I and is committed to amplifying globalization into full-blown, one-world government.

The Bilderberg Group

In This Chapter

- The origin of the Bilderberg Group
- The relation to the Council on Foreign Relations and Trilateral Commission
- The U.S. connection
- The globalism of David Rockefeller Sr.
- One-world aspirations

Much of what the Council on Foreign Relations (CFR) does is not only a matter of public record but actively publicized. Some of its proceedings and projects are confidential, even secret. Yet to call the CFR a "secret society"—as New World Order (NWO) conspiracy theorists do—is to invite immediate objection: *How can an organization that publishes a journal with nearly a quarter-million subscribers be secret?*

When it comes to the so-called Bilderberg Group, it is harder to object to the *secret society* label. The organization is so secret that it doesn't even have an official name. Bilderberg Group, Bilderberg Conference, Bilderberg Club—all are labels participants and others have casually applied to a yearly meeting of about 130 of the world's wealthiest and most influential people. The names came from the venue of the first meeting at the Hotel de Bilderberg on May 29, 1954, in the Dutch town of Oosterbeek. The hotel's own literature describes the town as "an idyllic village located in what is known as Europe's greenest borough."

The meetings are closed to the public and the press; the group has never issued a press release; and even though confidential minutes of meetings are recorded, no names are ever attached to the proceedings. On March 10, 2001, Denis Winston Healey, Baron Healey, founding member of the Bilderberg Group, breached the silence ever so tantalizingly. "To say we were striving for a one-world government is exaggerated," he told Manchester (UK) *Guardian* reporter Jon Ronson, "but not wholly unfair. Those of us in Bilderberg felt we couldn't go on forever fighting one another for nothing and killing people and rendering millions homeless. So we felt that a single community throughout the world would be a good thing."

"To Plan Events That Later Appear Just to Happen"

In December 1956, Józef Retinger (1888–1960), a Polish political adviser and founding member of the European Movement—that led to the creation of the European Union—and initiator of the first Bilderberg conference, sent invitations for the group's fourth meeting, to be held on St. Simon's Island off the Georgia coast. "The object of this conference," Retinger wrote, "will be to study common and divergent elements in the policies of the Western world."

Daniel Estulin, who has written a history of the Bilderberg Group (from the outspoken point of view of an NWO conspiracy theorist), puts the purpose of all the meetings quite differently: "to gather yearly in a luxurious hotel somewhere in the world to try to decide the future of humanity." In 1977, the usually staid *Times* of London described the effect of the Bilderberg's secret meetings as planning "events that later appear just to happen."

PASSWORDS

"[The Bilderberg Group is] a clique of the richest, economically and politically most powerful and influential men in the Western world, who meet secretly to plan events that later appear just to happen."

—*The Times* (London), April 22, 1977

Founding Fathers

When he cofounded the Bilderberg Group with Józef Retinger, Denis Healey was a Labour Party member of Parliament. He was also a councilor of the Royal Institute of International Affairs—Chatham House, the British counterpart of the U.S. Council on Foreign Relations. He was also councilor of the International Institute for Strategic Studies, a British think tank in the area of international affairs, with a strong military slant. He was also a member of the Fabian Society, a British political organization that, beginning in the late nineteenth century, has worked toward instilling social democracy (some would put it more frankly as socialism) in government through gradual, systematic reform rather than revolution. The Fabians laid the foundation of the British Labour Party.

SECRET LIVES

Denis Healey (b. 1917) became a member of Parliament in 1952, secretary of state for defense from 1964 to 1970, and chancellor of the exchequer (roughly equivalent to the U.S. secretary of the treasury) from 1974 to 1979. Healey was secretary of the International Department of the Labour Party and served as adviser to Labour Party leaders. He also served in the "Shadow Cabinet" (in British politics, an informal cabinet that functions as part of the "loyal opposition" to the party in power) when the Labour Party was out of power.

His globalist orientation motivated him to become one of the founding fathers of the Bilderberg Group in 1953–1954. Whereas fellow Labour Party members hailed him as "the best prime minister we never had," more conservative political figures have seen him as overly eager to merge British identity with the rest of Europe.

Born in Krakow, Poland, in 1888, Retinger became the youngest person to receive a Ph.D. from the Sorbonne in Paris. He traveled to revolution-wracked Mexico in 1917 to advise President Plutarco Elias Calles and during World War II was an adviser to the Polish government in exile. In 1944, the 56-year-old Retinger covertly parachuted into Nazi-occupied Poland to consult with the Polish underground and deliver money to the resistance. His war experience persuaded Retinger that only European unification could guarantee an end to armed conflict on the continent, and he became an energetic advocate of the movements that led to the present-day European Union. This was a step toward one-world government, conspiracy theorists believe.

Both Retinger and Healey claimed concern over anti-American sentiment in Western Europe and wanted to counter it by promoting greater understanding between American and European culture through a high-level but off-the-record international conference. Given Retinger's desire to unify Europe and Healey's Fabian objective of bringing about evolutionary change in global politics, it is possible to discern a one-world agenda in the very inception of the group.

Retinger approached Prince Bernhard of Lippe-Biesterfeld (1911–2004), prince consort to Queen Juliana of the Netherlands, for endorsement or sponsorship of the conference. Apart from his noble birth, Bernhard possessed a curious resumé. He was a hero in World War II, a leader of Dutch resistance during the early part of the German occupation, and a pilot with the British RAF from 1942 to 1944. In 1944, he was named to command of the Dutch armed forces and was present in May 1945 at the surrender of the Germans occupying Holland.

INTEL

The Fabian Society was founded in London and took its name from the Roman general Quintus Fabius Maximus, whose sobriquet, "Cunctator"—literally, "the Delayer"—was earned on account of his strategic avoidance of all-out frontal attacks against Hannibal Barca's Carthaginians in favor of harassment and attrition designed to wear down the enemy.

The most famous early member of the Fabians was playwright George Bernard Shaw, and the modern incarnation of the society is the cutting-edge think tank of the Labour Party, advancing its globalist perspective.

After the war, Bernhard was vigorous in his leadership of reconstruction efforts and generous in his assistance to postwar recovery groups as well as individuals in need. An environmentalist, he was involved in the creation of the World Wildlife Fund (today the World Wide Fund for Nature), and was a cofounder of Rotary International, the well-known global service organization.

Enormously popular with the Dutch people, he would have been an obvious and uncontroversial choice to help found the Bilderberg organization were it not for his connection to the very Nazis he himself fought in World War II. In the 1930s, before the outbreak of war, his younger brother publicly proclaimed his approval and support of Hitler, and Bernhard himself was made an honorary SS cavalryman. He also was employed by the giant German chemical conglomerate I. G. Farben, which became infamous as a chemical munitions manufacturer and the creator of Zyklon-B, the cyanide gas used to murder millions in Hitler's death camps. When Bernhard's brother became an active officer in the Wehrmacht (German regular armed forces), the prince was widely suspected of espionage—though nothing of the kind has ever been proven.

Bernhard chaired the Bilderberg Group until 1976, when it was discovered that he had taken a $1.1 million bribe from U.S. aircraft manufacturer Lockheed. In return he used his influence to persuade the Royal Dutch Air Force to purchase the firm's fighter jets. In the scandal that followed, the public at large learned of his SS connections, and he lost his place not only at the head of the Bilderberg Group but on the boards and committees of no fewer than 300 Dutch national and international corporations. This in itself revealed how closely connected the Bilderbergs were not only to various national governments, but to global business interests.

PASSWORDS

"[Prince] Bernhard has occasionally crossed the grain of his ardently democratic adopted [Dutch] countrymen. In 1971 former Dutch Prime Minister Barend Biesheuvel publicly told him to button his royal lip after the prince suggested that the Cabinet should be freed periodically from parliamentary interference so that the 'government could really get down to business without having to spend half its time answering questions.'"

—*Time,* February 23, 1976

U.S. Involvement

The participation of the United States was obviously vital to a conference whose stated purpose was promoting Euro-American mutual understanding. Of all the American government officials Bernhard might have contacted, he chose Walter Bedell Smith, head of the CIA. Although it is true that Smith and Bernhard became well-acquainted during World War II, conspiracy theorists suggest that, from the beginning, the Bilderberg Group was a covert operation that naturally reached out to the chief covert agency of the U.S. government.

This view is bolstered by the fact that Smith brought in Charles Douglas Jackson (1902–1964), a specialist in psychological warfare who served in the CIA's World War II precursor, the Office of Strategic Services (OSS), and was a special assistant to President Dwight Eisenhower, advising the administration on matters of *psychological warfare* and propaganda. Jackson eagerly embraced the Bilderberg idea, as he would later global initiatives, becoming active in the United Nations.

DEFINITION

Psychological warfare, also called PSYWAR or PSYOPS in military circles, is defined by the U.S. Department of Defense as "the planned use of propaganda and other psychological actions having the primary purpose of influencing the opinions, emotions, attitudes, and behavior of hostile foreign groups in such a way as to support the achievement of national objectives." Conspiracy theorists charge that PSYOPS have been used not only against "hostile foreign groups," but domestically as well, to promote the New World Order agenda, among others.

The Organization Is Born

After the Eisenhower administration was on board, invitations to the first conference went out to 50 delegates from 11 Western European countries and 11 from the
United States. After the first conference, a rudimentary organizational structure was
put together, which included a chairman, an honorary secretary-general, a Steering
Committee, and a body known only as the advisory group.

An Unofficial CFR

Although the Bilderbergers have never issued a press release, in 2008, an organization
called the American Friends of the Bilderberg issued a statement to the press intended
to counter charges of global conspiracy: "Bilderberg's only activity is its annual
Conference. At the meetings, no resolutions are proposed, no votes taken, and no
policy statements issued."

Nevertheless, noting that many Bilderbergers also hold membership in the CFR,
Neal Wilgus (author of *Illuminoids: Secret Societies and Political Paranoia*, 1978) characterized it as "a sort of unofficial CFR, expanded on an international scale." This
view is typical of NWO conspiracy theorists, who see the Bilderberg's international
membership and perspective as a means by which the American-based CFR globally
disseminates its one-world philosophy.

Bilderbergers and the Trilateral Commission

The American membership of the Bilderberg Group overlaps with that of the
exclusively American CFR. Both the Bilderberg Group and the CFR share a number
of members with the Trilateral Commission, a private organization founded in 1973
ostensibly to foster cooperation among the United States, Japan, and Europe (see
Chapter 4). James P. "Big Jim" Tucker Jr., a right-wing journalist who has focused
on exposing the Bilderberg Group since the 1970s, claims that the agendas of the
Bilderbergers and the Trilateral Commission are "much the same," and that the two
groups have an "interlocking leadership and a common vision of the world."

The Rockefeller Connection

It does not take a conspiracy theorist to see at least one connection among the three
organizations. David Rockefeller Sr. (b. 1915) is the son of John D. Rockefeller Jr. and

the grandson of Standard Oil founder John D. Rockefeller. The Rockefeller family has long funded charitable, educational, social, and political institutions—some with a frankly globalist orientation, particularly those funded under the leadership of David Rockefeller.

A banker by profession, Rockefeller also has ties to the International Monetary Fund. He was the longtime chairman of Chase Bank, which was closely associated with the World Bank. Influenced by his father, he became a globalist, joining the CFR in 1949 as its youngest director ever. He was present at the first meeting of the Bilderberg Group and attended regularly thereafter.

At a Bilderberg meeting in 1972, influenced by fellow Bilderberger Zbigniew Brzezinski (who later served as President Jimmy Carter's national security adviser), Rockefeller proposed creating the Trilateral Commission (TC). By including Japan, the TC expanded the reach of the globalist movement from America (CFR) and Europe (Bilderberg) to Asia. The organization was created the following year.

PASSWORDS

"For more than a century ideological extremists at either end of the political spectrum have seized upon well-publicized incidents ... to attack the Rockefeller family for the inordinate influence they claim we wield over American political and economic institutions. Some even believe we are part of a secret cabal working against the best interests of the United States, characterizing my family and me as 'internationalists' and of conspiring with others around the world to build a more integrated global political and economic structure—one world, if you will. If that's the charge, I stand guilty, and I am proud of it."

—David Rockefeller Jr., *Memoirs* (2002)

Rockefeller's associates have included some of the world's most influential people in politics, government, industry, finance, media, and the arts. He has also met with less savory world leaders such as Fidel Castro, Nikita Khrushchev, Mikhail Gorbachev, and Saddam Hussein. Conspiracy theorists are most intrigued by his long association with the U.S. intelligence community, which dates to World War II and the OSS (he was a personal friend of both Dulles brothers, Allen Welsh and John Foster) and continued through much of the Cold War–era CIA.

The Roster Includes ...

The list of Bilderberg participants over the years is long and constitutes a veritable *Who's Who* of global policymakers and influence brokers. It has included royalty (Britain's Prince Charles and his father, Prince Philip, are Bilderbergers) and world leaders from Belgium, the Netherlands, France, the United Kingdom, Portugal, Finland, Iceland, Germany, Poland, Sweden, Canada, Norway, and the European Union (EU) as well as NATO, the United Nations, and the World Trade Organization (WTO). Gerald Ford and Bill Clinton were both Bilderbergers before they became presidents; Ford attended the 1964 and 1966 meetings, Clinton the 1991 meeting.

A number of U.S. senators and governors have participated in meetings, as have a host of bankers, including current Federal Reserve chairman Ben Bernanke and former Fed chairman Paul Volcker, as well as Barack Obama's secretary of the treasury, Timothy Geithner (in 2004, when he was president of the Federal Reserve Bank of New York).

Numerous corporate CEOs and chairmen have been Bilderbergers, among them leaders of BP, IBM, H. J. Heinz, PepsiCo, Shell Oil, and Unilever. Among media figures, the late conservative pundit William F. Buckley Jr. and George Stephanopoulos, communications director of the Clinton administration and currently anchor of ABC's *Good Morning America*, have attended Bilderberg meetings.

What the Bilderbergers Want (Maybe)

The Bilderberg Group has never advertised itself or its intentions, although those participants who have commented, as well as the American Friends of the Bilderberg, claim that the purpose of the organization is to promote free, informal discussion of world affairs outside both the public spotlight and official government or corporate constraints and obligations. Others—and by no means exclusively NWO conspiracy theorists—have observed that Bilderbergers are often associated with international and transnational initiatives that have not merely been discussed but have actually come to pass. The assumption is that these initiatives and their implementation have in some measure flowed directly from Bilderberg meetings as cause and effect.

Bilderberger George McGhee (1912–2005), U.S. ambassador to Turkey (1952–1953) and West Germany (1963–1968), observed that "the Treaty of Rome, which brought the Common Market into being, was nurtured at Bilderberg meetings." The *European Common Market* was the precursor of the European Economic Community (EEC) and the European Union (EU). Another Bilderberg member, Amalgamated Bank chairman

Jack Sheinkman, was quoted (April 30, 1990) in *The Spotlight*, a controversial and now defunct U.S.-based right-wing weekly newspaper, as having observed that the "idea of a common European currency was discussed" at a Bilderberg meeting years before the Euro became a reality. He also claimed that the Bilderbergers "had a discussion about the U.S. establishing formal relations with China before Nixon actually did it."

DEFINITION

The **European Common Market,** also called the European Economic Community, was an association among Belgium, France, Germany, Italy, Luxembourg, and the Netherlands to create the economic integration of Europe, including a single market. Created in 1958, it was supplanted in 1993 by the European Economic Community (EEC) and the European Union (EU). The EEC was created in 1992 and quickly gave rise to the EU, which is an economic as well as political union among 27 European states.

In those Bilderberg discussions that were followed by implementation, NWO conspiracy theorists identify hints of the group's ultimate agenda. Having achieved to a significant degree the unification of European government (one-Europe government), the group wants to push toward one-world government. This would, of course, require the populace of the planet's nations to abandon such notions as patriotism and national sovereignty—a tall order.

In his *Rule by Secrecy*, Jim Marrs suggested that a 1998 Bilderberg meeting may have begun the process by influencing British Prime Minister Tony Blair not only to bring the UK into the EU, but also to "dissolve the House of Lords." Marrs claims that although the Lords were widely viewed as "unenlightened idlers," some "saw the wealthy, but patriotic, Lords as a bulwark against the erosion of English sovereignty by supporters of the 'New World Order.'"

INTEL

It is a distortion to claim that Prime Minister Tony Blair proposed the outright dissolution of the House of Lords; nevertheless, he did usher through Parliament in 1999 the House of Lords Act, which removed the hereditary peerage and made membership in the House of Lords subject to some combination of appointment and election. As of 2009, the proportion of appointed Lords to elected Lords has yet to be agreed upon, and Socialist members of Parliament have repeatedly voted against all proposals short of abolition of the Lords altogether.

Measuring the Motive

Objectively viewed, it seems a stretch to identify Blair's reform of the House of Lords, whether inspired by a Bilderberg discussion or not, as a deliberate step in a scheme to undermine and ultimately destroy British sovereignty. Nevertheless, many Bilderbergers consider themselves globalists either by philosophical orientation or financial necessity (a CEO of a multinational corporation must by definition be a globalist). Many are world political leaders or leaders in finance and industry (or have the ear of such leaders). It is reasonable to assume, therefore, that a wide range of globalist subjects, among them European unification, have been discussed at Bilderberg meetings. Given the lofty status of many members, it is also likely that matters discussed among them have become and will continue to become implemented matters of policy.

The ambition of the Bilderberg Group extends beyond Europe. If you take founding fathers Retinger, Healey, and Prince Bernhard at their word, the organization wishes to aid Europe and America to understand one another on a cultural level. Does this suggest a broader agenda—a desire to unite Europe and then join the United States to a united Europe? And, if so, how deep would such a union go? Would it require the nations of Europe and the United States to relinquish their sovereignty?

For most one-world conspiracy theorists, the answer is yes. Any step toward globalism is a step along a slippery slope to the ultimate submergence of nationhood. Moreover, the one-world government supplanting nationhood would not be a democratic commonwealth, but an oligarchy ruled by the rich, privileged, and powerful people who meet yearly in the world's posh resorts to design a future that will protect and continue to grow their wealth, privilege, and power.

The Secrecy Syndrome

The truth is that we can attribute practically any motive to the Bilderberg Group and can make practically any assumption about the organization's power to implement whatever its members advocate.

Why? Because the Bilderberg Group has cloaked itself in secrecy. The founders and everyone associated with the organization have justified the necessity of secrecy to ensure that all discussion will be free and uninhibited. Yet the very fact of secrecy promotes speculation about conspiracy.

We do not know what the Bilderbergers discuss, what they decide (or even if any decisions are actually made), and how (or even if) what happens in the sealed meetings manifests itself in the laws, actions, and policies of any nations. All we know is that very powerful people get together every year "to study common and divergent elements in the policies of the Western World." It is difficult to believe that the discussions are so much intellectual spitballing and that no action results.

And if secrecy promotes boundless speculation—practically *demands* the creation of conspiracy theories—it also raises disturbing questions among people who are not inclined to embrace conspiracy theories—those who do not object to the EU and other initiatives that develop positive global relationships and unite for common goals. Democracy is fundamentally transparent, and secrecy is fundamentally undemocratic. Each of us must therefore ask whether a nation can claim to be a democracy if its citizens are routinely unaware of what their political leaders are discussing—with their counterparts from other nations, as well as with financiers, industrialists, and others who control the bulk of the world's wealth.

The Least You Need to Know

- The Bilderberg Group was founded in 1954, ostensibly to improve Euro-American relations and to discuss various aspects of international affairs with European and American leaders (chiefly in politics, government, finance, and industry).
- Citing the globalist orientation of Bilderberg members, NWO conspiracy theorists believe the group has been instrumental in creating the European Union and is ultimately dedicated to submerging the nationhood of states into a one-world government.
- NWO conspiracy theorists believe that the Bilderberg group is a European extension of the American-based CFR, and that, in turn, the Trilateral Commission is an extension of both groups into the Asian sphere.
- At its inception, leaders in the U.S. intelligence and psychological warfare community were associated with the Bilderberg Group.
- Many conspiracy theorists regard the globalist banker and philanthropist David Rockefeller Sr. as the nexus formally linking the Council on Foreign Relations, the Bilderberg Group, and the Trilateral Commission.

The Trilateral Commission

In This Chapter

- Founding of the Trilateral Commission
- Relationship among the TC, CFR, and Bilderberg Group
- David Rockefeller, Zbigniew Brzezinski, and other founding members
- The Trilateralist agenda: official and alleged
- Trilateralists in the Carter, Reagan, George H. W. Bush, and Clinton administrations

For most New World Order (NWO) conspiracy believers, the Council on Foreign Relations (CFR) and the Bilderberg Group are the first two elements of the trinity at the heart of the movement toward one-world government. The third is the Trilateral Commission (TC), the first meeting of which was convened by David Rockefeller Sr. at Pocantico, the Rockefeller family's Hudson Valley compound, in July 1972.

Although the three organizations have overlapped chronologically and all are currently active, writers on the NWO conspiracy see their founding as evolutionary steps toward one-world government. The CFR is based in the United States, its membership restricted to American citizens or those intending to become American citizens. The Bilderberg Group was founded ostensibly to foster greater understanding between Europe and America, in effect extending the reach of the CFR into Europe. The TC was founded to extend the combined CFR-Bilderberg reach into Asia.

Birth of a Commission

According to a variety of accounts, the Trilateral Commission's (TC) origin was in a conversation between Zbigniew Brzezinski and David Rockefeller at a Bilderberg meeting. The two agreed that the reach of the CFR and Bilderberg Group should be extended to a group that would include Japan. Others trace the birth of the TC to the 1972 Chase Manhattan International Forums in London, Brussels, Montreal, and Paris. Rockefeller, the bank's chairman, proposed creating an International Commission of Peace and Prosperity, which would consist of delegates from Europe, the United States, and Japan. Only when the idea failed to strike sparks at the forums did Rockefeller take it to the Bilderberg.

Whereas attendees at the International Forums had been indifferent to the idea of the commission, the Bilderbergers enthusiastically embraced it. Both a Bilderberger and a member of CFR, Brzezinski in 1970 published *Between Two Ages: America's Role in the Technetronic Era.* This book argued that a fully coordinated policy among developed nations was vital to counteracting the global instability that was an inevitable byproduct of increasing economic inequality—especially between the developed and nondeveloped (Third World) nations.

From the perspective of NWO conspiracy writers, this was clearly a call for one-world government. Certainly the International Commission of Peace and Prosperity—about to be renamed the Trilateral Commission—harmonized perfectly with Brzezinski's *Between Two Ages* thesis. He was so enthusiastic about the idea that he left his professorship at Columbia University to serve as the first director of the TC.

Zbigniew Brzezinski

Zbigniew Kazimierz Brzezinski (b. 1928) was born in Warsaw, Poland, into the family of a diplomat. Fortunately for the Brzezinskis, Zbigniew was posted to Canada in 1938, the year before Germany's invasion of Poland started World War II. In Montreal, Brzezinski received a B.A. and M.A. from McGill University, and then earned a Ph.D. at Harvard in political science in 1953. Five years later, Brzezinski was naturalized as a U.S. citizen. He served from 1966 to 1968 on the Policy Planning Council of the Department of State and in 1973 collaborated with David Rockefeller to create the TC, becoming its director. He served Jimmy Carter as foreign policy advisor during his 1976 presidential campaign. After winning the White House, Carter appointed Brzezinski to national security adviser.

In 1988, Brzezinski crossed the aisle, endorsing fellow Trilateralist George H. W. Bush for president and serving during his campaign as co-chair of the Bush National Security Advisory Task Force. Although Brzezinski opposed the Gulf War of 1990 and 1991, he was also critical of many of the foreign policies of the next president, Bill Clinton, as well as George W. Bush. He was and remains a strong advocate for an expanded NATO role and continues as a member of the TC.

More on the Bilderberg-TC Connection

Even those who don't buy into the NWO conspiracy thesis must admit the extensive overlap in membership among the CFR, Bilderberg Group, and the TC. Of course, even having acknowledged this, one can still plausibly deny the suggestion of conspiracy. If all three groups are forums for discussing world affairs, they will obviously be populated by prominent persons interested in foreign affairs; hence the overlapping membership of the three groups. The people in these groups discuss the world's problems and their possible solutions, and some of the solutions these powerful and experienced people discuss may actually be put into effect. It only makes sense, and doesn't necessarily imply any causal relationships.

Even if this is taken as a satisfactory nonconspiratorial explanation of the connection among these groups, one intriguing question mark hangs over the relationship between the Bilderberg Group and the TC: Bilderbergers who have spoken out consistently deny that any binding decisions or concrete government policies are made or planned in Bilderberg meetings. Yet it seems quite clear that a Bilderberg meeting gave birth to the TC.

It is true that the TC is a private organization, funded exclusively by David Rockefeller, the Charles F. Kettering Foundation (which describes itself as a nonpartisan research foundation), and the Ford Foundation (established in 1936 by Henry Ford and his son Edsel "to receive and administer funds for scientific, educational and charitable purposes, all for the public welfare"). It therefore has no financial ties with any government. Nevertheless, Rockefeller believed the TC could "be of help to government by providing measured judgment." In short, it is not unreasonable to interpret the commission as a body created by the Bilderberg Group (which itself had been inspired, even spawned, by the CFR) to directly influence the creation of government policy.

The TC claims to be a nongovernmental organization (NGO), a legally constituted organization without the participation or representation of any government. Many NGOs receive government funds but maintain their NGO status by excluding government officials and representatives from membership. Because the TC accepts no government funding, it does not need to reject government representatives as members, albeit in a nonofficial capacity.

All Aboard

In addition to Rockefeller and Brzezinski, two of the world's highest-profile globalists, other founding members of the TC include the following:

- Robert R. Bowie, director of the Harvard Center for International Affairs and a member of the Foreign Policy Association. Founded in 1918 (three years before the CFR), it educates Americans on global issues to encourage them to "participate in the foreign policy process."

- George S. Franklin, a U.S. foreign-policy expert who (according to his *New York Times* obituary, March 7, 1996) "urged better relations with the Soviet Union and China long before such talk was fashionable," held "various Federal Government posts from 1940 to 1944," and worked for the CFR from 1945 to 1971 as its executive director and then on its board into the 1980s.

- Alan Greenspan, chairman of the Federal Reserve from 1987 to 2006.

- Marshall Hornblower, founding partner of the Washington law firm of Wilmer, Cutler, and Pickering. Clients included major U.S. corporations as well as such government agencies as the U.S. Railway Association (which oversees Conrail) and Comsat (the federally created provider of satellite telecommunications), as well as the Carnegie Institution of Washington.

- Max Kohnstamm, of the European Policy Centre (an independent, Brussels-based think tank committed to the success of the European Union and European integration).

- Henry D. Owen, Foreign Policy Studies Director of the Washington-based Brookings Institution think tank.

- Edwin Reischauer, a Harvard-based scholar of Japanese and East Asian history and culture, and U.S. ambassador to Japan from 1961 to 1966.

- Gerard C. Smith, a Rockefeller in-law and disarmament advocate who, beginning in 1969, helped negotiate the SALT I (Strategic Arms Limitation Treaty) between the United States and the Soviet Union, and became the first North American chairman of the TC.

- William Scranton, governor of Pennsylvania from 1963 to 1967 and U.S. ambassador to the United Nations during 1976 and 1977.

- Paul Volcker, Federal Reserve chairman from 1979 to 1987 and (as of 2009) chairman of President Obama's Economic Recovery Advisory Board.

By any measure, this was a distinguished group, all of whom share a globalist point of view. Most of them also have a strong connection to the government policy-making apparatus as well.

PASSWORDS

"The 'growing interdependence' that so impressed the founders of the Trilateral Commission in the early 1970s has deepened into 'globalization.' That interdependence also has ensured that the current financial crisis has been felt in every nation and region. It has fundamentally shaken confidence in the international system as a whole. The Commission sees in these unprecedented events a stronger need for shared thinking and leadership by the Trilateral countries, who (along with the principal international organizations) have been the primary anchors of the wider international system."

—"About the Organization," www.trilateral.org/about.htm

The Public Record

The first meeting at Pocantico, in July 1972, brought together 250 prominent scholars, government advisers, financiers, and business leaders. In October 1973, an Executive Committee met in Tokyo, and the TC was officially launched.

1975 Full Meeting, Kyoto

At the first full meeting, in Kyoto in 1975, a so-called "Trilateral Commission Task Force" issued a report sweepingly titled *An Outline for Remaking World Trade and Finance*. It did not use the phrase "global government," but did advocate "close Trilateral cooperation in keeping the peace, in managing the world economy, and in fostering economic development and in alleviating world poverty" for the purpose of improving "the chances of a smooth and peaceful evolution of the global system."

NWO conspiracy theorists widely regard "global system" as code for one-world government. And the fact is that other documents from 1975 added fuel to the conspiratorial fire by defining the TC's "overriding goal" as making "the world safe for interdependence." The phrase obviously echoed Woodrow Wilson's famous "make the world safe for democracy" justification for America joining a European alliance to fight World War I. As a TC document explained, this "interdependence" would be secured "by protecting the benefits which it [interdependence] provides for each country against external and internal threats which will constantly emerge from those willing to pay a price for more national autonomy."

The CFR and (in their few public statements) the Bilderbergers had already spoken of international cooperation and collaboration, but never of "interdependence." They certainly never directly opposed "interdependence" and "national autonomy." The TC seemed to be drawing a proverbial line in the sand: global interdependence would come—and *should* come—at the price of national autonomy. Indeed, the tone that emerged from Kyoto approached militancy in announcing that it would "frequently" become necessary to check "the intrusion of national government into the international exchange of both economic and noneconomic goods."

1976 Plenary Meeting of Regional Groups, Kyoto

The May 1976 meeting of all the TC regional groups was attended by President Jimmy Carter. It solidified a structure consisting of 300 to 350 "private citizens"—corporate CEOs, politicians, academics, labor leaders, and representatives of philanthropic nonprofits—not just from Europe, the United States, and Japan, but representing Europe, all North America, and the Asia/Pacific region. The official TC magazine, the *Trialogue*, was also launched at the 1976 meeting.

Present Day

Today, the TC includes members from the United States, Canada, Mexico, Austria, Belgium, Cyprus, Czech Republic, Denmark, Estonia, Finland, France, Germany, Greece, Hungary, Ireland, Italy, the Netherlands, Norway, Poland, Portugal, Romania, Russia, Slovenia, Spain, Sweden, Turkey, the United Kingdom, Japan, South Korea, Australia, New Zealand, Indonesia, Malaysia, Philippines, Singapore, Thailand, China, and Taiwan.

The leadership of the TC is by any measure distinguished.

Joseph S. Nye Jr., who is chairman of the organization's North American Group, is University Distinguished Service Professor at Harvard University and from 1995 to 2004 served as dean of the Harvard Kennedy School. Before this, he was U.S. assistant secretary of defense for international security affairs and was awarded two Distinguished Service medals. Nye also chaired the National Intelligence Council. He originally joined the Harvard faculty in 1964, serving as director of the Center for International Affairs and associate dean of arts and sciences. From 1977 to 1979, he was deputy to the undersecretary of state for security assistance, science, and technology and chaired the National Security Council Group on Nonproliferation of Nuclear Weapons.

The European Group is chaired by Peter Sutherland, who became chairman of the board of Goldman Sachs International in 1995 and, beginning in 1997, of BP (British Petroleum) as well. In 2008, he was appointed chairman of the London School of Economics and is currently UN special representative for migration and development. Sutherland was the founding director-general of the World Trade Organization, having previously served as director-general of GATT. Before this, he was chairman of Allied Irish Banks from 1989 to 1993 and chairman of the Board of Governors of the European Institute of Public Administration (Maastricht) from 1991 to 1996.

The Pacific Asian Group's chairman, Yotaro Kobayashi, serves as chief corporate advisor of Fuji Xerox Co., Ltd. (Tokyo), of which he was formerly chairman of the board of directors. He is also a member of the board of directors of Callaway Golf Company, Nippon Telegraph and Telephone Corporation (NTT), American Productivity & Quality Center, and Sony Corporation, and is chairman of the International University of Japan. Kobayashi received a B.A. in economics from Keio University and an MBA from the University of Pennsylvania's Wharton School of Finance and Commerce. He joined Fuji Xerox in 1963, becoming executive vice president in 1976, president and CEO in 1978, and chairman and CEO in 1992. He served as chairman of the board from 1999 and became chief corporate advisor in April 2006.

North American Deputy Chairman Allan E. Gotlieb is senior adviser of Bennett Jones LLP, Toronto, Ontario; Chairman of Sotheby's, Canada; and the former Canadian ambassador to the United States. Lorenzo Zambrano, also a North American Deputy Chairman, is chairman of the board and chief executive officer of CEMEX in Mexico. Herve de Carmoy, European Deputy Chairman, is the chairman of ETAM, Paris; honorary chairman of Banque Industrielle et Mobilière

Privée, Paris; and former chief executive of the Société Générale de Belgique. Andrzej Olechowski, also European Deputy Chairman, founded the Civic Platform organization and was formerly Chairman of Bank Handlowy; he served the Polish government as minister of foreign affairs and of finance. Han Sung-Joo, Pacific Asian Deputy Chairman, chairs the Asian Institute for Policy Studies and is the former president of Korea University, Seoul, as well as former Korean minister for foreign affairs and former Korean ambassador to the United States. His fellow Pacific Asian Deputy Chairman, Shijuro Ogata, was formerly the deputy governor of the Japan Development Bank and has served as deputy governor for international relations for the Bank of Japan.

The TC claims as its "major project work" the creation of reports, known as "Triangle Papers," by "teams of authors from our three regions working together for a year or so." The reports are made to the TC, which takes no formal positions on them, but issues them for publication. Recent Triangle Report titles have included *Engaging Iran and Building Peace in the Persian Gulf Region* (2008); *Energy Security and Climate Change* (2007); *Engaging with Russia: The Next Phase* (2006); *The New Challenges to International, National, and Human Security Policy* (2004); *The "Democracy Deficit" in the Global Economy: Enhancing the Legitimacy and Accountability of Global Institutions* (2003); and *Addressing the New International Terrorism: Prevention, Intervention, and Multilateral Cooperation* (2002).

The TC Conspiracy Theory

Despite the official claim that the TC's major work consists of study and reports, the organization has sent mixed messages in the unapologetically globalist pronouncements of David Rockefeller Sr. and in its stated goal of promoting global interdependence at the cost of suppressing national autonomy.

Moreover, although the TC is less secretive than the Bilderberg Group (like the CFR, it is difficult to call the TC a secret society), its very name suggests something more than a mere study group. *Trilateral Commission* sounds like an official government agency—and although it is not, the TC certainly has the ear of many U.S. government officials, up to and including the president of the United States.

Four Goals

Most NWO conspiracy theorists agree that the TC has four major objectives:

1. To create a world monetary system.

2. To use U.S. funds to support and empower Third World ("have-not") nations.

3. To increase trade with the communists (primarily China).

4. To exploit the global energy crisis to consolidate more centralized international control of resources and energy-related policy.

Theorists claim that the TC has succeeded in furthering this agenda, and typically cite the following:

1. The emergence of the European Community and the North American Free Trade Agreement (NAFTA).

2. U.S. and other First World subsidies of Third World nations.

3. U.S. technological support of Soviet and Chinese industry, which opened up trade and made China a world economic superpower that threatens to eclipse the United States.

4. The emergence of a series of energy crises, especially centered on Middle Eastern oil.

Criticism from the Right ...

In his 1979 memoir, *With No Apologies*, Arizona senator and conservative icon Barry Goldwater put the conspiratorial interpretation concisely: "In my view, the Trilateral Commission represents a skillful, coordinated effort to seize control and consolidate the four centers of power: political, monetary, intellectual, and ecclesiastical."

Goldwater conceded, "All this is to be done in the interest of creating a more peaceful, more productive world community," but he continued: "What the Trilateralists truly intend is the creation of a worldwide economic power superior to the political governments of the nation-states involved." Most provocatively, Goldwater defined the means by which this global superiority was to be attained: "They believe the abundant materialism they propose to create will overwhelm existing differences."

In other words, instead of positing the Wilsonian goal of making the world safe for democracy, the Trilateralists (in Goldwater's analysis) propose to make the world safe for profit. Their vision of globalism offers such material benefits that the peoples of the world will throw over old ideas of national identity and sovereignty to reap the economic benefits of globalism. As for the Trilateralists themselves, "As managers and creators of the system they will rule the future."

... and from the Left ...

Those whose political orientation tends toward left-leaning liberalism typically embrace globalist initiatives, whereas many right-leaning conservatives or libertarians not only oppose them but see in such initiatives the seeds or even the fruits of conspiracy.

The TC is rare among globalist organizations in that it has drawn fire from the conservative right as well as the liberal left. Noam Chomsky, whose credentials as a left-wing political dissident are long established, included in his 1981 collection of political essays, *Radical Priorities*, "The Carter Administration: Myth and Reality." In this piece, Chomsky identified as "perhaps the most striking feature of the [Carter] Administration" the "role played in it by the Trilateral Commission."

Chomsky observed that "all of the top positions in the government—the office of President, Vice-President, Secretary of State, Defense, and Treasury—are held by members of the Trilateral Commission, and the National Security Advisor [Brzezinski] was its director." Additionally, Chomsky wrote, "Many lesser officials also came from this group. It is rare for such an easily identified private group to play such a prominent role in an American Administration." Like the right-wing critics, the leftist Chomsky objected to the influence of an insular elite, who seemed to work in an opaque and secretive environment.

... as Well as the Center

Chomsky asserted that the "mass media had little to say about" the preponderance of Trilateralists in the Carter administration. Actually, the *Washington Post, U.S. News and World Report*, and other mainstream media outlets took note of the extraordinary presence of TC members in the Carter administration. *U.S. News* also noted that not only Carter Democrats but many prominent Republicans were TC members. These include Nixon and Ford's Secretary of State Henry Kissinger and four other Nixon-Ford cabinet members, including Caspar Weinberger, secretary of health, education, and welfare under Nixon and Ford and secretary of defense under Ronald Reagan.

There were more. As of 1971, George H. W. Bush, former CIA director and future president, was identified as a Trilateralist, as was William Cohen, who would become President Clinton's secretary of defense. President Carter appointed Trilateralist, CFR member, and Bilderberger Paul Volcker to chair the Federal Reserve, who would be replaced on his retirement in 1987 by Alan Greenspan, likewise a Trilateralist (as well as a CFR member and Bilderberger).

The Reagan Revolution?

Those who attempt to paint the political landscape exclusively in the primary colors of blue and red would surely be disturbed by the NWO conspiracy theorists' take on the rise of another icon of Republican conservatism, Ronald Reagan.

During his 1980 bid for the Republican presidential nomination, Reagan attacked the Trilateralist influence operating in the Carter White House and also criticized his chief Republican rival, George H. W. Bush, pointing out that he was not only a Trilateralist but also a member of the CFR. At one point, candidate Reagan even promised voters that Bush would earn no position in his White House.

Yet when delegates to the Republican National Convention began talking of fielding a "dream ticket" consisting of Reagan for president and, as vice president, the popular Gerald Ford (who became president in 1974 upon the Watergate-driven resignation of Richard Nixon), Reagan turned a stunning about-face. Understandably opposed to sharing power with a former president, Reagan suddenly recommended that the convention nominate as his running mate none other than George H. W. Bush. From that point forward, candidate Reagan never again criticized (or even mentioned) the TC—or, for that matter, the CFR.

Ronald Reagan, of course, defeated Carter and his Trilateralist-laden administration, but NWO conspiracy writer Jim Marrs points out that of the 59 members of the Reagan presidential transition team, 28 had membership in the CFR, 10 were Bilderbergers, and at least 10 were Trilateralists. In addition to Caspar Weinberger, already mentioned as a Trilateralist, whom Reagan appointed as his secretary of defense, the new president's secretary of state, Alexander Haig, and his treasury secretary, Donald Regan, were TC members. Also members were Reagan's White House chief of staff, James A. Baker III, and, of course, his vice president. Lou Cannon of *The Washington Post* (March 18, 1981) took notice in an article titled "The Trilateralists Are Coming, The Trilateralists Are Coming":

> *Remember those dreaded three-sided Trilateralists, the international conspirators headed by David Rockefeller who were going to take over the world? Jimmy Carter*

was one. George Bush used to be one, too, and it cost him dearly in his campaign last year against Ronald Reagan …. Well, guess who's coming to the White House. Guess who invited them …. The Trilateralists are coming. President Reagan has asked them to come …. The Trilateralists have landed and the conspiracy theorists will no doubt be close behind.

The election of Ronald Reagan was widely seen as a rejection of the globalism of Jimmy Carter. Yet, as many of the right, left, and center observed, one Trilateralist White House replaced another. Conspiracy writers see this as clear evidence that the NWO not only transcends but is superior to the opposed political parties and the opposed political philosophies they supposedly represent. The NWO in the form of the TC has infiltrated the U.S. government and intends to stay, regardless of who is elected.

INTEL

Passed in 1799, the Logan Act states: "Any citizen of the United States, wherever he may be, who, without authority of the United States, directly or indirectly commences or carries on any correspondence or intercourse with any foreign government or any officer or agent thereof, with intent to influence the measures or conduct of any foreign government or of any officer or agent thereof, in relation to any disputes or controversies with the United States, or to defeat the measures of the United States, shall be fined under this title or imprisoned not more than three years, or both."

Critics of the TC claim that at least some members of the organization have been in violation of the act; however, whereas TC critics cite the reference to unauthorized "correspondence or intercourse," TC defenders point out that the restriction specifically applies to the intent to exert influence "in relation to any disputes or controversies with the United States, or to defeat the measures of the United States" and assert that TC members do nothing of the kind.

Some conspiracy theorists have linked the TC to any number of historical secret societies, especially the Illuminati (see Chapter 13), but Goldwater, in his *With No Apologies*, hammered home his less romantic theory, arguing that the TC, "David Rockefeller's newest international cabal," had only one overriding purpose: "to be the vehicle for multinational consolidation of the commercial and banking interests." He and his family had a massive stake—"by seizing control of the political government of the United States."

The Least You Need to Know

- The Trilateral Commission was an outgrowth of the Bilderberg Group and was founded chiefly by David Rockefeller and Zbigniew Brzezinski, both Bilderbergers and globalists.
- NWO conspiracy theorists assert that the TC was founded purposely to extend the reach of the Bilderberg Group into Asia, just as the Bilderberg Group had been founded to extend the reach of the U.S.-based CFR into Europe.
- The official Trilateralist agenda is to promote international understanding, peace, and productivity through expert studies of global issues and high-level discussion thereof.
- Conspiracy theorists assert that the real TC agenda is to create a global economic power superior to the governments of the world's individual nation-states, citing the preponderance of Trilateralists throughout the U.S. government and others.

Around the Round Table

In This Chapter

- Cecil Rhodes's imperialist globalism
- From Round Table to Chatham House
- The controversial Chatham House Rule
- Chatham House: a return to imperial globalism?
- The questionable relevance of Chatham House in the NWO

From the point of view of most American New World Order (NWO) conspiracy theorists, the Council on Foreign Relations (CFR), the Bilderberg Group, and the Trilateral Commission (TC) are, taken together, the incubators of a covert one-world government movement. Go wider than the American focus, however, and you must take in Chatham House—formerly known as the Royal Institute of International Affairs—and the Round Table movement that preceded it. It may have grown out of the Society of the Elect, a genuine secret society that was the brainchild of one of the most remarkable, powerful, and mysterious men of the late nineteenth century.

Cecil Rhodes made a fortune in diamonds and used it to advance the British Empire in Africa "from the Cape to Cairo." He did this not entirely as a selfless patriot, but with the intention of putting himself and his principal investors, the first of whom was N. M. Rothschild and Sons, at the center of it all. When those who believe in an NWO conspiracy step back for a view beyond America and the founding of the CFR in 1921, they see Cecil Rhodes as the late nineteenth-century leader of the globalist march toward a one-world government.

The Philosopher Magnate

In the December 10, 1892, issue of the British humor magazine *Punch*, Edward Linley Sambourne published one of his most famous cartoons. Entitled "The Rhodes Colossus," it caricatured Cecil Rhodes in a bush get-up that suggested the British army field uniform of the era, rifle slung on his right shoulder, one booted foot planted in Cairo, the other on the Cape. Bestriding the entire African continent, he held aloft a single wire connecting the north to the south, symbolic of the Cape Town-to-Cairo telegraph and rail line he proposed to build. Sambourne pictured Rhodes as the British people and much of the world thought of him: bringer of Civilization to dark places; builder of Empire; and ruthless man who cared not where his heavy boots landed as he scratched out of the African earth an unimaginable fortune in diamonds and oil.

Colossus with Asthma

The circumstances of Rhodes's birth and upbringing made him a most unlikely Colossus, magnate, and builder of empire. He was born in 1853 at Bishops Stortford, in Hertfordshire, England. He was the fifth son of an Anglican vicar whose chief claim to noble achievement was the merciful brevity of his sermons, none of which (he claimed) ever exceeded 10 minutes in length. Unlike his strapping brothers, Cecil was severely asthmatic and became so sickly that he had to be withdrawn from grammar school. His parents decided to get him out of Hertfordshire's cold, wet climate and sent him to live with his brother Herbert, who owned a cotton farm in arid Natal, South Africa.

Rhodes branched out from the farm to the diamond fields in 1871, taking a break in 1873 to return to England and Oriel College, Oxford. He stayed for only a single term before returning to the farm and the diamonds of South Africa for three years, then came back to Oxford in 1876 for a second term. He continued to alternate between Africa and Oxford for eight years, until he earned his degree.

Formative Influences

At Oxford, Rhodes had three life-changing encounters. The first was his transformative contact with John Ruskin. If Rhodes's delicate health made him an unlikely candidate for empire builder, Ruskin's reputation as an aesthetician, an art critic, an architectural historian of exquisite sensibilities, and as one of the great Victorian

masters of English prose hardly seemed to qualify him as an instigator of revolutionary social change. For Rhodes, however, he was just such an instigator.

Ruskin combined an intense interest in modern utopian and socialist thought with a
passion for Plato, whose *Republic* posited an ideal society founded not in democracy
but in a top-down government flowing from an elite ruling class trained to achieve
the highest excellence. As Rhodes shuttled between South Africa and Oxford, he
came to revere Ruskin as his mentor.

Rhodes's second encounter was with the majesty of Oxford itself, which he quickly
concluded produced the best-educated men (other than scientists) in the world. This
would lead him to bequeath a fortune to endow the coveted Rhodes Scholarships.

INTEL

The Rhodes Scholarships were endowed with funds Rhodes bequeathed in the
last of several wills he drew up before he died in 1902. As his will provided,
the scholarships were intended to fund study at Oxford for students from the
British colonies, the United States, and Germany. In the words of the will, "a
good understanding between England, Germany, and the United States of
America will secure the peace of the world."

Conspiracy theorists say that Rhodes intended his scholarships to create an
Anglo-centric, imperialist intellectual elite throughout the British colonies, the
United States, and Germany.

These first two encounters, with Ruskin's Platonic utopianism and the so-called
"Oxford system," persuaded Rhodes of the supremacy of English civilization. It
helped inspire in him the ambition to sow the seeds of British imperialism throughout Africa.

The third encounter was with Freemasonry (see Chapter 15). Rhodes became a
Freemason in Oxford's Apollo University Lodge and made powerful connections
through it. He remained a Mason for the rest of his life.

A Diamond Empire

As he divided his time between Oxford and Africa, Rhodes combined a modest loan
from his aunt with financing from the Rothschild family of bankers and entrepre-
neurs to buy diamond mining operations throughout the Kimberley region. In 1880,
he and a business partner founded the De Beers Mining Company and within eight
years most of the Kimberley mines were consolidated under the De Beers banner.

In 1889, Rhodes hammered out a partnership with the powerful London-based Diamond Syndicate, with whom he colluded to exert absolute control over the world diamond supply and raise and maintain the highest possible prices. This monopoly became the main source of a fabulous fortune, which eventually encompassed South African oil, South African gold, and a massive fruit export business in addition to diamonds.

Rhodes's Round Tables

Although he was a Freemason, Rhodes believed "the Craft" would never reach anything like its true potential, at least not in England. In the right hands, he thought, such an organization could transform the world, and he therefore designed a quasi-secret society of his own. It would be known as the Round Tables. Rhodes hoped that it would bring the entire planet into the orbit of English civilization and British imperial government.

As we will learn in Chapter 8, believers in the NWO conspiracy identify the Rothschilds (along with the Morgans and Rockefellers) as a financial dynasty that has bankrolled a number of secret societies dedicated to advancing one-world government schemes while also growing and protecting their own dynastic wealth and power.

Researcher Jim Marrs has drawn on *Conspirators' Hierarchy,* an obscure book by John Coleman, a former British intelligence officer, for evidence that Rhodes acted as an agent for the Rothschilds in South Africa and used Rothschild money to found the first Round Table group in South Africa. It is impossible to determine if this is true because the origin of the Round Table movement is shrouded in obscurity.

Origin

Some students of secret societies believe that Rhodes first founded a group called the Society of the Elect, from which the Round Tables subsequently developed. Others believe that the Round Tables came first, were structurally divided into an inner and an outer circle, and that the inner circle was known as the Society (or Circle) of the Elect (or Initiates) and the outer as the Association of Helpers.

Whether or not the Round Table idea was preceded by the Society of the Elect, it was itself an association of *the elect*—the social, financial, and intellectual elite, the bearers of the best in civilization. Rhodes saw the members as the equivalent of the legendary King Arthur's knights, an inner circle of supermen gathered in perfect equality with one another around the famed Round Table.

DEFINITION

The elect is a term used by Calvinist Christians (including, for example, the Puritans) to identify those marked for salvation and deliverance into Heaven versus those who are doomed by Original Sin to suffer the torments of Hell. As an Anglican vicar's son, Rhodes must have been familiar with the theological implications of the term, which was intended to distinguish members of his secret society as blessed above all common men.

Early Growth

John Coleman wrote that the Round Tables (they were soon established in many countries) used wealth derived from diamonds, gold, and other Rhodes-Rothschild South African enterprises to send influential men across the globe for the purpose of assuming "control of fiscal and monetary policies and political leadership in all countries where they operated."

Even the most ardent of NWO conspiracy theorists must regard Coleman's interpretation with skepticism; however, it is a fact that, with the Round Table idea, Rhodes instigated a movement that outlived his own rather brief span on Earth. He died in 1902 at the age of 49, having never shaken the ill health that perpetually shadowed him.

Building on Rhodes's prototype, and funded in some measure by the Rhodes trust, the so-called "Round Table movement" was established in 1909 as a confederation of organizations dedicated to promoting a closer union between Britain and its self-governing colonies. Conspiracy writers interpret "closer union" as code for an agenda intended to return Britain's self-governing colonies—in 1909, South Africa, Canada, Australia, New Zealand, and India—to something like the full colonial status that existed in the heyday of the British Empire.

After Rhodes: The Round Table Movement

The meeting that created the Round Table movement was convened at Plas Newydd, the Welsh estate of Lord Anglesey, during September 4 to 6, 1909. It was presided over by Lord Milner and Lionel Curtis.

Alfred Milner, 1st Viscount Milner (1854–1925), was a British colonial administrator in South Africa, who gathered about himself a group of British colonial civil servants that became known as "Milner's Kindergarten." One of the members of the Kindergarten was Lionel Curtis (1872–1955), who, like Milner, advocated transforming the British Empire as it existed at the beginning of the twentieth century into an "Imperial Federation." London could then maintain central control over a realm that was rapidly becoming self-governing. By the end of his life at the middle of the twentieth century, Curtis was actively advocating not merely a British Imperial Federation, but some form of world state.

The Movement Spreads

What John Coleman characterized as a conspiracy intended to spread across the globe and gain control of national governments seems never to have gotten beyond a set of discussion and lobbying groups in many of the world's major cities.

It is true that the activities of these groups were centrally coordinated from London headquarters, and, in 1910, those headquarters began publishing *The Round Table Journal: A Quarterly Review of the Politics of the British Empire*. The editor was Lord Milner, and the periodical was staffed and largely written by alumni of his Kindergarten. The chief purpose of the journal was to impose doctrinal unity on the far-flung Round Table groups. Yet it is difficult to trace any concrete achievement, program, policy, or law back to the Round Tables.

INTEL

The relationship between the three British government–sponsored Round Table Conferences that took place in London during 1930 to 1932 and the Round Table movement is uncertain. The conferences were intended to address Indian agitation for home rule or outright independence by formulating a transition from colonial to dominion status. This effort met so much resistance that the organizers of the conferences never even completed the reports of their activities. If these conferences were indeed an outgrowth of the movement Rhodes had started, it would suggest a dead end.

As for *The Round Table Journal,* it is still published, although it received a new subtitle after World War II—*A Quarterly Review of British Commonwealth Affairs*—a notably nonconspiratorial concession to the actual state of the postwar world.

By 1915, there were active Round Table groups in Britain, South Africa, Canada, Australia, New Zealand, India, and the United States. The most famous member of the American group was Walter Lippmann (1889–1974), a high-level political adviser, an academically respected political philosopher, and a popular political journalist.

Curtis and Lippmann

By the conclusion of the Paris Peace Conference that ended World War I, Curtis seemed to have outgrown the Round Table, or perhaps concluded that the rush of international events had outrun an organization rooted in Rhodes's quaint Arthurian metaphor. In June 1920, with Robert Cecil, 1st Viscount Cecil of Chelwood, undersecretary of state for foreign affairs during most of World War I, Curtis founded the Royal Institute of International Affairs (counterpart of the American CFR). He took many of the Round Table members with him.

SECRET LIVES

Robert Cecil, 1st Viscount Cecil of Chelwood (1864–1958), served as British undersecretary of state for foreign affairs from 1915 to 1919. In September 1916, he sent a circular through the government in which he made several proposals for mechanisms by which future wars might be avoided. Cecil claimed that this was the beginning of "British official advocacy of the League of Nations," and, after the war, he became a principal architect of the League. For this work, he was awarded the Nobel Peace Prize in 1937. When the League was finally extinguished after World War II, however, Cecil ended his last speech as an official of that body, "The League is dead; long live the United Nations!"

The idea for the institute originated in meetings with the American delegates to the Paris Peace Conference (see Chapter 2). The founding of the British organization, however, preceded the creation of its American counterpart by a year.

It was no surprise that the British were ahead of the Americans, because Cecil was on the cutting edge of globalism. In September 1916, when Europe was focused on the ongoing war, Cecil sent a circular through the British government with a list of proposals for avoiding future wars. Cecil always proudly claimed that this was the document that kindled official British advocacy of the League of Nations—the first major globalist organization of the twentieth century and a precursor to the United Nations.

The degree to which Cecil sought to merge national identities into a global identity may be gauged by his passionate advocacy of *Esperanto*, an attempt to disseminate a universal tongue, as the official language of the proposed league.

DEFINITION

Esperanto is the most widely spoken "constructed international auxiliary language," an invented tongue intended to serve as a universal language. It was developed in the late 1870s and early 1880s by Dr. Ludovic Lazarus Zamenhof, who wrote under the name Doktoro Esperanto ("One Who Hopes").

Among President Woodrow Wilson's handpicked members of the study group known as The Inquiry and subsequently renamed the American Commission to Negotiate Peace at the Paris Peace Conference (see Chapter 2) was Walter Lippmann (1889–1974). Born and raised in New York, he entered Harvard when he was only 17 and graduated in just three years with a degree in philosophy and languages. Highly successful and respected in academic circles, Lippmann could have carved out a university career, which might have led, as Woodrow Wilson's did, to political office. Instead, he became primarily a journalist, thoughtfully defining *journalism* as an intelligent conduit between policymakers and the public.

In 1913, with fellow political intellectuals Herbert Croly and Walter Weyl, Lippmann founded *The New Republic* magazine. Its name deliberately echoed *The Republic* of Plato, the very philosopher whose vision of an ideal government and society had inspired Cecil Rhodes. The purpose of Lippmann's magazine was to educate—to mold—public opinion and thereby compel policymakers to hold themselves accountable to the people they serve.

Through *The New Republic* and other journalistic projects, Lippmann sought to facilitate democracy. His critics, however, accused him of skewing democracy toward his own liberal, globalist perspective by creating what he called "public opinion" in his own image. No matter—he became so influential so quickly that Woodrow Wilson enlisted him as an adviser, a member of The Inquiry, and a source for his famous Fourteen Points. Wilson's Fourteen Points were the substance of a presidential address to Congress (January 8, 1918) in which Wilson set forth the goals of victory in the world war, among them the creation of the League of Nations.

PASSWORDS

"What each man does is based not on direct and certain knowledge, but on pictures made by himself or given to him .... The way in which the world is imagined determines at any particular moment what men will do."

—Walter Lippmann, *Public Opinion* (1922)

At the Paris Peace Conference, Lippmann became one the prime figures in meetings with Curtis, Cecil, and the other Round Tablers who were in the process of creating Chatham House. Lippmann not only joined the Chatham House group when it was founded, but served as the link between it and the CFR (of which he was also a founding member). Thus Lippmann became the highest-profile American political intellectual in the great wave of globalism that followed World War I.

Chatham House

Chatham House occupies the eighteenth-century building of that name in St. James's Square in London's exclusive St. James's district of the City of Westminster. It was the home of three British prime ministers, beginning with the 1st Earl of Chatham, William Pitt the Elder (1708–1778), and is at the heart of the former British empire. The prime location of the organization's headquarters, its early association with bankers Paul M. Warburg (CFR's first director and a founding advocate of the Federal Reserve System) and Bernard Baruch (the "Lone Wolf of Wall Street" and an influential presidential adviser), its ties to the legacy of Cecil Rhodes, and its ongoing support by major banks and corporations—not to mention its royal patronage—all suggest the same kind of "establishment elite" exclusivity that characterizes the CFR, the Bilderberg Group, and the TC. However, membership in Chatham House is open to anyone—although not all meetings are.

Chatham House Rule

Today, Chatham House is probably best known for having originated the Chatham House Rule. It is put forth in the organization's by-laws:

> *When a meeting, or part thereof, is held under the Chatham House Rule, participants are free to use the information received, but neither the identity nor the affiliation of the speaker(s), nor that of any other participant, may be revealed.*

The CFR and Bilderberg Group have similar rules, as do many other organizations, some doubtless inspired by the Chatham House precedent. In addition, Chatham House discourages publishing any list of meeting attendees. Like the CFR and Bilderberg Group, Chatham House justifies the secrecy as a measure that "allows people to speak as individuals, and to express views that may not be those of their organizations"; the Chatham House Rule "therefore … encourages free discussion. People usually feel more relaxed if they don't have to worry about their reputation or the implications if they are publicly quoted."

Critics, however, are quick to pounce on the secrecy, especially in an organization that brings together government policymakers, financiers, industrialists, and other representatives of special interests.

Influence of Chatham House

In 2009, the CFR's *Foreign Policy* magazine named Chatham House the most important political think tank outside of the United States. Both admirers and critics of the organization claim that much of British foreign policy is formulated within the organization. The organization itself claims only to be a "world-leading source of independent analysis, informed debate and influential ideas on how to build a prosperous and secure world for all."

Today, NWO theorists tend to criticize Chatham House less as a center of globalist thought than as an organization dedicated to resurrecting some aspects of the old British Empire. To the extent that Chatham House members seek one-world government, critics point out that they seem to do so with the object of putting Great Britain at its controlling center. Far from joining hands with the United States, for example, recent Chatham House research reports and briefing papers have criticized UK foreign policy for its subordination to that of the United States, especially in regard to combating terrorism. A widely read 2005 report, *Security and Terrorism in the UK*, called Great Britain a mere "passenger" in the United States' war on terror. A 2006 briefing paper retrospectively blasted the administration of former Prime Minister Tony Blair for tying the United Kingdom to the United States instead of Europe.

Place in NWO Conspiracy Theory

Conspiracy writers are more interested in the ancestry of Chatham House, its origin in the self-centered and exploitive imperialism of Cecil Rhodes and his financial associates (especially the Rothschilds), its incubation in the Round Tables, and its founding connection to the CFR, than they are in the present-day organization. The lingering aura of a connection with the lost cause of British Empire has prompted the most widely read conspiracy writers, such as Jim Marrs and Daniel Estulin, to pay relatively little attention to Chatham House. However, it continues to loom in the background of many accounts of the one-world government movement, if only because it's a gathering place of the elite and powerful whose words are cloaked in the secrecy of the Chatham House Rule.

The Least You Need to Know

- Diamond magnate Cecil Rhodes attempted to act on an imperialist vision of Great Britain as the superior civilization that should be at the controlling center of an expanded empire.
- Rhodes laid the foundation of a Round Table movement in which men of superior intellect, ability, and wealth would decide the fate of the British Empire and, ultimately, the world.
- Years after Rhodes's death, the Round Table movement spread to many of the world's major cities and, in the aftermath of World War I, gave rise to the Royal Institute of International Affairs, or Chatham House, associated with and founded a year before the U.S.-based CFR.
- Today, Chatham House claims to be a major policy think tank, but, unlike the CFR and the Bilderberg Group, its membership is open to anyone interested in international affairs. However, its controversial Chatham House Rule imposes a layer of secrecy on everything that is discussed during meetings.

The United Nations

In This Chapter

- War drives the creation of the United Nations
- The Dumbarton Oaks Conference
- Overcoming the "sovereignty fetish"
- The CFR's role in creating the United Nations
- The United Nations System as a global government

The men who founded the Council on Foreign Relations (CFR; see Chapter 2) and Chatham House (see Chapter 5) in 1921 and 1920, respectively, were the forefront of the creation of the League of Nations in 1919, following World War I. Although U.S. President Woodrow Wilson was a driving force behind the league, whose handpicked advisers were the future members of the CFR, the Republican-controlled U.S. Senate refused to ratify American membership in the world body. The League of Nations was thereafter doomed to impotence. It was powerless, certainly, to stop the aggression that led to World War II just 20 years after the Treaty of Versailles.

Planning for the League of Nations began, mainly in Britain, during World War I. In 1939, planning began within the U.S. Department of State for something to replace the ineffectual League of Nations. World War II had just started, with Germany's invasion of Poland in September, but more than two years would pass before the United States entered the war. It was President Franklin D. Roosevelt who first used the phrase "united nations" to describe the countries allied against the Axis (Germany, Italy, and Japan). The term was put into writing in the "Declaration by the United Nations," which was signed on January 1, 1942, by 26 nations dedicated to the defeat of the Axis.

By the time World War II was drawing to a close in 1945, "United Nations" had become not only a familiar phrase, but a highly positive label for an alliance dedicated to saving the world from a manifest evil. Selling the American people on the idea of a new world organization called the United Nations was far easier than persuading them to join a League of Nations.

At the Heart: War

As with the League of Nations, the United Nations (UN) was promoted to the world as a means of avoiding future catastrophic wars. However, the Preamble to the Covenant of the League of Nations put the objective of promoting "international cooperation" before that of achieving "international peace and security." The Preamble to the United Nations Charter not only gave top billing to the avoidance of war, but put its objective far more dramatically: "to save succeeding generations from the scourge of war, which twice in our lifetime has brought untold sorrow to mankind."

Who could argue with this objective, especially when it was expressed in this manner?

NWO conspiracy theorists can and do argue. They take the position that war and the threat of war—especially civilization-destroying thermonuclear war—is the very reason for the existence of the UN. Only to avoid the possibility of global annihilation would people willingly subordinate patriotism, national identity, and nationhood itself to an idea of one-world government. Peace did not "sell" the UN to America and the world. War and the threat of war did. For conspiracy theorists, the implication is that the UN's real mission is to perpetuate war in order to keep national leaders afraid of war and thereby willing to subordinate sovereignty to membership in the globalist UN.

This being the case, it follows that war had long been an instrument of conspiracies and movements toward one-world government (see Part 3).

 PASSWORDS

"… the New World Order will require an Army, and it will be formed under the UN banner."

—Daniel Estulin, *The True Story of the Bilderberg Group,* 2009

The United Nations' Genesis

What conspiracy theorists call the "mainstream" view of the UN depicts it as a noble and enlightened attempt to avoid repeating the tragic errors of the Treaty of Versailles. It was also supposed to bring into being something better than the feckless League of Nations, which had failed to "unite" the world in peace. Those who take a different view, however, see the UN as a renewed attempt at what the League of Nations intended to create: the firm foundation of a one-world government.

They point to the language of the Preamble to the UN Charter. Whereas the Preamble to the Covenant of the League of Nations began with the traditional language of international treaties, referring to "the High Contracting Parties"—that is, the signatory nations—the UN Charter *begins* by negating individual nations or nationalities: "We the peoples of the United Nations ...." The words unmistakably echo the Preamble to the U.S. Constitution—"We the people of the United States ...." It seems to conflate the idea of nation with world-nation, supplanting the first with the second. The Preamble goes on to use phrases such as "unite our strength," "common interest," and the employment of "international machinery." That machinery is to be used "for the promotion of the economic and social advancement of all peoples"—not governments, not sovereignties, not nations.

SECRET LIVES

The Preamble to the Charter of the United Nations was largely the work of Archibald MacLeish (1892–1982), an American poet who received the Pulitzer Prize three times. In 1939, President Franklin D. Roosevelt appointed MacLeish Librarian of Congress, where he served for five years through most of World War II. Simultaneously, he served as director of the War Department's Office of Facts and Figures, and assistant director of the Office of War Information (OWI), producing propaganda.

In 1944, MacLeish was appointed assistant secretary of state for cultural affairs, then, after World War II and the creation of the United Nations, MacLeish was appointed to the governing board of the United Nations Educational, Scientific, and Cultural Organization (UNESCO).

Those who see the UN as an instrument of one-world government thus argue that the very idea of the world body, from its inception, has been marketed to America and the rest of the world through a massive propaganda campaign. Fueled by war, the United Nations was presented as a vehicle of peace—its very name drawn from a wartime alliance freighted with positive, world-saving connotations. Yet embedded in the language that opens its charter is the replacement of national governments with one-world rule.

Dumbarton Oaks

The outbreak of World War II proved once and for all that the League of Nations had failed in its mission to maintain world peace. As NWO conspiracy theorists see it, far from invalidating the idea of a global governing body, the new war provided cover and distraction for many of the same people who had advocated the league to now work toward a new, more powerful organization.

John Foster Dulles was instrumental in organizing the Dumbarton Oaks Conference. Years earlier, President Wilson had appointed him legal counsel to the American Commission to Negotiate Peace—the think tank formerly dubbed The Inquiry, which accompanied the president to the Paris Peace Conference in 1919 (see Chapter 2). Subsequently, he became a charter member of the CFR.

The Dumbarton Oaks Conference convened in Washington, D.C., from August 21 to October 7, 1944, and was attended by representatives from the United States, the Soviet Union, the United Kingdom, and the Republic of China (noncommunist "Nationalist China," led by Chiang Kai-shek). Its purpose was to plan the structure of the United Nations, addressing such issues as who would be invited to membership, how the Security Council (effectively the UN's inner circle) would be constituted, and what right of veto Security Council member states would have.

INTEL

Like Chatham House (see Chapter 5) and the CFR's Harold Pratt House, an elegant mansion on Manhattan's Upper East Side, Dumbarton Oaks was a storied residence associated with wealth, exclusivity, and power. It was built in 1800 in the wealthy Georgetown neighborhood of the nation's capital and was the Washington residence of John C. Calhoun (1782–1850), a U.S. senator, cabinet officer, vice president of the United States, and architect of the doctrines of nullification and states' rights, which laid the foundation for the secession of the Confederate states that precipitated the Civil War. In 1920, Robert Woods Bliss (1875–1962), a U.S. diplomat, and his heiress wife, Mildred Barnes Bliss (1875–1969), purchased it then donated it 20 years later to create the Dumbarton Oaks Research Library and Collection, under the auspices of Harvard University.

Yalta—and the Korean Connection

The Dumbarton Oaks Conference was followed in February 1945 by the Yalta Conference, at which the "Big Three" of the World War II United Nations—Franklin Roosevelt, Winston Churchill, and Joseph Stalin—agreed on the division of Germany for postwar occupation, the postwar status of Poland and Yugoslavia, and the entry of the Soviet Union into the war against Japan. The Big Three also hashed out further details concerning the United Nations that were left unresolved at Dumbarton Oaks.

Such was the public business of the Yalta Conference. Privately, Roosevelt and Stalin also discussed the fate of Korea. Occupied by the Japanese during the war, it would soon be liberated, leaving a pro-Western, pro-democracy regime in the southern portion of the country and a pro-Communist regime, under Soviet-trained Kim Il-sung (1912–1994) in the north. FDR proposed that liberated Korea be administered as a trusteeship by the United States, the Soviet Union, and China. Stalin advocated also including Great Britain as a trustee. None of this was put into writing, but a secret protocol Roosevelt and Stalin drafted at Yalta, and to which Churchill agreed, provided for unspecified territorial concessions to the Soviet Union in the Far East as a condition for Soviet entrance into the war against Japan after the defeat of Germany.

The Korean trusteeship had, in fact, been recommended a year earlier, in the April 1944 issue of *Foreign Affairs*, the journal of the CFR. In his 1985 *The Unseen Hand*, A. Ralph Epperson, a leading advocate of the so-called *conspiratorial view of history*, wrote that the CFR members recognized that the American public might not agree to go to war to defend a Korean trusteeship were it threatened. If the public was not behind a war, Congress would not declare one. Epperson claims that an "internal CFR memo" addressed what it called the "sovereignty fetish"—that is, the "difficulty ... arising from the Constitutional provision that only Congress may declare war." The memo speculated that the treaty creating the Korean trusteeship could be written in language that would "override" the constitutional barrier. Instead of going to war to defend the Korean trusteeship, the United States would commit itself to "such police action as might be recommended by [an] international security organization." This police action "need not necessarily be construed as war."

DEFINITION

The **conspiratorial view of history** holds that historical events occur by design, as a result of conspiracy among a powerful few and for reasons generally kept secret. Advocates of this view typically oppose it to the mainstream, or accidental, view of history, in which events are seen as occurring by accident rather than by design.

Thus, according to conspiracy theory, the Yalta Conference set up the means by which an international security organization (namely the future United Nations) would "override" the U.S. Constitution and, by so doing, overcome the "sovereignty fetish." The anticipated conflict in Korea (which President Truman called a "police action") would compel the United States to act in obedience to the United Nations and in contravention of its own constitutional sovereignty. A precedent for the subordination of nationhood to a one-world government was thus created.

San Francisco Launch

On April 25, 1945, the United Nations Conference on International Organization began in San Francisco. Its purpose was to draft a charter, the work of representatives of the member nations as well as several nongovernmental organizations (NGOs) such as Rotary International and the service organization that Bilderberg co-founder Prince Bernhard had founded (see Chapter 3). The Charter of the United Nations was ready for signing on June 26, 1945. Initial membership consisted of 50 nations. Upon ratification of the charter by the five permanent members of the Security Council—the Republic of China, France, the Soviet Union, the United Kingdom, and the United States—and a majority of the other 46 signatories on October 24, 1945, the United Nations came into existence.

INTEL

In 1947, the UN General Assembly resolved to declare October 24 "United Nations Day," and in 1971, the General Assembly adopted UN Resolution 2782, which declared United Nations Day an international holiday and additionally recommended that it should be observed as a public holiday by all United Nations member states.

Critics of the UN point to both resolutions as evidence that the United Nations presents itself as a super-state with a super-national holiday it tries to impose on all nations. Although presidents of the United States have routinely issued annual United Nations Day proclamations since 1946, the day has never been observed as a national holiday.

Throughout the process of creating the charter, the U.S. delegation, which included no fewer than 47 CFR members, was guided by John Foster Dulles, who was senior adviser. With good reason, when Dulles subsequently assumed the office of secretary of state under Dwight Eisenhower in January 1953, he did so in the belief that he, not the president, was expected to originate foreign policy and that this foreign policy would be globalist in nature.

The headquartering of the United Nations in the United States was by no means the work of any CFR clique or cabal but, rather, came at the unanimous invitation of both houses of Congress. After accepting the invitation, UN officials considered a variety of sites in Queens and Manhattan, but settled on the present East River site when John D. Rockefeller Jr.—globalist father of globalist David Rockefeller—donated $8.5 million to purchase the land.

The United Nations System

Officially, the five major operating entities of the United Nations—which include the General Assembly, Security Council, Economic and Social Council (ECOSOC), Secretariat, and International Court of Justice—are the principal constituents of the "United Nations System." NWO conspiracy writers interpret "system" as code language for "government." They argue that the UN is not merely a step toward one-world government but already is itself a kind of global government, replete with deliberative bodies, an extensive bureaucracy, and a justice apparatus.

PASSWORDS

"We shall have world government whether or not we like it. The only question is, whether world government will be achieved by conquest of consent."

—James Warburg (banker son of CFR founding member Paul Warburg), testimony before the U.S. Senate, February 17, 1950

The General Assembly

The main *deliberative assembly* of the United Nations, the General Assembly consists of delegates from member states and meets in regular annual sessions. Members observe parliamentary procedure to discuss and debate issues, which are divided into "important questions" and other questions. Important questions, such as recommendations on peace and security, are decided by a two-thirds vote, whereas all other questions require only a simple majority.

Except for matters of budget, General Assembly resolutions are recommendations only and not binding on the members. Moreover, votes are apportioned by state and are not proportionate to population. Each member state gets one vote. Conceivably, then, this could result in a case in which members representing just 8 percent of the world's population impose their will on the rest of the world's people by producing the required two-thirds majority. However, because the resolutions are nonbinding, there is virtually no chance of this occurring.

DEFINITION

A **deliberative assembly** describes any organization that discusses, debates, and decides issues according to the rules of parliamentary procedure.

The Security Council

The nonbinding nature of General Assembly resolutions combined with the fact that votes are apportioned to sovereign states rather than made proportionate to population argues against assertions that the UN wields the super-national powers of a one-world government. Critics of UN authority readily concede that the power of the General Assembly is limited and therefore point to the Security Council as the repository of genuine one-world governing powers.

Article 25 of the UN Charter provides that Security Council resolutions, unlike those of the General Assembly, are binding on all members. NWO conspiracy theorists contend that by signing the UN Charter and thereby assenting to this article, all UN member nations have made a de facto agreement to compromise their individual sovereignty in the interests of one-world rule.

In addition to the five permanent members—China, France, Russia, the United Kingdom, and the United States—the Security Council consists of 10 nonpermanent members, voted in by the General Assembly on a regional basis for two-year terms. The presidency of the Security Council is rotated alphabetically each month. Any of the five permanent members may veto any substantive resolution but may not veto a procedural resolution. That is, any permanent member can block a resolution for action, but no one member can suppress debate about it.

Security Council resolutions concern the gravest decisions nations typically make, including the imposition of sanctions on other nations and the authorization of military action. Therefore, agreeing to be bound by these resolutions requires each nation to yield sovereignty in a manner that, as some interpret it, in itself constitutes one-world government.

The United Nations Secretariat

The Secretariat is housed in the largest building of the New York UN headquarters. Much of its work resembles that of the CFR, Bilderberg Group, and TC in that it conducts research, produces studies, and furnishes other information that the General Assembly, Security Council, and other UN entities request, albeit always under the direction of the secretary-general.

In principle, the Secretariat reports exclusively to designated UN officers and entities and is immune to outside influence. The UN Charter forbids the Secretariat staff from soliciting or following instructions from any source other than the UN. In signing the charter, the member countries agree not to influence the staff.

The Economic and Social Council

The Economic and Social Council (ECOSOC) promotes international economic and social cooperation and development by gathering data, advising member nations, and making recommendations. It works closely with the UN financial and social agencies that conspiracy theorists believe greatly extend the global reach of the United Nations' quasi-governmental authority: the International Bank for Reconstruction and Development (the World Bank), the International Monetary Fund (IMF), the International Labor Organization (ILO), the Food and Agriculture Organization (FAO), the World Health Organization (WHO), and the United Nations Educational, Scientific, and Cultural Organization (UNESCO).

The International Court of Justice

The International Court of Justice (ICJ) is headquartered in the Peace Palace at The Hague, Netherlands. The ICJ hears and adjudicates cases related to war crimes, ethnic cleansing, and *contentious issues* among nations.

Related to the ICJ is the recently established (2002) International Criminal Court (ICC), which tries individuals accused of the gravest crimes under international law, such as genocide and war crimes.

The decisions of the ICJ (but not the ICC) are subject to veto by permanent members of the Security Council. Critics see this as a major flaw in the international justice system; however, many who fear the establishment of one-world government object to virtually any concept of international law and international judgments held to be binding on a sovereign state.

DEFINITION

As used to define the jurisdiction of the International Court of Justice, **contentious issues** are major legal disputes between nations that are not likely to be solved easily, expeditiously, or amicably by the parties themselves.

The "World Moderator"

The secretary-general is the public face of the United Nations. Although the charter defines the office as that of "chief administrative officer"—not *executive* officer—the fact that he or she is also empowered to bring before the Security Council (in the language of the charter) "any matter which in his opinion may threaten the maintenance of international peace and security" certainly makes the office something more than administrative. President Franklin D. Roosevelt imagined the secretary-general as what he called a "world moderator"—precisely the kind of terminology that NWO conspiracy theorists find provocative.

The UN Charter specifies only that the secretary-general is to be appointed by the General Assembly on the recommendation of the Security Council, any member of which may veto the selection. In practice, the office has observed a two-term limit (each term is for five years) and appointments have been based on geographical rotation, excluding (by mutual informal agreement) candidates from any of the five permanent Security Council member states.

End or Means?

Some writers on the NWO point to the United Nations as a manifestation of one-world government that exists not in some nightmare future, but right here and right now. For them, the UN is in and of itself a form of one-world government. The UN may seek to further enhance its authority and power, but it already possesses a significant amount of both.

Others—the majority of conspiracy theorists—see the UN as just one stage in an incremental or *gradualist* implementation of an NWO based on one-world government. Typically, gradualists trace the march toward the one-world destination to roots in any number of ancient secret societies (see Part 2). They believe it seriously got underway with such modern secret societies as Rhodes's Round Tables at the end of the nineteenth century, through the introduction of the U.S. Federal Reserve in 1913, the League of Nations in 1919, the CFR in 1921, and the United Nations in 1945.

> **DEFINITION**
>
> **Gradualism,** in the context of the alleged NWO conspiracy, describes a process by which one-world government is introduced incrementally over time rather than suddenly, as by revolution.

The United Nations, in turn, gave rise to the United Nations System, including the powerful Security Council and such globalizing institutions as the World Bank, the International Monetary Fund, and the World Health Organization. All either threaten national sovereignty or actually usurp it. Beyond the UN and the varied constituents of the United Nations System are such gradualist steps toward one-world government as the creation of the European Union, the adoption of the Euro as a universal European currency in 1993, the signing of the North American Free Trade Agreement in 1994, and the formation of the World Trade Organization in 1995.

Thus, although all NWO theorists regard the United Nations as an organization dedicated to one-world government, there is a wide range of thought concerning how the UN fits into the movement. Is it an *end*, or perhaps one of many ends? Or is it no more than a gradual *means* to an end that will bring a much more comprehensive purge of national sovereignties and their replacements by a thorough implementation of global government in the hands of a cadre of the corporate and financial elite?

The Least You Need to Know

- The idea of the United Nations was promoted in part as a continuation of the "United Nations" alliance that defeated the Axis in World War II, and in part as an improved version of the League of Nations, intended to avert a third world war and possible nuclear holocaust.

- NWO conspiracy theorists contend that war is the engine that drives the UN; that is, an organization empowered to keep the peace perpetuates itself by the continual presence of armed conflict. Therefore, the UN foments conflict (as in the Korean War).

- The UN was founded mainly by members of the CFR and other globalists, so it is essentially an institutionalized extension of the CFR and related secret societies dedicated to one-world government.

- NWO conspiracy theorists debate whether the United Nations is a gradualist means toward the end of creating a one-world government, or if it is itself a powerful manifestation of one-world government.

Bonesmen

In This Chapter

- Colleges and fraternities as incubators of a "power elite"
- Skull and Bones origin, founding, and history
- Skull and Bones as a secret society
- Notable members
- Rivals to Skull and Bones

"Hidden in plain sight." The phrase Edgar Allan Poe used in his pioneering detective story, *The Purloined Letter* (see Chapter 1), could be applied to the globalist secret societies most writers identify as the core of the New World Order (NWO). The Council on Foreign Relations (CFR), the Bilderberg Group, the Trilateral Commission (TC), and Chatham House—all are hidden in plain sight. Of course, the organ of one-world government that has the biggest footprint and highest profile of all is the United Nations (UN).

Yet although NWO conspiracy writers acknowledge that UN activities are highly visible, they assert that the leading motive of the organization is not. They assert that UN leaders and supporters talk a lot about *international collaboration, coordination,* and *cooperation,* words that hide in plain sight the *real* objective: the dissolution of national sovereignties in one global government ruled by a cadre of the wealthy elite.

This brings us to yet another category of institution that (according to conspiracy writers) hides secret motives in plain sight—the university.

Alma Mater

Richard Milhous Nixon grew up poor, the son of a failed Southern California lemon-orchard owner who became a small-time grocer. Even though he won a full scholarship to Yale University, his family could not afford to send him. He had to settle for a local school, Whittier College, so that he could live at home and help out in the store. For the rest of his life, Nixon resented the *Ivy League* as an exclusive club—the club of the Kennedys and the Rockefellers and the whole "East Coast Liberal Establishment"—from which he had been excluded.

Throughout his political climb, Nixon carried that chip on his shoulder. As a congressman and senator, it drove him to see a communist in virtually anyone with a Yale, Harvard, Princeton, or Columbia degree, and it made his rivalry with Harvard-educated John and Robert Kennedy far more personal than a simple matter of Republican versus Democrat.

DEFINITION

Originally, **Ivy League** referred to the college athletic conference consisting of eight private schools in the American Northeast. Today, the term refers more generally to the oldest private, most prestigious, and most selective colleges and universities in the United States—all of which are in the Northeast. These include: Brown, Columbia, Cornell, Harvard, Princeton, and Yale universities, plus the University of Pennsylvania and Dartmouth College. Many NWO conspiracy theorists identify the Ivy League as an exclusive group of institutions dedicated to perpetuating a privileged power elite.

Although Nixon's resentment of Ivy League exclusivity was particularly dramatic and consequential, it was neither unusual—many people have harbored similar sentiments—nor entirely without justification.

In plain sight, the great flagship universities—the Ivy League in the United States, Oxford and Cambridge in the United Kingdom—are places of inquiry and learning, and by definition open to the world. In plain sight, they also share some key characteristics of secret societies: they are exclusive, requiring for membership a varying combination of academic achievement, wealth, and family connection (and not necessarily in that order). In turn, they disseminate to members certain bodies of knowledge and create or reinforce certain social connections that promise some degree of power, wealth, and prominence.

Frat Boys

Many colleges and universities have another feature in common with most secret societies. They have an outer circle and an inner circle.

These days, most of us think of college fraternities and sororities as social clubs, places to live, and places to party hearty. They are all that, of course; but defenders of the "Greek system" proudly point to statistics showing that Greek alumni generally enjoy higher income levels after graduation than students who did not join a frat or a sorority. Membership has its privileges. Who hasn't heard of the bank president who brings aboard his numbskull frat brother as VP?

Since at least the days of the Flat Hat Club, founded at the College of William and Mary in 1750 and believed to be the first American frat, fraternities and sororities have been the inner circle of university life.

The Next Level

But there are college fraternities, and then there is Skull and Bones. To begin with, unlike a typical fraternity, Bonesmen—as members call themselves—meet not in a friendly residence, but in a nearly windowless building on High Street on the Yale campus. Skull and Bones Hall looks like a Greco-Egyptian mausoleum and for that reason is universally called "the Tomb." Many fraternities are selective, but the Order of Skull and Bones (initiates call it "the Order") is downright exclusionary. It "taps" (that's their word) for membership just 15 seniors annually, who become lifetime members. There are, therefore, only about 800 Bonesmen living at any time.

Of this small number, a remarkable proportion go on to hold some of the most influential jobs in the country. Cynics call Skull and Bones the ultimate old boy's club. Conspiracy theorists call it an incubator of the power elite, the nursery of the secret clique who pulls the strings of great wealth, national influence, and international ambition. The Tomb is the womb of the NWO.

PASSWORDS

"I think Skull and Bones has had slightly more success than the Mafia in the sense that the leaders of the five families are all doing 100 years in jail, and the leaders of the Skull and Bones families are doing four and eight years in the White House."

—Ron Rosenbaum, *New York Observer* columnist, in a *60 Minutes* interview, June 13, 2004

Conspiracy Theories

Although Yale became coeducational in 1969, the Order remained exclusively male until the Class of 1991 ignored the provisions of the Russell Trust (which funds the society) and tapped seven women for membership in 1992. Conservative journalist, publisher, and political pundit William F. Buckley (1925–2008), an alumnus Bonesman, brought suit to block their admission, but dropped it when Bonesmen reaffirmed by vote their desire to admit women. Nevertheless, members are still generally referred to as Bonesmen—and Bonesmen, male or female, refer to nonmembers as barbarians.

Among the barbarians who chronically pound on the gates of the Tomb are a host of conspiracy theorists who link the Order with the CIA, CFR, Bilderberg Group, TC, and the Third Reich as well as the Fourth (see Chapter 20).

Memento Mori

The Latin phrase *memento mori*, meaning "Remember, you will die," is commonly applied to various objects and artifacts intended to remind us of death and mortality. Everything about Skull and Bones, from its name to its emblem—a skull over crossed bones under which is inscribed "322"—to the Tomb, and to what little is publicly known of its initiation ritual veritably screams, "Memento mori."

First, the business of the "322." Nobody seems to be able to pin down the significance of the number. One theory is that the first two digits, 32, refer to the year of the Order's founding, 1832, and that the final digit, 2, signifies "Second Corps." This means that the American Skull and Bones is related to a "First Corps," which exists— or existed—in some unnamed, unknown, never-identified German university. Another interpretation is that 322 is a reference to the year of the death of the Greek orator Demosthenes, 322 B.C.E., which signifies that the ancestry of the Order long predates 1832 and reaches back to "Anno-Demostheni," the year of Demosthenes's death.

Alexandra Robbins, author of *Secrets of the Tomb: Skull and Bones, the Ivy League, and the Hidden Paths of Power*, elaborated on this in a January 22, 2004, radio interview:

> *So, according to Skull and Bones lore … in 322 B.C.E., a Greek orator died. When he died, the goddess Eulogia, whom Skull and Bones called the goddess of eloquence, arose to the heavens and didn't come back down until 1832, when she happened to take up residence in the tomb of Skull and Bones. Now Skull and Bones does everything in deference to this goddess. They have songs or … sacred anthems that they sing. When they are encouraged to steal things—some remarkably valuable*

items, supposedly—they are said to be bringing back gifts to the goddess. They begin each session in the Tomb, and they meet twice weekly by unveiling a sort of a guilt shrine to Eulogia. That's the point of the society. They call themselves the Knights of Eulogia. That's where the 322 comes in.

Now to the apparent fascination with death. Bonesmen neither confirm nor deny the popular rumor that initiates are obliged, as Bonesmen look on, to masturbate in a coffin while confessing their sexual exploits. By way of reward, they are not only admitted to membership but also presented with a gift of $15,000.

There is also a tradition of ritual theft attached to Skull and Bones, a practice reputedly called *crooking* by members of the Order. There are stories of Bonesmen having stolen a number of skulls, including those of President Martin Van Buren, Pancho Villa, and, most infamously, Geronimo.

Nothing is known for certain about Van Buren's skull—the body has never been officially exhumed—but no one disputes that *somebody* purloined the skull of the charismatic Mexican revolutionary guerrilla leader Pancho Villa shortly after he was murdered in 1923. Skull and Bones researcher Alexandra Robbins reported in her 2002 book *Secrets of the Tomb: Skull and Bones, the Ivy League, and the Hidden Paths of Power* that the Order paid $25,000 for the skull in the 1920s, but later retracted the claim, having concluded that the payment of such a sum at such a time was highly implausible. Others have also cited the story as an unfounded myth.

The Geronimo caper is more complicated. In 1986, Ned Anderson, former chairman of the San Carlos Apaches, received an anonymous letter accompanying a photograph and a copy of a 1918 Skull and Bones ledger page recording the acquisition of the skull of the Apache war chief Geronimo, stolen from Fort Sill, Oklahoma, during World War I. Anderson met with representatives of the Order, including the group's attorney, Endicott P. Davidson, who formally denied that the Order possessed the skull. He explained that the ledger was a hoax; however, Skull and Bones offered to give Anderson a glass case containing the skull of a 10-year-old boy. Understandably, Anderson declined the offer.

In 2006, a letter dated 1918 turned up, purportedly written by Bonesman Winter Mead to one F. Trubee Davison. It reported that members of the Order had "exhumed" Geronimo's skull from Fort Sill and that the relic resided in the Tomb. This prompted former U.S. Attorney General Ramsey Clark to bring suit in 2009, on behalf of persons claiming to be Geronimo's descendants, against President Barack Obama, Secretary of Defense Robert Gates, Skull and Bones, and others, demanding the return of Geronimo's remains. Pressed by *The New York Times*, Clark admitted he had "no hard proof" that the Order stole or possessed the skull. Yet while several sources have called the tale a hoax—one authority pointed out that Geronimo's grave was unmarked in 1918—others have labeled it as plausible. Some have even claimed that the ringleader of the Bonesmen who took the skull was Prescott Bush (1895–1972), father of the forty-first president of the United States and grandfather of the forty-third.

Mumbo Jumbo, Metaphor, or Conspiracy?

New York Observer columnist Ron Rosenbaum, a non-Bonesman Yale alumnus, spent three decades investigating Skull and Bones. In a 2004 *60 Minutes* interview, he described the initiation ceremony:

> *[The Tomb is] this sepulchral, tomblike, windowless, granite, sandstone bulk that you can't miss. And I lived next to it [on the Yale University Campus] …. I had passed it all the time.*

> *And during the initiation rites, you could hear strange cries and whispers coming from the Skull and Bones tomb …. A woman holds a knife and pretends to slash the throat of another person lying down before them, and there's screaming and yelling at the neophytes …. There is a devil, a Don Quixote and a Pope who has one foot sheathed in a white monogrammed slipper resting on a stone skull. The initiates are led into the room one at a time. And once an initiate is inside, the Bonesmen shriek at him. Finally, the Bonesman is shoved to his knees in front of Don Quixote as the shrieking crowd falls silent. And Don Quixote lifts his sword and taps the Bonesman on his left shoulder and says, "By order of our order, I dub thee knight of Eulogia."*

Fraternities, lodges, and other so-called secret societies have always had initiation ceremonies, many of them involving bizarre or morbid elements as well as embarrassing or humiliating acts. Outsiders typically dismiss all of this as mumbo jumbo—nonsensical and even childish.

Perhaps. But those sympathetic to Skull and Bones see the rituals of initiation and the omnipresence of memento mori as deliberately metaphorical. The obsession with death, they say, is to remind initiates and members that life is short and therefore not to be wasted. Pointing to the privileged social position most members enjoy, they suggest that the death imagery is intended to inspire dedication to a life of service, a life that makes all it can out of what little time is allotted. As for the humiliating aspects of the initiation and the general aura of secrecy surrounding the Order, sympathetic commentators believe that these serve to create lifelong bonds among members. These bonds help members achieve the levels of influence necessary for a more effective and far-reaching life of service.

Others, far less sympathetic, see the imagery of Skull and Bones as deliberately crafted to intimidate, and the secrecy as intended to do neither more nor less than conceal and deceive. The silence of Skull and Bones, they say, is the same as that surrounding the Mafia. It is the silence that covers activities that would be stopped if they were more widely known.

History of the Mystery

There are at least two versions of Skull and Bones history. The first is generally accepted, and the second conspiratorial.

Version 1: The Standard Story

Skull and Bones came into being in 1832 in response to a disagreement among the debating societies then active at Yale: Linonia, Brothers in Unity, and Calliope. The subject of the dispute was that season's Phi Beta Kappa awards. In the course of the argument, some members of all three societies broke away to create Skull and Bones. The new organization operated only on the Yale campus until a separate chapter was created at Wesleyan University in 1870, called the Beta Chapter of Skull and Bones. Within two years, however, it severed ties with the Yale group over the issue of adding yet more chapters; the Wesleyan offspring wanted to, the Yale originals objected. The Beta Chapter renamed itself in conventional Greek letters as Theta Nu Epsilon.

In the meantime, there were also disputes on the Yale campus. In 1841, disagreements over who should be elected to Skull and Bones gave rise to a rival secret society, the Scroll and Key, and, in 1884, 300 members of the senior class sought to counteract the dominance of the Skull and Bones by creating yet another rival, Wolf's Head. Both Scroll and Key and Wolf's Head continue to exist, and both have had some highly distinguished members.

Scroll and Key boasts CIA official Cord Meyer Jr.; Secretary of State Dean Acheson; Secretary of State, Secretary of the Army, and Federal Reserve Chairman Cyrus Vance; Peace Corps founder Sargent Shriver; first U.S. Ambassador to the Soviet Union William C. Bullitt; Mellon Bank fortune heir and philanthropist Paul Mellon;

Chicago Tribune publisher Robert McCormick; *Newsweek* editor and writer Fareed Zakaria; Vanderbilt heir Cornelius Vanderbilt III; First National City Bank of New York chairman James S. Rockefeller; and famed childcare guru Dr. Benjamin Spock.

Wolf's Head alumni include poet and essayist Stephen Vincent Benet; architectural historian and critic Paul Goldberger; University of Chicago president Robert Maynard Hutchins; and avant-garde composer Charles Ives. Whereas conspiracy theorists have been quick to cite influential members of Skull and Bones, they have for the most part said little about the prominent members of rival societies.

SECRET LIVES

Scroll and Key member Cord Meyer Jr. (1920–2001) graduated from Yale University in 1942. After World War II, he was an outspoken proponent of world government. He helped found United World Federalists in 1947, a globalist organization that counted Albert Einstein and Kurt Vonnegut as members. It gave rise to the currently active Citizens for Global Solutions, dedicated to a "future in which nations work together to … solve the problems facing humanity that no nation can solve alone." Meyer joined the CIA in 1951 under Allen Dulles. Six years after Meyer's death, the son of E. Howard Hunt (1918–2007), former CIA agent and convicted Watergate "plumber," presented tape recordings of his father's deathbed claim that Meyer had organized the JFK assassination at the behest of Vice President Lyndon B. Johnson.

Similar to both Scroll and Key and Wolf's Head, Skull and Bones is a property-owning senior society. In addition to the Tomb on the Yale campus, it owns Deer Island, an upstate New York campground on an island in the St. Lawrence River intended as a gathering place of Bonesmen.

Version 2: The Conspiratorial Story

Those who believe that Skull and Bones exists first and foremost as an incubator of a power elite dedicated to establishing a one-world government say that it was imported from Germany in 1832 by businessman, educator, and politician William H. Russell and Alphonso Taft, who became President Ulysses S. Grant's attorney general and then secretary of war. His son, William Howard Taft (also a Bonesman), was elected as the twenty-seventh president of the United States and subsequently appointed Chief Justice of the U.S. Supreme Court.

Conspiracy theorists believe the German connection to be of paramount importance. Through it, they trace Skull and Bones to the Bavarian Illuminati, the progenitor (according to some) of virtually every important modern secret society. This includes the so-called "Illuminized Freemasons," the most politically influential branch of Freemasonry (see Chapters 13 and 15). Some conspiracy writers believe Skull and Bones is not merely rooted in the Illuminati, but is a modern incarnation of that secret society and shares with it a belief in uniting the world through rationality or "reason." It does so by whatever means are necessary, including deceit, theft, murder, and war.

Roll Dem Bones

One can dispute the purpose and motives of Skull and Bones endlessly, but there is no denying that the Order has had more than its share of very prominent members. Until 1971, Skull and Bones published its annual membership lists, which are in the Yale library collection. Other rosters were published through 1982, after which no official lists were kept. An extensive representative list may be found by searching for "Skull_and_Bones_members" in Wikipedia.

It includes, for example, Walter Camp (1880), generally considered the founder of American football; Henry L. Stimson (1888), U.S. secretary of war; Percy Rockefeller (1900), director of Brown Brothers Harriman (investment bankers), Standard Oil, and Remington Arms; George L. Harrison (1910), president of U.S. Federal Reserve; Averell Harriman (1913), financier, railroad baron, and U.S. ambassador to the Soviet Union; Archibald MacLeish (1915) poet and librarian of Congress; Prescott Bush (1916), financier, senator, father of President George H. W. Bush and grandfather of George W. Bush; Henry Luce (1920), co-founder of Time-Life Enterprises; H. J. Heinz II (1931), heir to the Heinz Company; McGeorge Bundy (1940), national security adviser to Presidents Kennedy and Johnson; David McCullough (1955), Pulitzer Prize–winning historian; Winston Lord (1959), CFR chairman and U.S. ambassador to China; and John F. Kerry (1966), senator and presidential candidate defeated by fellow Bonesman George W. Bush (1968) in 2004.

Fraternity brothers are supposed to look out for one another in life after graduation, so there should be little wonder that so many Bonesmen have enjoyed power and influence. In helping one another out, Bonesmen (in this view) are no more conspiratorial or sinister than the members of any other fraternal organizations. Conspiracy theorists point out, however, that whereas making connections is incidental to ordinary frat life, it is the very reason for the existence of Skull and Bones.

They cite none other than the case of George W. Bush. As a young man, he was (by his own admission) what a later generation would have called a slacker, with little interest in academic achievement and without particularly distinguished intellectual aptitude. Indeed, despite the fact that his father was a Yale alumnus—which made his son a candidate for "legacy admission"—his grades at Andover (where he prepped) were sufficiently poor to disqualify him for admission. Three of the seven members of the admissions committee that voted W. in were Bonesmen. For conspiracy theorists, this constitutes an "enough said."

Criteria

Skull and Bones has never commented officially on its membership criteria, although informally it has been said that the Order looks for "campus leaders" and others who are in some way "notable," including those who have achieved academic distinction or who are star athletes. Delta Kappa Epsilon ("Deke") members are often prime candidates; indeed, like Bonesmen, Dekes often go on to become prominent in business, politics, media, and the military. The Yale Political Union and the school newspaper, the *Yale Daily News*, are also well represented.

Beyond this, it is difficult to make a persuasive case that the Order seeks out individuals who possess special qualifications as candidates for elevation to the "power elite." It is important to bear in mind that the student body at Yale University is already highly select, both intellectually and socially.

The Cement of Secrecy

As with other groups conspiracy theorists associate with the NWO, much of the Skull and Bones mystique emanates from the secrecy surrounding the organization. Secrecy, of course, makes it difficult, perhaps impossible, to assess the true nature, motives, and influence of any group.

Secrecy also implies something to hide, which, in turn, suggests something harmful, underhanded, or conspiratorial. If the purpose of Skull and Bones were really to do no more than cultivate the best and the brightest to encourage and prepare them to pursue lives of service, why all the skulking and hocus pocus? Why hide behind grotesque images of death? Why meet in a "tomb"? Why invent secret names (Bonesman Averell Harriman was called Thor; McGeorge Bundy, Odin; George H. W. Bush, Magog; and so on)?

Skull and Bones is a *senior society*. Membership is restricted to one's last year in college. Obviously, therefore, the relationships established here are intended to extend beyond graduation. Shared secrets create bonds, which may last for life. When the secret sharers become influential and powerful in disproportionate numbers—many claiming high-profile public roles in a government founded on democratic principles of transparency—the secrecy naturally takes on an aura of the sinister.

DEFINITION

In colleges and universities, a **senior society** is a fraternity, sorority, or other organization in which membership is restricted to fourth-year (senior) undergraduate students.

Whatever specific allegations the conspiracy theorists make concerning Skull and Bones, there is one question they raise that everyone must consider pondering: To whom does a powerful public figure answer first, foremost, and above all—the public he or she serves, or the fraternity brother/sorority sister with whom he or she shares a bundle of secrets?

The Least You Need to Know

- Many conspiracy theorists believe that Skull and Bones, a highly selective senior society at Yale University, is a kind of incubator for a "power elite," who attain positions of great influence in government and industry, from which they plan an NWO.

- The mainstream view of Skull and Bones is of a rarified college fraternity; the conspiratorial view depicts it as a secret society rooted in the Illuminati of the eighteenth century and dedicated to cultivating power and confining it to a select few.

- Bonesmen (as Skull and Bones members are called) are bound to each other through pledges of secrecy sealed with humiliating, perhaps sexually compromising, initiation rituals.

- Notable members of Skull and Bones have included captains of industry, media figures, statesmen, and politicians, including the two presidents Bush.

The Oligarchs

In This Chapter

- The rise of the military-industrial-congressional complex
- The "power elite" and the NWO conspiracy
- The role of war in creating and maintaining national power and sovereignty
- The principal oligarch families: the Rothschilds, Morgans, and Rockefellers
- The Rockefeller family's global initiatives

"There are no nations! There are no peoples! There are no Russians. There are no Arabs! There are no third worlds! There is no West! There is only one holistic system of systems, one vast and immane, interwoven, interacting, multivariate, multinational dominion of dollars! Petro-dollars, electro-dollars, multi-dollars, Reich marks, rubles, rin, pounds, and shekels! It is the international system of currency that determines the totality of life on this planet! That is the natural order of things today! ... There is no America. There is no democracy. There is only IBM and ITT and AT&T and DuPont, Dow, Union Carbide, and Exxon. Those are the nations of the world today .... We no longer live in a world of nations and ideologies .... The world is a college of corporations, inexorably determined by the immutable by-laws of business .... The world is a business .... It has been since man crawled out of the slime, and our children ... will live to see that perfect world in which there is no war and famine, oppression and brutality—one vast and ecumenical holding company, for whom all men will work to serve a common profit, in which all men will hold a share of stock, all necessities provided, all anxieties tranquilized, all boredom amused."

These are the words of one Arthur Jensen—or, rather, actor Ned Beatty playing Arthur Jensen, the fictional chairman of the fictional multinational conglomerate that owns the fictional Universal Broadcasting System (UBS) in the 1976 classic film *Network*. But for believers in the New World Order (NWO) conspiracy, this Hollywood fantasy could just as easily have been billed as a documentary and Jensen's rant taken for the gospel of modern life.

Military-Industrial-Congressional Complex

Surprisingly few presidential farewell speeches are memorable. Two exceptions are George Washington's, with its admonition to "avoid foreign entanglements," and Dwight D. Eisenhower's. That we should remember the latter is remarkable for two reasons. Ike was a great general, but as a president he was notable for his numbing lack of eloquence and smilingly bland association with a complacently prosperous postwar America dedicated to preserving the status quo.

DEFINITION

Military-industrial-congressional complex describes the close and massive interdependence of the military with the private sector that supplies it with the technology of war. Some fear that the demands of the military drive industry and industry in turn shapes the military's demand for its products, so that, together, the military and industry exert undue influence on government and national policy, especially where war and peace are concerned.

All the more reason to be shocked by what he broadcast to the nation on January 17, 1961, three days before he turned the White House over to John F. Kennedy: "A vital element in keeping the peace is our military establishment," he said. "Our arms must be mighty, ready for instant action, so that no potential aggressor may be tempted to risk his own destruction …." No surprise so far. But then Ike turned contemplative:

> *This conjunction of an immense military establishment and a large arms industry is new in the American experience. The total influence—economic, political, even spiritual—is felt in every city, every statehouse, every office of the federal government. We recognize the imperative need for this development. Yet we must not fail to comprehend its grave implications. Our toil, resources and livelihood are all involved; so is the very structure of our society. In the councils of government, we must guard against the acquisition of unwarranted influence, whether sought or unsought, by the military-industrial complex. The potential for the disastrous rise of misplaced power*

*exists and will persist. We must never let the weight of this combination endanger
our liberties or democratic processes. We should take nothing for granted. Only an
alert and knowledgeable citizenry can compel the proper meshing of the huge industrial and military machinery of defense with our peaceful methods and goals so that
security and liberty may prosper together.*

The military-industrial complex? Was *this* the status quo—an unholy alliance between
the nation's war-making and industrial apparatus so powerful that it threatened
democracy itself? The message was that of a latter-day Jeremiah, a radical prophet,
not the avuncular figure who seemed more comfortable on the golf course than in the
Oval Office. And as startling as the message was, Ike planned to make his valedic-
tory warning even stronger. The second-to-final draft of the speech used the phrase
military-industrial-congressional complex, thereby linking the legislature, constitutionally
answerable only to the people, directly with the masters of war, industry, and finance.

SECRET LIVES

Although President Eisenhower is generally credited with coining the phrase
military-industrial complex, it was really the brainchild of two presidential
speechwriters. Born in Pecos, Texas, Ralph E. Williams (1917–2009) became a
member of President Dwight D. Eisenhower's White House staff in 1958, serving as assistant to the president's naval aide, Captain Evan P. Aurand.

Williams did double duty as Aurand's assistant and a presidential speechwriter,
collaborating with another White House staff writer, Malcolm Moos (1916–
1982), to coin the famous military-industrial complex phrase. Moos worked for
the *Baltimore Evening Sun* as an associate editor, and his popular political writings brought him to the attention of Sherman Adams, an Eisenhower assistant.
Moos became Ike's chief speechwriter in 1958. President of the University of
Minnesota from 1967 to 1974, he was also executive director of the Center for
the Study of Democratic Institutions, Santa Barbara, California, from 1972 until
his death.

The *Real* Status Quo

President Eisenhower called the "conjunction of an immense military establishment
and a large arms industry ... new in the American experience." But there is ample
evidence that it was not actually all that novel.

The influential sociologist C. Wright Mills (1916–1962) described in his much-discussed 1956 study of power and class, *The Power Elite*, the cadre of military, industrial, and political leaders, united by mutual interests involving money and power, who had become the actual leaders of government and were beyond the force of the Constitution and democracy's control.

Although Mills saw the rise of the power elite as a post–World War II phenomenon, some of the greatest and wealthiest industrialists built their fortunes on the great wars of the nineteenth and early twentieth centuries. In Germany, Alfried Krupp (1812–1887) turned his family's steel-making firm to manufacturing superb heavy artillery to enable the Kaiser to realize his imperial ambitions. In the United States, Eliphalet Remington (1793–1861) and Samuel Colt (1814–1862) founded companies that supplied many of the rifles and revolvers that were used to fight the U.S.-Mexican War, the Indian Wars, the Civil War, and the Spanish-American War, among others. In Sweden, Alfred Nobel (1833–1896) created a range of explosives that made war increasingly destructive and himself fabulously wealthy.

 PASSWORDS

"We Krupps never cared much about [political] ideas. We only wanted a system that worked well and allowed us to work unhindered. Politics is not our business."

—Arms manufacturer and Hitler supporter Alfried Krupp (1907–1967), pleading his innocence of war crimes at the Nuremburg Tribunals, 1947

We take for granted that war brings ruin. In fact, it also creates wealth—and probably always has. Armies have to be equipped and paid, and weapons are first and foremost industrial goods. All of this requires finance. The great Rothschild fortune was founded on financing the final phase of the British war effort against Napoleon in 1813 through 1815. In America, J. P. Morgan and other financiers were instrumental in funding many aspects of the Civil War.

By the late nineteenth century, in Britain, France, and Germany, alliances among the military, government, finance, and industry became more pervasive, especially as the industrial requirements of war became bigger and more complex—bigger, more sophisticated guns; bigger, more destructive warships; and so on. Most historians see the Franco-Prussian War of 1870 as the watershed event in the creation of the world's first true military-industrial complexes. This war was fought with advanced industrial weaponry, and it created a national sentiment in Britain and France that Germany's imperial ambitions had to be stopped at any cost, while also creating in Germany a national will to continue to act upon those very ambitions. During the years leading up to World War I (1914–1918), between Britain and Germany in particular, the competition to build bigger, faster, and more heavily armed warships in substantial quantity grew fierce and fed the need for a military-industrial complex.

By the outbreak of World War I, the major powers had come to believe that victory in any large-scale modern war depended on an effective partnership among the government, the military, and the so-called "private" enterprise.

Report from Iron Mountain

From its founding in 1923, Dial Press had a reputation for publishing cutting-edge and controversial authors, ranging from James Baldwin to Norman Mailer. In 1967, during the Johnson administration, it put out a blockbuster. *The Report from Iron Mountain* was presented as a top-secret document leaked by a Midwestern university professor known only as "John Doe." He was purportedly one of a 15-member "Special Study Group" assembled by National Security Adviser McGeorge Bundy, Secretary of State Dean Rusk, and Secretary of Defense Robert McNamara to explore the consequences of both war and peace in the nuclear age. (All three men were CFR and Bilderberg members; Bundy was also a Bonesman, and McNamara a Trilateralist.)

The appointees to the Special Study Group, all of whom remained anonymous, were reportedly prominent historians, economists, scientists, and at least one active industrialist. They met at "Iron Mountain," said to be a subterranean bunker near Hudson, New York, which reputedly housed auxiliary offices for a number of major banks as well as Standard Oil of New Jersey (a Rockefeller company) and Dutch Shell Oil (chaired by Bilderberg founder Prince Bernhard). The introduction to the *Report* noted that it was designed to survive thermonuclear war.

According to John Doe, the "Iron Mountain Boys" submitted their report in March 1966. Its major conclusion was that, even if lasting peace "could be achieved, it would almost certainly not be in the best interests of society to achieve it." War, the *Report* claimed, was "itself … the basic social system," which had "governed most human societies of record." War was essential to the economy and was the very reason for the existence of nation-states. Eliminate war, and "national sovereignty" will come to an immediate end. "The basic authority of the modern state over its people resides in its war powers." Additionally, war served to divert dangerous collective aggression.

PASSWORDS

"As I would put my personal repute behind the authenticity of this document *[The Report from Iron Mountain],* so would I testify to the validity of its conclusions. My reservations relate only to the wisdom of releasing it to an obviously unconditioned public."

—John Kenneth Galbraith, "Book World," *The Washington Post,* November 26, 1967

According to the report, war was so vital to the continuation of the sovereign state that alternatives to war had to be found to fill any intervals of peace. These included massive state-run social-welfare programs, never-ending state-run research programs (such as the space race), international military and police operations (such as UN weapons inspections and peacekeeping missions), rumors of an extraterrestrial threat (UFOs, alien invasion), global environmental pollution requiring massive global programs to combat, demonized enemies (at the time of the report, Mao Zedong, perhaps; more recent examples would include Saddam Hussein and Osama bin Laden), national service (Peace Corps, VISTA, etc.), reinvigorated religions (the Christian Right, for instance), and public "blood" sports (such as professional football). The report even suggested some "sophisticated" form of slavery, but did not specify what this would mean.

INTEL

Although most NWO writers believe *The Report from Iron Mountain* to be authentic, Leonard C. Lewin (1916–1999), a writer and former labor organizer, wrote in the March 19, 1972, issue of *The New York Times Review of Books* that he had written the report as a hoax. This claim started a controversy that has yet to be fully resolved.

Famed Harvard economist and presidential adviser John Kenneth Galbraith (1908–2006) wrote in a 1976 *Washington Post* article that he knew the report was real because he had been invited to participate in its creation. (Although he declined the invitation, he said he served as a consultant to the project from time to time.) In later comments, Galbraith hinted that Lewin was the author; he did not say whether or not what Lewin wrote was authentic or a hoax.

The Report from Iron Mountain concluded that government required more or less continuous warfare or some substitute to maintain its power and authority. NWO conspiracy theorists use this assertion as a springboard to another conclusion, arguing that if war is at the heart of government, then those who possess the wherewithal to finance and profit from war (that is, "the power elite") inevitably hold sway over the government. Regardless of election results, *they* are the power behind any presidential administration or Congress.

Moreover, although history might record that a certain government decided to go to war and therefore turned to certain bankers and financiers to help finance the endeavor, more often the impetus for war has come not from the legally constituted leaders of the government, but from the financiers themselves. Because war means profit and more profit means more power, the great financiers have fomented war whenever and wherever they wanted. The initiative lies with them, not a president, not Congress, not some dictator, and not a king.

Family Affairs

NWO conspiracy theorists generally identify three prominent families as the great financiers/fomenters of war. First to reach prominence were the Rothschilds, followed by the Morgans and the Rockefellers. Members of these dynasties are, in effect, oligarchs—the true wielders of governing power, though they hold no elective, appointed, or legally inherited government office.

The House of Rothschild

Mayer Amschel Rothschild (1744–1812) was born in the Jewish ghetto of Frankfurt am Main to Amschel Moses Rothschild, a money changer. As a youth, Mayer apprenticed in a banking house and proved so adept at handling money that he was appointed a royal financial agent. With his rise in prominence came an invitation to join the Freemasons (see Chapter 15), a secret society whose inner circle consisted of men of influence in the community. Wealth and power earned a man admission into the Masonic inner circle, and membership in that inner circle, in turn, meant acquiring even more wealth and power.

The secret to Mayer Rothschild's success as a financier was his determination to retain absolute control over his affairs by keeping all business interests firmly in family hands. This required careful management over the expansion of his family, so that, like a king, he arranged marriages for all his sons, pairing them exclusively with members of the extended Rothschild clan. In this way, five sons, each with a dynasty of his own, came to occupy the chief cities of Europe: in Frankfurt was Amschel Mayer Rothschild (1773–1855); in Vienna, Salomon Mayer Rothschild (1774–1855); in London, Nathan Mayer Rothschild (1777–1836); in Naples, Calmann Mayer Rothschild (1788–1855); and in Paris, Jakob Mayer Rothschild (1792–1868). They established great, interlocking banking concerns in each of the countries in which they lived and, like a royal family, adopted a coat of arms. Theirs featured five arrows tightly clenched in a fist.

The first great leap in the family's fortune beyond what the patriarch Mayer Rothschild had accumulated came in the last years of the Napoleonic Wars. Between 1813 and 1815, Nathan Mayer Rothschild—the London son—was the single largest financier of the culminating British war effort.

PASSWORDS

"Give me control of a nation's money and I care not who makes the laws."

—Mayer Amschel Rothschild

Based on the wealth this activity generated, the Neapolitan, Austrian, French, and English Rothschilds collaborated in creating a trans-European financial and mercantile network. This facilitated the family's business not only by providing an extensive proprietary transportation system, but also a means of acquiring and transmitting information rapidly. Thanks to the Rothschilds' advance knowledge of Wellington's victory at the Battle of Waterloo (June 16–19, 1815), the family was able to buy certain British stocks in the knowledge that their value would rise dramatically when the rest of the world heard news of Napoleon's final defeat. As a result, the family made another enormous profit.

Within a few years of Waterloo, the Rothschilds had many of Europe's governments and royal families in their debt. Their status as de facto nobility was officially ratified in 1816 when four of the brothers were ennobled by Austria's Emperor Franz I. Two years later, Nathan was similarly elevated. In 1822, the four were made barons (given the Austrian title of "Freiherr"). Later, in 1885, Nathan Mayer Rothschild II (1840–1915), a member of the London family, was created (titled) Baron Rothschild, thereby entering into the British Peerage. A number of NWO theorists have studied the Rothschilds and their investments, concluding that their financial interests trumped any patriotic allegiance to their country of residence. Indeed, they claim, the family typically financed both or all sides of any given armed conflict, including the Union *and* the Confederacy in the U.S. Civil War (1861–1865).

PASSWORDS

"When your patient is desperately sick, you try desperate measures, even to bloodletting."

—Baron Jacob Rothschild, to U.S. minister to Belgium Henry Sanford regarding the Civil War

Financing the North as well as the South brought in tremendous war profits for the Rothschilds, who also enjoyed favor from the governments of France and Britain. Concerned that the economic power of the United States had become overwhelming, these governments were eager for Rothschild money to perpetuate a war that promised to break up the union and thereby diminish America as a commercial competitor.

The House of Morgan

John Pierpont (J. P.) Morgan (1837–1913) was probably the most famous American tycoon of the nineteenth century's *Gilded Age*. This titan of industrial consolidation and corporate finance was the son of Junius Spencer Morgan (1813–1890), who built a dry goods business into a fortune of staggering proportions. In the 1850s, he began an association with George Peabody (1795–1869), an American financier living in England. His British banking establishment, George Peabody & Co., did extensive business with the English Rothschilds. J. S. Morgan joined Peabody to create Peabody, Morgan & Co., which brokered many loans to the Union during the Civil War (some of them from the Rothschilds). Some historians, including NWO conspiracy theorists, go so far as to call the Morgans covert American agents of the British Rothschilds.

Although J. P. Morgan's father may have linked his son to the Rothschilds, his mother, Juliet Pierpont Morgan, was the granddaughter of a Yale University founder. This fact does not escape conspiracy writers, who see in this a direct link to the home of Skull and Bones.

DEFINITION

The **Gilded Age** refers roughly to the period 1865–1901 in American history when the upper class not only accumulated great wealth but did not hesitate to exhibit it extravagantly. The Morgans and the Rockefellers are prime examples of Gilded Age financiers and industrialists.

Although he was closely connected with the Rothschilds, who financed both sides, J. S. Morgan backed only the Union. However, his son J. P. made no pretense to a display of patriotism. In May 1861, he concluded a deal with the Union commander at St. Louis to sell him 5,000 rifles at the grossly inflated price of $22 each. Desperate to arm his men, the commander agreed, only to refuse payment when he discovered that all the rifles were obsolete and many nonfunctioning. Morgan responded by filing suit against the U.S. Army and won a judgment in the amount of $109,912. This prompted a congressional investigation, which discovered that Morgan had not only acquired the substandard weapons for a mere $3.50 each, but hadn't even used his own money to buy them at this fire-sale price. Instead, he posted his army purchasing contract as collateral against a loan for the purchase money. He had thus sold to the army, at $22 each, weapons it had already purchased for $3.50—without risking a penny of his own cash. And, at that, most of the weapons were useless. (The results of the investigation notwithstanding, Morgan kept the judgment settlement he had won in court.)

Beyond the reach of national allegiance and even conventional ethics, J. P. Morgan came to rule a financial empire that controlled many of the biggest U.S. corporations. This gave him a great deal of leverage over representatives, senators, and presidents, and it put him in position to participate in the creation of the U.S. Federal Reserve System, which some NWO conspiracy theorists describe as a super-state controlled by international bankers (see Chapter 9).

The House of Rockefeller

John Davison Rockefeller (1839–1937) founded Standard Oil in 1870 and built it into a vertical monopoly—for a time controlling most of the American oil business from drilling, through refining, through distribution—that made him the first U.S. billionaire and the richest man on the planet. When his wealth is adjusted for inflation, he may well stand as the wealthiest man in history.

 PASSWORDS

"John D. Rockefeller sleeps eight and one-half hours every night, retiring at 10:30 and rising at 7. Every morning when he gets up he is $17,705 richer than he was when he went to bed. He sits down to breakfast at 8 o'clock and leaves the table at 8:30, and in that short half hour his wealth has grown $1,041.50."

—"Rockefeller's Enormous Income," *The Wise County* (Texas) *Messenger,* May 26, 1897

Although he devoted much of his fortune to a wide range of philanthropic works, ranging from huge gifts to prominent American universities (especially the University of Chicago), to medical research, to the promotion of "eugenics" (genetic selection intended to "improve" the human race), Rockefeller's wealth and influence made him among the most reviled men in America. Yet even though many Americans hated him, they could at least point to his remarkable story as a distinctly American product of American capitalism—or so they thought.

When Rockefeller's monopolistic practices finally triggered congressional investigation during the administration of "trust buster" Theodore Roosevelt early in the twentieth century, it was revealed that the National City Bank of Cleveland, which financed Standard Oil's early monopolization efforts, was a Rothschild bank. Thus Rockefeller was, from the beginning, tied into a global financial system controlled by the most famous financial dynasty in the modern world.

INTEL

Many conspiracy theorists believe that the NWO will include centrally administered population control as a means by which the activities and movement of individuals can be more effectively regulated. Some see "pro-choice" organizations such as Planned Parenthood as advocates of abortion to limit population growth. Some believe that deliberately engineered plagues, tainted vaccines, programs to influence climate, and even water fluoridation will be used in genocidal campaigns. Those who pull the strings of one-world government are believed to be interested in selective human breeding—eugenics—to produce citizens with various traits considered desirable.

According to NWO conspiracy writers, the second and third generations of Rockefellers used the family fortune most extensively to move the world toward one-world government. Riding the tide of internationalism that followed World War I, John D. Rockefeller Jr. (1874–1960) launched the Interchurch World Movement (IWM) in 1919 in an attempt to consolidate the world's Christian denominations along the lines of a great corporate monopoly. (Both John D. Rockefeller Jr. and his father were devout Baptists who avidly supported the church and its activities.)

Although the movement was not long lived, it spurred Samuel Zane Batten to write *The New World Order*, which was published in 1919 by the American Baptist Publication Society. Batten called not only for a world religion, but for a "World Federation" that would create an "international mind" and generate "world patriotism," which would supplant national allegiance and therefore purge humanity of the chief cause of war.

It is easy to see the connection between Batten's World Federation and the League of Nations, which came into being in 1919 as a condition of the Treaty of Versailles. It is no coincidence (conspiracy theorists point out) that John D. Rockefeller Jr. donated the Manhattan land on which the headquarters of the successor to the League of Nations, the United Nations, was built.

All of the junior Rockefeller's five sons became prominent in national and international affairs. His eldest, John D. Rockefeller III, chaired the Rockefeller Foundation, which underwrote a variety of international organizations and agencies. Nelson Rockefeller served in the administration of President Franklin D. Roosevelt in the unofficial capacity of "coordinator for inter-American affairs," a kind of liaison between the United States and Latin America, before he went on to four terms as governor of New York and vice president under Gerald Ford. Laurence Spelman Rockefeller became a great venture capitalist, who financed Eastern Airlines and the company that became McDonnell-Douglas, a major builder of commercial and military aircraft. He was also a pioneering global environmentalist. As for Winthrop Rockefeller, his ambitions were more narrowly confined to the oil industry and Arkansas state politics.

Of all the third-generation Rockefellers, David (b. 1915), the youngest, is most extensively associated with organizations and initiatives NWO conspiracy theorists identify as aspects of a one-world government movement. His chairmanship of Chase Bank led to his connection with the World Bank and the International Monetary Fund. An unapologetic globalist, he joined the CFR in 1949 as the youngest-ever director, subsequently becoming chairman of the CFR board (see Chapter 2). He was present at the first Bilderberg meeting in 1954 and has remained active in the Bilderberg inner circle (see Chapter 3). With Zbigniew Brzezinski, he founded the Trilateral Commission in 1973 and has also remained a member of its leadership (see Chapter 4). Rockefeller was a prime mover behind the planning, financing, and construction of the World Trade Center, destroyed in the terrorist attacks of September 11, 2001.

Ultimate Stewardship or Rule of the Many by the Few?

The political activism and global philanthropy of the Rothschilds, Morgans, and, above all, the Rockefellers may be seen as selfless, socially responsible expressions of what another fabulously wealthy magnate, Andrew Carnegie, called the "gospel of wealth": the obligation of the rich and powerful to give back to society. There is ample reason to look at the many cultural, scientific, educational, and charitable institutions endowed by the select circle of the world's wealthiest families as social stewardship on a scale both ambitious and selfless.

Those who believe in an NWO conspiracy, however, see the "philanthropy" as cover for one-world government intended to produce profit and power for the benefit of the privileged few. For them, the Rothschilds, Morgans, and Rockefellers are the most prominent of the people who have connected themselves to one another by blood, marriage, business associations, and memberships in various secret societies (or the inner circles of more public organizations) for the purpose of controlling the global corporations and financial institutions that dominate modern life. The power and influence of these corporations and institutions transcend patriotic allegiance and national sovereignty, thereby functioning as an invisible world government at work behind our legally and democratically constituted national governments.

As you will see in the chapters of Part 2, students of the NWO conspiracy regard these families as links in a great chain of conspiracy that stretches back to the time and mysteries of the ancients.

The Least You Need to Know

- The rise of the military-industrial-congressional complex is the modern product of generations of powerful industrialists and financiers who have grown their wealth by fomenting wars from which they profit.
- NWO conspiracy theorists regard war as a means of creating and maintaining national sovereignty—or seizing and transcending it to create one-world government.
- Beginning with the Rothschilds and continuing through the Morgans, Rockefellers, and other powerful dynasties, legally constituted sovereign governments have been supplanted by oligarchies.
- Among all the families NWO conspiracy theorists identify as one-world oligarchs, the Rockefellers have been most ambitious and least secretive in developing and presenting sweeping global initiatives, which they pass off as philanthropy.

Secrets of the Federal Reserve

In This Chapter

- The 1910 meeting on Jekyll Island
- Manipulating the American economy
- Central banking in the United States
- The Federal Reserve Act of 1913
- The Fed: official purpose versus "real" purpose

On the night of November 22, 1910, seven men who among them controlled perhaps a quarter of the planet's wealth approached the end of a journey that began when they boarded a private railroad car in Hoboken, New Jersey, and rode south to the small coastal-Georgia town of Brunswick. Here they boarded a private launch for Jekyll Island, 7 miles long by a mile and a half wide, part hard-packed sand, part tidal marshland, the seat of J. P. Morgan's vacation "cottage" and the enormous Queen Anne–style duck hunting club Morgan shared with the likes of Rockefeller and Vanderbilt.

The club—in fact, the entire island—had been cleared out of guests as well as staff, save for a handful of trusted servants. Its only guests for the next several days would be the seven men. The historians conspiracy writers call "mainstream" generally depict the meeting as a gathering of financial leaders dedicated to reforming the basics of the U.S. money and banking system. Conspiracy writers portray the meeting as the hijacking of those financial systems, a seizure of the nation's economy, and a bid to determine the destiny, in perpetuity, of untold millions in America and abroad.

Secret Planners, Secret Plans

Had anybody asked the seven men where they were going, they would have answered duck hunting. Had anybody asked why they were conspicuously calling each other by first names only, perhaps they wouldn't have answered at all.

The seven men were:

- Frank A. Vanderlip, representing the investment firm of Kuhn, Loeb & Company, controlled by William Rockefeller and Jacob Schiff

- Abraham Piatt Andrew, assistant secretary of the treasury

- Henry P. Davison, senior partner at J. P. Morgan & Co.

- Charles D. Norton, president of the Morgan-dominated First National Bank of New York

- Benjamin Strong, J. P. Morgan's right-hand man

- Paul Warburg, of Kuhn, Loeb & Company

- Senator Nelson W. Aldrich of Rhode Island, chairman of the National Monetary Commission

But even their full names didn't always say everything there was to say about them. Senator Aldrich, the nation's single most important financial legislator, was also in business with J. P. Morgan and was father-in-law to John D. Rockefeller Jr. Paul Warburg not only represented a major American investment house, but was the confidential agent of the European Rothschilds and the brother of Max Warburg, who, as head of the Dutch-German financial consortium M. M. Warburg, was one of the most powerful bankers in the Old World.

SECRET LIVES

Paul Mortiz Warburg (1868–1932) was born in Hamburg, Germany, to a major European banking family, married the daughter of investment banker Solomon Loeb, then moved permanently to New York and was naturalized as a U.S. citizen in 1911.

Warburg was a champion of central banking and was appointed to the first Federal Reserve Board by President Woodrow Wilson. Warburg joined the CFR at its founding in 1921 and became a member of the advisory council of the Federal Reserve Board the same year. At his death in 1932, he was chairman of the Manhattan Company and a director of many banks and major international corporations.

Reform Agenda

Ostensibly, the men were meeting to plan a banking system that would put an end to the ruinous financial panics that had dogged the unregulated American economy since the eighteenth century. It was a noble undertaking that many in both the government and business sector had been clamoring for. Woodrow Wilson, governor-elect of New Jersey at the time of the secret meeting, had even publicly remarked on how the nation might avert all its financial "trouble" if only "six or seven public-spirited men like J. P. Morgan [would volunteer to] handle the affairs of our country."

Engineered Panic

Although *financial panics* had long been an unwelcome part of American life, the Jekyll Island meeting was most immediately spurred by the severe jolt of the Panic of 1907. Like many such panics, this one began with a run on a major bank—in this case, the Knickerbocker Trust in New York.

> **DEFINITION**
>
> **Financial panic** is a somewhat vague term to describe a situation in which stocks, currency, or other assets suddenly lose a significant portion of their value, typically sending financial institutions as well as individual investors or account holders into crisis.

According to the New World Order (NWO) conspiracy authors Ralph Epperson and Jim Marrs, the Knickerbocker run was not a random event. J. P. Morgan returned to the United States from a European grand tour in 1907 and immediately started a rumor that the Knickerbocker was insolvent. This was sufficient to send key depositors running. When the mighty Knickerbocker tottered, other runs on other banks followed. Epperson, Marrs, and others believe that the Panic of 1907, like the two major U.S. panics that preceded it in 1873 and 1893, had been engineered. Morgan not only spread rumors, but he and his business associates pulled deposits from the bank and sold their Knickerbocker stock. Whereas conspiracy theorists pin the 1907 panic largely on Morgan, it was London-based international bankers who were behind the two earlier panics.

The rollercoaster of boom and bust brought on a collective national nausea. After suffering through 1873, 1893, and 1907, Americans were ready for relief. The Jekyll Island seven were prepared to give them just what they wanted.

Or, rather, they intended to give the people what the people *thought* they wanted. According to NWO conspiracy theorists, the price of an apparently stable banking system would be nothing short of a shadow government wholly controlled by Morgan, Rockefeller, Rothschild, and a few others who were given the power to regulate billions upon billions of dollars year in, year out.

INTEL

With his distinctively florid mustache, bald pate, and impeccably formal habit of dress, Paul M. Warburg cut a striking and widely known public figure. In 1924, when cartoonist Harold Gray (1894–1968) created his famed *Little Orphan Annie* comic strip for the *Chicago Tribune* syndicate, he modeled Oliver "Daddy" Warbucks, who adopts Annie, on Warburg. An idealization of a captain of industry, Daddy Warbucks wears a tuxedo and a diamond stickpin. Similar to Warburg, he is bald. Although his name clearly echoes that of Warburg, it also suggests that he made his fortune as a result of the Great War (1914–1918)—an event that also added to Paul Warburg's vast wealth.

A History Lesson

From an economist's perspective, the central theme of American history is a see-saw struggle between an economy unregulated by any central financial authority, agency, or bank, and one that is regulated, moderated, and perhaps even controlled by such an institution.

The promise of an unregulated economy is the freest of free enterprise. The hazard of the same is a whipsaw cycle of boom and bust that can bring wealth or ruin in the interval of a heartbeat. The promise of a regulated economy is stability, a flattening of the boom-bust rollercoaster. The hazard is a loss of democratic capitalist opportunity and (under certain circumstances) the concentration of financial control, wealth, and therefore inordinate political power in the hands of very few.

The Function of a Central Bank

The promised benefit of a central bank is greater economic stability. If the central bank has authority to manipulate the value of the *currency*, it can encourage boom times to boom even louder, while providing an economic cushion to make crash landings softer and more survivable. This manipulation is carried out chiefly by increasing or decreasing the money supply. When credit is tight, a boom can be stimulated by increasing the money supply. But when growth looks to be overly speculative and therefore unsustainable, the money supply can be tightened—by raising the cost of credit—which, in turn, forces investors to rein in speculation. A crash may still come, but it will have less impact and be more recoverable.

> **DEFINITION**
>
> **Currency,** in the modern sense, is the equivalent of so-called "fiat money"—signifying value yet intrinsically valueless. For example, a paper dollar bill does not consist of a dollar's worth of paper. Currency may be contrasted with *specie*, which is money (typically coins) that has intrinsic worth in addition to a monetary face value.

That, at least, is the theory. NWO conspiracy theorists are hardly alone in pointing out that central banks—most notably the Federal Reserve—often fail to sustain, let alone enhance, booms and, even more often, fail to stave off, control, or otherwise moderate busts.

A Revolutionary Cause

The same people who, in the throes of a financial panic, clamor for central regulation are also capable of rebelling against such regulation when they feel it is pinching their lives and limiting their financial growth.

Just consider the run-up to the American Revolution, when people rose in arms against authoritarian economic legislation from the British crown. Although many certainly resented the taxes Parliament imposed on various goods, it was the Currency Act of 1764 that triggered the greatest outrage of all. Lacking gold and silver mines, the colonies were chronically short on currency and so began printing their "bills of credit"—in effect, their own paper money. This freed up trade, but also created wild fluctuations in exchange rates, which prompted Parliament to forbid colonial banks, cities, and governments from printing their own money.

A Counterrevolutionary Response

The Founding Fathers of the United States were well aware of the consequences of attempting to centrally regulate the money supply as well as the consequences of failing to regulate it. When American independence was won, they wrestled with the issue. The debate came to a head during the administration of George Washington, with Secretary of the Treasury Alexander Hamilton arguing for a strong central bank, and Secretary of State Thomas Jefferson arguing against it.

Hamilton prevailed, and the First Bank of the United States was chartered to pay off war debts and thereby establish the good credit of the new country. Most historians have traditionally agreed that this was a good thing, and dismissed Jefferson's argument that the bank was unconstitutional; however, few historians have paid much attention to Jefferson's expressed fear that the central bank would remove competition among banks and therefore bind the American people to the *national bank*. The bank is "free to refuse all arrangement, but on their own terms," whereas the public would have no option "to employ any other bank."

 DEFINITION

Today, in the United States, a **national bank** is a banking institution that operates under a charter granted by the Office of the Comptroller of the Currency (OCC), a U.S. Treasury Department agency responsible for certifying that the bank meets certain standards. Not all modern banks are national; some are chartered by the states in which they operate.

In short, Jefferson feared that individual banks would scramble to gain favor with the central bank rather than with their potential depositors and seekers of credit. The result would be centrally administered collusion rather than free-market competition.

 PASSWORDS

"A national debt, if not excessive, will be to us as a national blessing."

—Secretary of the Treasury Alexander Hamilton

"I believe that banking institutions are more dangerous to our liberties than standing armies. If the American people ever allow private banks to control the issue of their currency, first by inflation, then by deflation, the banks and corporations that will grow up around [the banks] will deprive the people of all property until their children wake up homeless on the continent their fathers conquered. The issuing power should be taken from the banks and restored to the people, to whom it properly belongs."

—Attributed to Thomas Jefferson

The Monster

In effect, the First Bank of the United States was a counterrevolutionary response to a revolution that was successfully fought, in part, to end central control of the national economy. By law, the bank's charter expired after only five years. Central banking was renewed, however, as the Second Bank of the United States in 1816 during the administration of President James Madison. A protégé of Jefferson, Madison was fundamentally opposed to the idea of a central bank, but faced with massive economic instability following the ruinous War of 1812, he gave in to the idea.

This pleased the East Coast establishment, who were associated with banks that enjoyed favorable relations with the Second Bank of the United States. It outraged the rising class of inland settlers and frontiersmen—so-called westerners—whose growth and prosperity were hobbled by tight credit and scarce currency. In 1828, this class sent Andrew Jackson to the White House. He campaigned as a foe of the Second Bank, which he called "the Monster." Installed in office, Jackson killed the bank by withdrawing all federal deposits from it and letting its charter expire.

From National *Bank* to National *Banks*

Jackson's policy of decentralization freed up credit and cash but, predictably, also destabilized the economy, subjecting it to wild fluctuations. Northerners repeatedly tried to reinstitute a central banking system, but southerners resisted.

Only after the defeat of the South in the Civil War (1861–1865) did a new American banking system emerge. Certain banks were chartered not by the individual states but by the federal government, which provided a unified national currency that brought new stability, but by no means completely ended the boom-bust cycle. Moreover, lack of rigorous central regulation exposed the entire banking system to fraud and manipulation.

The Power of One

Those who held major interests in national banks, including J. P. Morgan and his cronies, were eager for the federal government to guarantee liquidity in times of crisis. This would give their banks a competitive edge on state and private banks.

Hence the assault Morgan and others mounted against the private Knickerbocker Trust in 1907. When this ballooned into a general panic, Morgan stepped in with an offer to provide liquidity to keep banks solvent and thereby control the panic. His condition was assistance from the federal government, which President Theodore Roosevelt provided in the form of $25 million in government funds. This brought an end to the panic, but it also made J. P. Morgan effectively a one-man central bank, free to decide who would survive and who would not.

In an era already bedeviled by monopolistic "trusts" in industries of every description, the onset of a one-man banking trust was too much for the public to swallow. A demand arose for genuine, disinterested government regulation in the form of a much stronger central bank.

Undaunted by the public clamor, which was in large part directed against *him*, Morgan convened the secret meeting at Jekyll Island. He wanted to hammer out what would become the Federal Reserve—the strongest central banking system in the nation's history—but (NWO conspiracy theorists argue) one that serves the interests of a handful of the most powerful bankers and financiers in the world.

The Federal Reserve Act of 1913

Like most people, Americans often tend to see things in terms of black and white, evil and good, and when the Federal Reserve Act was passed in 1913, a majority of them saw it as the triumph of selfless government over selfish—indeed, rapacious—big business. Indeed, Wall Street—Morgan included—made a great show of opposing the act, condemning it as anti-capitalist, anti-democratic, socialist, and simply unworkable.

Woodrow Wilson was elected in 1912, and his secretary of state (who was also his son-in-law), William McAdoo, noted that the bankers had fought the act "with the tireless energy of men fighting a forest fire," yet later observed that, "through all the haze and smoke of controversy," it was clear that "the banking world was not really as much opposed to the bill as it pretended to be."

PASSWORDS

The Federal Reserve System "establishes the most gigantic trust on earth … [an] invisible government …."

—Congressman Charles A. Lindbergh Sr., 1913

Official Function of the Fed

The Federal Reserve was created to provide a safer, more flexible banking and monetary system for the United States. This function has greatly expanded over the years to include the objectives of facilitating economic growth, maintaining a high level of employment, ensuring stability in the purchasing power of the dollar, and maintaining a reasonable balance in transactions with foreign countries.

To achieve both its original and expanded objectives, "the Fed" takes action to influence money and credit in the economy, largely by regulating the supply of monetary reserves and adjusting the interest rate at which the U.S. Treasury loans funds to banks that are members of the Federal Reserve. By no means is the Fed the sole regulator of the U.S. economy, but it is without doubt one of the most powerful.

Proof of the Pudding

Does the Fed work? Historically, its record is mixed at best. One has only to point to the Great Depression that began in 1929 (16 years *after* the Federal Reserve had been established) and endured throughout the 1930s to find evidence of its failure.

What happened in this case? Established in part to rein in the unregulated money "trusts" and "interlocking directorates"—boards of directors of the nations supposedly independent and competing financial institutions that were actually closely related and often in collusion—the Fed actually endowed national banks with more freedom and power. These included the right to establish overseas branches and offer a host of new, sometimes highly speculative banking services. Most of all, the Fed served as a vast pool of loan money, which encouraged banks to put more of their depositors' and investors' funds at risk.

Throughout the 1920s, the monetary supply rapidly expanded, feeding a frenzied economic growth that, based on unwarranted speculation, proved tragically unsustainable. The result was the crash of 1929 and the beginning of the worst economic depression in modern history.

Similarly, the Fed did nothing to avert the "housing bubble" and catastrophic economic "meltdown" of 2007 and 2008. Conspiracy theorists are not alone in suggesting that these and other "failures" through the years have not been entirely accidental. Some believe they are, at least in part, the products of the deliberate application of a policy not of prudent regulation, but of reckless license: the empowerment of big money speculators—the wealthy few who, in the 1990s, took to calling themselves the "masters of the universe," embracing the satirical tag novelist Tom Wolfe applied to them in his 1987 book, *The Bonfire of the Vanities*.

"Invisible Government"

The governing body of the Federal Reserve is a seven-member Board of Governors, located in Washington, D.C. The president of the United States appoints each member to a 14-year term, subject to Senate confirmation. The president appoints a chairman and vice-chairman from among the members, again with the consent of the Senate.

The leadership of the Federal Reserve has traditionally been highly academic and long-serving. As this book was being written, Ben S. Bernanke, Ph.D., was chairman of the Board of Governors of the Federal Reserve System, having been appointed on February 1, 2010. He had also served earlier, beginning on February 1, 2006. Although his second term as chairman will end on January 31, 2014, he will continue to serve on the board until January 31, 2020.

Before he was appointed to his first term, Bernanke had chaired the President's Council of Economic Advisers from June 2005 to January 2006 and was associated with the Federal Reserve System in several roles. He had been a member of the Board of Governors of the Federal Reserve System from 2002 to 2005; a visiting scholar at the Federal Reserve Banks of Philadelphia (1987–1989), Boston (1989–1990), and New York (1990–1991, 1994–1996); and a member of the Academic Advisory Panel at the Federal Reserve Bank of New York (1990–2002).

Bernanke became a professor of economics and public affairs at Princeton University in 1985, and from 1994 to 1996, he was the Class of 1926 Professor of Economics and Public Affairs at Princeton University. He was the Howard Harrison and Gabrielle Snyder Beck Professor of Economics and Public Affairs and Chair of the Economics Department at the university from 1996 to 2002.

Before coming to Princeton, Bernanke taught at the Graduate School of Business of Stanford University, at New York University (1993), and at the Massachusetts Institute of Technology (1989–1990). He earned a B.A. in economics (summa cum laude) from Harvard in 1975 and a Ph.D. in economics four years later from the Massachusetts Institute of Technology.

The vice chairman of the Board of Governors, Donald L. Kohn, took office as a board member on August 5, 2002, and was sworn in as vice chairman for a four-year term ending June 23, 2010. Like Bernanke, Kohn had a long association with the Federal Reserve System. Before becoming a member of the Board, he served on its staff as Adviser to the Board for Monetary Policy (2001–2002), Secretary of the Federal Open Market Committee (1987–2002), Director of the Division of Monetary Affairs (1987–2001), and Deputy Staff Director for Monetary and Financial Policy (1983–1987). He also worked for the Board's Division of Research and Statistics going back to 1970.

Kohn earned his Bachelor's degree in economics at the College of Wooster in 1964 and his Ph.D. in economics in 1971 from the University of Michigan.

Whereas the organization of the Board of Governors is straightforward, the rest of the structure of the Federal Reserve System gets rather weird. The president appoints the Board of Governors, yet that board is not part of the administration or even the executive branch. Instead, it functions as an entirely independent agency of the federal government. And although the Board of Governors is a federal agency—albeit answerable to no other federal agency or authority—the Federal Reserve System itself is not truly part of the federal government. It describes itself as "an independent entity within the government, having both public purposes and private aspects."

Neither the Federal Reserve nor its component banks are owned by anyone or any entity, including the government or the people of the United States; however, its 12 component Federal Reserve Banks are privately held by private investors.

INTEL

Each Federal Reserve Bank is the headquarter institution of one of the 12 Federal Reserve Districts into which the United States is divided.

1st: Boston
2nd: New York City
3rd: Philadelphia
4th: Cleveland, Ohio
5th: Richmond, Virginia
6th: Atlanta, Georgia
7th: Chicago
8th: St. Louis, Missouri
9th: Minneapolis
10th: Kansas City, Missouri
11th: Dallas, Texas
12th: San Francisco

Nominally independent, the 12 banks are nevertheless dominated by the Federal Reserve Bank in New York City (Second District). Some NWO conspiracy writers claim that the stockholders of the New York Federal Reserve Bank are mostly the stockholders of the major New York City–based banks—that is, the members of the few families who have long held or controlled an inordinate proportion of the nation's wealth. Among them are the Morgans, the Rockefellers, and those related by marriage to these families.

In short, the Federal Reserve System puts the most powerful central bank in U.S. history—perhaps the most powerful central bank in global history—in private hands.

The Money Cult

By means of the Federal Reserve, according to conspiracy theorists, a select group of oligarchs exerts direct control over the U.S. economy and, through it, the global economy. Moreover, because the Fed effectively underwrites private banks doing business in the United States, the American taxpayer even provides coverage for any losses the oligarchs might incur.

This, it would seem, would be a sweet enough deal for even the most power-hungry of magnates. But there is more. The Federal Reserve System is so complex, its workings so esoteric, that it is no longer merely a financial institution, but a secret society, a cult—even a kind of religion, say conspiracy theorists. At the heart of this new faith is a "mystery" as potent as that of any religion.

Whereas the observant Catholic (for instance) accepts a bland wafer and a sip of ordinary red wine as the inherently sacred body and blood of Christ, millions in America and billions the world over accept as inherently valuable the paper currency the "priests" of the Federal Reserve pronounce as valuable. It is a power that no dictator, president, or monarch—and only a handful of prophets—have ever wielded anywhere and at any time.

The Least You Need to Know

- The outline of the Federal Reserve System was planned in secret by seven powerful financiers in a 1910 meeting on Jekyll Island, Georgia, under the sponsorship of J. P. Morgan.

- The Federal Reserve Act of 1913 was presented as an effort to centralize American banking to reduce the harmful effects of otherwise ruinous boom-and-bust cycles.

- NWO conspiracy theorists believe that a handful of the nation's wealthiest financiers promoted the creation of the Federal Reserve as a means of gaining greater control of the American economy. That way they could, at will, create booms and busts to increase their own wealth and power.

- The Federal Reserve System is a unique hybrid of government and private enterprise; conspiracy theorists believe that it puts the nation's central bank wholly in private hands.

New Age and End Time

In This Chapter

- The link between utopian socialism and New Age global government
- Globalism in the "Age of Aquarius"
- H. G. Wells and Ann Bailey as precursors of New Age globalism
- The conservative Christian critique of the NWO
- How New Age beliefs attempt to sabotage the End Time

It is possible to argue that organized religion was the very first New World Order (NWO) conspiracy and one-world government movement. After all, many who passionately espouse a particular religion believe that theirs and only theirs is the "one true faith" and therefore should be universal among humankind. Jihad, Crusade, Reformation, Counter-reformation—many great and terrible wars have been fought for the purpose of extinguishing one faith and propagating another.

But when most contemporary NWO conspiracy theorists talk about the role of religion in the one-world government movement, they zero in specifically on two current religious strains: the New Age movement and the End Time movement.

From Global Federation to Synarchy

Herbert George (H. G.) Wells (1866–1946) was born poor in Bromley, Kent, and might have stayed that way had he not broken his leg in 1874. Laid up for a long time, he started reading books from the local library and decided as a result to become a writer. He could not decide what kind of writing to specialize in, so he became a polymath, with remarkable command of a dazzling range of subjects. He produced in his lifetime a vast bibliography that includes at least 51 novels, some 30 short-story collections (published during his lifetime—many more have appeared posthumously), and more than 70 book-length works of nonfiction in many fields.

Although he is best known for his often remarkably prescient science fiction, including *The Time Machine, The Island of Doctor Moreau,* and *The War of the Worlds,* he was also a prolific *socialist* thinker and modern utopianist. He is the author of two important works that combine these two strains, *The Open Conspiracy* (1928, with revisions in 1930, 1931, and 1933) and *The New World Order* (1940).

DEFINITION

In the strictest sense, **socialism** describes a set of political and economic theories in which the workers own and manage all means of production and all members of society have access to resources allocated based on the amount of labor an individual performs. For NWO conspiracy theorists, socialism also implies the creation of a global authoritarian state that possesses the power and authority to control and distribute resources.

The Open Conspiracy

Wells's vision in *The Open Conspiracy* was of a world in which the most intelligent people of all nations assembled for the purpose of creating a global federation transcending nationality and state sovereignty but embodying democracy in socialistic global institutions. This "open conspiracy," Wells believed, would bring about a great "adjustment" of "our dislocated world," reconciling national, political, religious, social, cultural, and economic differences and producing a collaborative humanity.

PASSWORDS

"It seemed to me that all over the world intelligent people were waking up to the indignity and absurdity of being endangered, restrained, and impoverished, by a mere uncritical adhesion to traditional governments, traditional ideas of economic life, and traditional forms of behaviour, and that these awaking intelligent people must constitute first a protest and then a creative resistance to the inertia that was stifling and threatening us."

—H. G. Wells, *The Open Conspiracy,* 1928

The New World Order

If the idea of adjusting our dislocated world sounded like another way of talking about bringing a "new world order" into being, Wells himself made this connection explicit in his 1940 book, *The New World Order*. With Europe roiling in the second great war of the century—a war that would engulf virtually the entire world by the end of the following year—he elaborated on his earlier ideas of transcending nationalism and state sovereignty by means of a global federation.

Wells argued that such a one-world government was not only possible, but obviously beneficial as the only truly effective means of avoiding future war. That is, if war is usually a contest between states, then by transcending the concept of sovereign statehood, the greatest engine of war would thereby be dismantled.

The Failed Promise of the Socialist World State

Both *The Open Conspiracy* and *The New World Order* were popular and highly influential among socialist-minded reformers, who, after 1940, picked up on Wells's title and spoke frequently about creating a "new world order." They tended to regard Joseph Stalin's Soviet Union as a well-intentioned but failed attempt to create a socialist world state and argued that, had the Bolsheviks and Stalin maintained the purity of Karl Marx's original vision of communism, a genuine new world order would have been introduced. Class consciousness—a global union of all workers—would have replaced divisive and destructive allegiance to individual sovereign states.

Enter Alice Bailey

Alice Ann Bailey (1880–1949) was born Alice LaTrobe Bateman in Manchester, UK, but lived most of her life in the United States, to which she immigrated in 1907. Influenced by the theosophical writings of Madame Blavatsky, she created a body of *esoteric* writings that are often referred to as "neo-theosophy," a version of the idea that all religions are attempts to help humanity evolve to a greater degree of perfection.

DEFINITION

In spiritual and philosophical contexts, the adjective **esoteric** refers to bodies of thought and belief that turn inward and draw on mysticism and ancient wisdom. The secret societies and movements discussed in Part 2 are all aspects of esoteric belief.

Theosophy combines religion and broad spirituality with philosophy and what must be described as metaphysics to facilitate humanity's climb through a "Spiritual Hierarchy" that will bring people to a plane of greater spiritual and intellectual perfection. Theosophy is not a new religion, but an attempt to synthesize the best of existing religions in the belief that each of the world's faiths has a "portion" of the truth and is therefore a step up the Spiritual Hierarchy.

INTEL

Theosophy was established in 1875 in New York City by the Theosophical Society. It was founded by the movement's chief figure, Helena Petrovna Blavatsky (1831–1891), Henry Steel Olcott (1832–1907), and William Quan Judge. The Russian-born "Madame Blavatsky" (as she was known) was an earnest and charismatic figure who became widely regarded as a spiritual and philosophical teacher. Among them a variety of literary figures (including Irish poet William Butler Yeats), political reformers (such as Indian National Congress champion Allan O. Hume), philosophers, and, far more darkly, Adolf Hitler.

Bailey's writings are copious, complex, and, for many, maddeningly vague. For the purposes of the NWO, she is best known for advancing the idea that, due to the confluence of certain astrological influences sometime during the millennium beginning in 2001, humankind would enter the Age of Aquarius, marked by universal freedom and extraordinary advances in technology (especially electricity). This would usher in a global epoch of group consciousness. Although, astrologically, the Age of Aquarius was distant—estimates vary from early to mid to late in the millennium—its "dawning," Bailey believed, could be discerned in the twentieth century, and enlightened thinkers could act in ways that would anticipate the utopian transformations it would bring.

For some, Bailey's reputation was irreparably damaged by anti-Semitic and racist elements in her writings, but many regard her as the founder of the so-called New Age movement based on what she called *synarchy*. This refers to a one-world rule guided by a class of enlightened, esoteric, or ascended masters, who guide humanity to full acceptance and realization of the dawn of the Age of Aquarius, which Bailey sometimes associated with the mystical Second Coming of Christ.

DEFINITION

Synarchy describes one-world government guided by a class of enlightened, esoteric, or ascended masters, who lead humanity to greater perfection.

Although Bailey's vision was mystical and quasi-religious, she also deliberately harmonized her theory of the New Age and the dawning of the Age of Aquarius with the writings of H. G. Wells. She saw in his concept of global federation the hard-edged practical and political manifestation of her own occultism. Indeed, in the midst of World War II, she seized on Wells's *The New World Order* as a platform for her own prophecy that the Allies (mainly Britain and the United States) would defeat the Axis (Germany, Italy, and Japan) and would establish a new world order. Champions of Bailey's thought point to the United Nations, created by the victorious Allies, as the precursor of precisely this.

 SECRET LIVES

Under the aegis of the Theosophical Society, Alice Ann Bailey (1880–1949) began publishing on subjects encompassing astrology, esoteric thought, spiritual psychology, spiritual healing, meditation, the future—she was a self-described prophet—and utopian visions of society. She claimed that none of what she wrote was original, but was merely a transcription of wisdom she received telepathically from a figure she referred to variously as the "Master of the Wisdom," "the Tibetan," or "D.K." (Djwhal Khul, a Tibetan master revered by some Theosophists).

Her body of work always returns to the theme of unifying society through a global or universal "spirit of religion," which anticipates the quasi-millennial liberation and unification of spirit that will come with the astrological Age of Aquarius. Some NWO conspiracy writers condemn her ideas (along with New Age utopianism in general) as everything from anti-Christian to pro-communist to satanic.

New Age Beliefs as New World Order Conspiracy

Christians and others who espouse End Time theology (sometimes called *millenarianism*), believe that we live in a corrupt, wicked, and unjust civilization, which is on the verge of the apocalypse—in which the evil majority will be annihilated and the pious elect translated by the Rapture into the Kingdom of Heaven. Some millenarians and "End Timers" see the New Age belief in one-world government—and, indeed, any manifestation of the NWO conspiracy—as a fulfillment of the biblical prophecies in the Book of Ezekiel, the Book of Daniel, and Revelations concerning the End Time: namely that it will be heralded by false prophets and the coming of the Antichrist.

DEFINITION

Millenarianism is a belief primarily held by some Christians and among some Christian denominations that a golden age of heaven on Earth is approaching as the penultimate step toward the Final Judgment—that is, the end of the world.

Millenarians believe that New Agers and others who advocate one-world government are agents of Satan, who, in the End Time, will engage God in a final titanic evil-versus-good struggle for universal dominance. In this view, New Age advocates (including, according to some, Scientologists) are false prophets, and such figures as the secretary-general of the United Nations may be the Antichrist himself.

Successfully resisting the manifestations of the NWO conspiracy, whether in the form of some New Age religion, Scientology, the Council on Foreign Relations (CFR), the United Nations, or another globalist influence will not put off the end of the world, but it will position those who successfully resist on the side of God and good rather than in league with Satan and evil. It will confirm their faith, thereby preventing them from being "left behind" at the time of the Rapture—the transportation of the faithful into the kingdom of heaven.

One does not necessarily have to be a millenarian to regard New Age beliefs as aspects of an NWO conspiracy. Many conservative (so-called "fundamentalist") Protestants and conservative Catholics (whether or not they explicitly profess End Time beliefs) also see New Age doctrine in this light. Some Jewish writers have criticized the New Age body of thought, at least insofar as it is derived from Alice Ann Bailey's writings, as anti-Semitic. These writers assert that the one-world government it advocates excludes Jews and is therefore aimed ultimately at destroying Judaism.

The New World Order Conspiracy as an Imperial Cult

"You shall have no other gods before me" is the very first of the Ten Commandments. Those who condemn on religious grounds (typically conservative, evangelical Christians) various New Age movements, nonconventional global religions (such as Scientology), and ostensibly secular global movements (the CFR, the Bilderberg Group, TC, the UN, and so on) ultimately regard them all as manifestations of an *imperial cult*—that is, a secular religion in which some leader or even a set of principles is worshipped as a false god.

The conviction that various forms of globalist doctrine figure as false gods in an imperial cult, thereby breaking the First Commandment, is the common denominator of virtually all Christian-based NWO conspiracy theories. It matters little if the doctrine in question has actual and deliberate religious, spiritual, or theological content (as in New Age belief), or even if it's resolutely secular and makes no claim or reference to religion or theology (United Nations "global government," for example). From the conservative Christian perspective, *any* one-world "faith" is an obstacle standing sinfully between humanity and the "One True God" and is therefore an evil to be feared, shunned, and destroyed.

The Least You Need to Know

- According to some NWO conspiracy writers, nineteenth- and twentieth-century utopian socialist thought and New Age beliefs have conspired to create a movement toward global government.

- New Age doctrine blends a body of theosophist-derived spiritual theory with socialist utopian thought to create a vision of a world unified by a single government in which wise masters guide humanity to enlightenment and greater perfection.

- Some conservative Christians (and others) believe that the New Age doctrine first espoused by the Neo-Theosophist writer Ann Bailey in the first half of the twentieth century is part of a conspiracy to aid false prophets and the Antichrist in defeating the forces of good and God at the approaching End Time.

Roots

Those who believe they have exposed a New World Order conspiracy argue that it exists today and is growing in strength and influence as it moves toward the future. Nevertheless, the roots of the New World Order are ancient, and the chapters of Part 2 take you back—nearly a half million years—then forward, through the epoch before Christ, into the Middle Ages, through the Enlightenment and the Age of Reason, and into the heyday of Freemasonry. Many conspiracy theorists believe this is the most important force in Western history, and all the more powerful because so few of us know anything about it.

Ancient Secrets

In This Chapter

- Links between the modern NWO conspiracy and ancient history
- Constantine I and the fourth-century Christian Church as one-world government prototypes
- Gnostics and Essenes
- Secret wisdom coded in the Bible and Cabalistic texts
- Ultimate secrets as the ultimate knowledge

Although some people are inclined to see conspiracies in practically everything, others reject the very notion of conspiracy out of hand. Even so, if you define the "new world order conspiracy" as a group of the world's wealthiest people conspiring to preserve their wealth and build even more by controlling government, you stand a good chance of persuading even the most skeptical that at least some aspects of a powerful one-world government movement are plausible. Yet put it this way to those who already believe in such a conspiracy, and you will be told that your definition does not go far enough. Yes, the New World Order (NWO) conspiracy is about powerful people trying to become even more powerful, the true believers will tell you, but it hardly stops with this. There is a backstory—a very long one.

The three main historical pillars of the globalist conspiracy theory—the Council on Foreign Relations (CFR; see Chapter 2), the Bilderberg Group (see Chapter 3), and the Trilateral Commission (TC; see Chapter 4)—are all twentieth-century creations. However, these and the other modern manifestations of the NWO have ancient roots in certain pre-Christian cults and secret societies. The most important of these represent an ancient wisdom that is itself rooted in the very beginnings of civilization and maybe even in a reality that is, quite literally, out of this world.

Litmus Test

Being willing to sign on to the theory that the one-world government movement is rooted in ancient mysteries is the litmus test for the true NWO conspiracy believer. Even those whose instinctive response is to dismiss conspiracy theories as symptoms of faulty reasoning or outright paranoia can be persuaded to at least entertain the possibilities presented in Part 1 of this book. Nothing is more universally familiar than the profit motive and the tendency for the rich and powerful to crave greater wealth and more power. Therefore, it requires no great imaginative leap to believe that rich and powerful people might conspire to protect, enhance, and enlarge their place in the world. To believe this is really no different from believing that (for example) oil barons have, from time to time, secretly colluded to fix the price of oil.

But to believe in a globalist conspiracy that exists not merely to make more money, but also because it is joined to the distant past by mystical cords of secret tradition and ancient knowledge—*that* requires a commitment to conspiracy theory that far fewer readily make. Yet it is just such a belief that characterizes NWO conspiracy theories in their most complete and fully formed versions.

   PASSWORDS

"You will know the truth and the truth will make you free."

—John 8:32, frequently quoted by conspiracy believers

The New World Order Conspiracy, Old School

The Christian Church was 300 years old in the fourth century. That should have boded well for the continued longevity of any faith, especially one that was started by a renegade Jew scorned by both the mainstream religious authorities of the Middle East (where he preached) and the secular authorities. The all-powerful administrators of the Roman Empire summarily executed him when he was only 33. But the fact was that the fourth-century Christian Church was torn by competing sects and rival theologies, all vying for control of a faith that truly promised to bring a new order to the world.

Who Has the Power?

The Roman emperor Diocletian, who reigned from 303 to 305, unleashed the Great Persecution—also called the Diocletian Persecution—at the start of his reign. Under this pressure, some Christians renounced their faith, including some bishops, who, on demand, handed over sacred scriptures to be burned (and were therefore called *traditores*, "ones who had handed over"). Diocletian's successor, Constantine I, reversed the persecution policy in 313, proclaiming religious toleration throughout the Roman Empire. He was motivated by his desire to become the absolute and undisputed Augustus (emperor) over a unified Roman Empire, which had been split into a Western and an Eastern empire.

> **DEFINITION**
>
> *Traditore* (Latin, "one who had handed over") refers to the fourth-century Christian bishops who, persecuted by the Roman emperor Diocletian, handed over on demand sacred scriptures, which the Romans burned. The modern word *traitor* is derived from this Latin root.

Christians were grateful for an end to the persecution, but they were divided over the status of the *traditores* and others who had earlier renounced their faith. Whereas most Christians were willing to welcome these individuals back into the church and even reinstate the authority of *traditore* priests and bishops, the Donatists (named after their leader, Donatus Magnus) refused to accept them, especially the *traditores*. The Donatists appealed to Constantine to support their position. In response, he convened the Council of Arles in 314—a convocation of church authorities—which, far from supporting Donatus, excommunicated him, thereby ending the Donatist "heresy" and, even more importantly, identified Constantine I as an agent of the God of Christianity. This in effect conferred on him divine status (which would later be ratified by his canonization as a saint).

Eleven years after the Council of Arles, Constantine convened the First Council of Nicaea, the first *ecumenical* council in the history of the Christian Church. The word is significant. Derived from the Greek *oikoumenikos*, it means "worldwide" and reflects the intention of the council to establish Christianity as the single uniform governing faith of the world (equivalent at the time to the Roman Empire). The council produced the Nicene Creed, which remains the most widely accepted profession of the Christian faith. It also sealed the identification of Constantine with the one true church—thereby facilitating his own elevation to the position of uncontested Augustus over an empire that unified East and West.

DEFINITION

Ecumenical (from the Greek *oikoumenikos,* meaning "worldwide") is the adjective applied today to convocations of world religious leaders. It was first applied in 325 to the First Council of Nicaea, a gathering of Christian leaders from all over the Roman Empire (in effect, the known world). The word reflects the early church's effort to become, in effect, a global governing authority.

Suppressing Alternate Realities

With the First Council of Nicaea in 325, the Christian Church had taken a major step toward resolving internal dissent and establishing itself as the dominant faith throughout the Roman Empire, which included most of the known world. Moreover, Constantine I made himself the vast realm's undisputed emperor.

This required more than congenial and consensual resolution of all dissent. The Arians, followers of a priest named Arius (250–336), who denied the divinity of Jesus and thereby proposed the most dangerous alternative to the idea of a holy Trinity (Father, Son, and Holy Ghost), were declared heretical and ejected from the council and the church. A year after this, Constantine himself ordered the confiscation and destruction of all religious texts that questioned the new orthodoxy proclaimed by the First Council. In 331, he ordered that new copies of Christian texts be made.

Some NWO theorists interpret the actions of the First Council of Nicaea and Constantine's subsequent decrees concerning Christian texts as a conspiracy. Church and state authority acted to suppress ancient wisdom to promote the absolute spiritual authority of the newly established "orthodox" Christian Church and the secular authority of Constantine I. They point out that most of the early Christian texts had already been destroyed during the Diocletian Persecution, so Constantine recognized and exploited what was for him a golden opportunity to create Christian doctrine in a version that suited his one-world government agenda. Theorists argue that the New Testament, as it now exists, was edited to withhold from the masses the most important ancient wisdom and instead disseminate doctrine that served to unify the church and the state under one rule.

Esoteric Knowledge

In theory, the purpose of religion is to deliver the truth, and the ultimate truth concerns the origin of humankind and the place of the individual in the universe. In practice, however, religion is crafted and controlled by the wealthy and the powerful—men such as Constantine I—who want to protect and increase their wealth and power, even if that means withholding the ultimate truth from the people.

According to some NWO conspiracy writers, the Catholic Church was instrumental in creating part of a scheme to transmit to the masses a version of reality edited so as to enable church and emperor to achieve and maintain absolute control of the known world. What was edited out of this picture was certain ancient knowledge that threatened the power of the church and the state.

SECRET LIVES

Constantine I (ca. 272–337) became a Roman emperor (Caesar) in 306 in the Western Empire and proclaimed himself Augustus (absolute ruler) in 309. The Eastern Empire accepted him as Augustus in 310. Two years later, his status as Augustus was also undisputed in the West, and from 324 until his death in 337, he reigned as Augustus over a reunified Roman Empire.

Constantine I embraced Christianity, reunified the Roman Empire, and established the Christian Church as the "Catholic" Church, from the Greek *katholikos*, meaning "universal." In the context of the NWO, Constantine I created the prototype of a one-world government, putting most of the known world under a single political and spiritual authority.

The Gnostics

The Gnostics were religious groups—some concentrated in Persia, others in Syria and Egypt—whose members professed a personal and direct relationship with God, which, precisely because it was personal and direct, did not require the mediation of a priestly hierarchy, a church. It is one thing for a church to have to cope with internal dissent concerning specific articles of faith and theology, but absolutely nothing is more dangerous than people who claim to have no need for a church of any kind.

It is unclear whether or not the origins of Gnosticism preceded Christianity, but Gnostics not only claimed to be Christians, they claimed to be the only *true* Christians inasmuch as they were keepers of an ancient wisdom that had been wrongfully excluded from the New Testament.

Some Gnostics sought to introduce into Christianity the spiritual ideas of the ancient Greek philosophers, such as Socrates. Others introduced elements of belief from ancient Mesopotamia, including the idea that entities known as "aeons" were messengers between the heavens and the earth. Persian Gnostics sought to introduce into Christianity elements of Zoroastrian belief, with its dualistic vision of a universe in which dark and light, evil and good, perpetually contend.

Whatever specific doctrine various Gnostic groups attempted to introduce into Christian belief, the most important, according to influential Freemason/philosopher/historian Manly P. Hall (1901–1990), was the knowledge required for spiritual regeneration. Although conventional Christianity had suppressed this knowledge, Laurence Gardner (in *Genesis of the Grail Kings*, 1999) explained that modern Freemasonry (see Chapter 15) preserved it through its own hierarchy in which members ascend in rank through 33 degrees of initiation. According to Gardner, the Gnostic regeneration took place through the 33 vertebrae of the spinal column.

INTEL

Of various Gnostic terms, none has elicited more speculation from modern commentators than the *aeon*. Although the word is generally interpreted as a collective label for the various "emanations" of God, a number of modern writers speculate that *aeons* were actual beings of extraterrestrial origin, who perhaps 450,000 years ago visited the earth, bringing wisdom from another planet, solar system, or galaxy.

If one accepts aeons as aliens from other worlds, one must conclude that the ultimate secret knowledge is of extraterrestrial origin; indeed, some conspiracy theorists assert just this.

The Essenes

After Constantine, Christianity succeeded in withholding Gnostic wisdom from the great mass of humanity, but Gnosticism nevertheless persisted among the literate minority through the Middle Ages and formed the basis of many esoteric secret societies, including Freemasonry and the Illuminati (see Chapter 13).

Gnosticism also influenced the Essenes, a Jewish sect that flourished from the century before the birth of Christ through the first century following his birth. The theology of this group differed sharply from the Jewish mainstream, and some NWO writers believe that the Essenes preserved and developed Greek philosophical traditions. Included in these is the doctrine of Pythagoras (sixth century B.C.E.) that the universe is structured according to a system of celestial mathematics known as the "harmony of the spheres." These writers draw a line from Pythagoras (and subsequently Plato) via the Gnostic-influenced Essenes to Freemasonry and the Illuminati as well as those influenced by Freemasonry and Illuminism. One so influenced was Cecil Rhodes, founder of the Round Table movement, which helped shape the modern NWO conspiracy (see Chapter 5). The Essenes are also widely regarded as a source of the Rosicrucians, a group that, in turn, is often identified as a historical source of the modern one-world government movement (see Chapter 14).

As with Gnosticism, Essene belief was suppressed by the early Christian Church, and kept from the uneducated masses. Manly P. Hall (and others) believed that Jesus Christ had been educated by Essene rabbis and was thereby initiated into the Pythagorean wisdom.

PASSWORDS

"The Essenes were regarded as among the better educated classes of Jews. The fact that so many artificers were listed among their number is responsible for the order's being considered as a progenitor of modern Freemasonry."

—Manly P. Hall, *The Secret Teachings of All Ages* (1928)

Coded Revelation

Constantine and other promoters of early mainstream Christianity suppressed but did not destroy Gnostic, Essene, and other strains of ancient wisdom that threatened to undermine their control of spiritual and secular power. According to a number of recent writers—including Michael Drosnin, author of the 1997 bestseller *The Bible Code*—the Bible we know today emerged from Christian texts edited during the period of Constantine, replete with coded messages. Properly interpreted, these not only provide Nostradamus-like predictions of modern events (the Kennedy assassination, World War II, the Oklahoma City federal building bombing of 1995, and so on), they also point backward, toward the ancient past and a deeper understanding of deities suppressed by fourth-century Christianity.

Back to Sumer

Some who believe that embedded within the Bible is an extensively coded revelation argue that the message points far into the past, to ancient Sumer—the planet's earliest known civilization, dating to the sixth millennium B.C.E.

What great wisdom did these most ancient people possess that "modern" Christianity (that is, Christianity as it emerged in the fourth century) and "modern" central government (as personified in Constantine I) sought to suppress?

The answer will come at the end of this chapter, but, for now, it is important to know that those who trace the modern NWO conspiracy to the ancient secret societies regard the Essenes as, in effect, the oldest secret society. They believe that they were the guardians of a suppressed Mystic Christianity, which was based on "ancient mysteries" with origins in Sumer.

Cabala

Those NWO conspiracy writers who believe that the Essenes were the first genuine secret society and functioned as guardians of a wisdom dating back to the beginning of civilization in Sumer also believe that they were the first students of *Cabala*.

Scholars agree that the origins of the Cabala predate Jesus, and some trace it to the historical period of Genesis, to secrets passed from the sons of Adam to Noah and on to Abraham. Some NWO theorists believe that the knowledge contained within Cabala is Sumerian in origin, carried out of Sumer by Abraham. Others identify Cabala as a form of Gnosticism—that is, texts that aid humankind in finding divinity within themselves.

DEFINITION

Cabala (also spelled Qabala[h], Kabbala[h], and in other variant forms) may refer to a variety of systems of mysticism (all ultimately derived from Jewish mystical tradition) or to a body of Jewish religious texts (Torah, Heichalot, Sefer Yetzirah, Bahir, Sefer Raziel HaMalakh, Zohar, Pardes Rimonim, and Etz Hayim) that embody these mystical teachings.

The Cabalistic texts are obscure and have been the subject of centuries of study and commentary. Some interpret the obscurity of the texts as deliberate code—or, rather, the revelation of codes that are embedded within the Old Testament and other Jewish texts. What all authorities agree on is that the texts convey the mystical aspect of

Judaism and are esoteric teachings concerning the inherently mysterious and para-doxical relationship between finite and mortal humankind and infinite and immortal divinity. In short, Cabala is the secret of life's meaning and, as such, has long figured as a kind of metaphor for the ultimate esoteric or secret knowledge, the possession of which implies utmost secrecy and conspiracy. The English word *cabal* is a synonym for a group of secret conspirators.

Because Cabala is the very essence of secret wisdom, it is understandable that those who delve into the deep background of the NWO conspiracy believe that the Knights Templar (see Chapter 12)—the secret society associated with the ultimate prize of Christianity, the Holy Grail—brought Cabalistic lore with them from the Holy Land to Europe during the Crusades. Moreover, the Templars imparted this lore to the Masonic guilds (precursors of the Freemasons) with which the Templars were allied (see Chapter 15).

Not that the Freemasons obtained a European monopoly on Cabalistic wisdom. Many secret societies, including the Rosicrucians (see Chapter 14) and various modern groups, are interested in Cabala. Moses Mendelssohn (1729–1786), the prominent German Jewish philosopher and the grandfather of composer Felix Mendelssohn, was a Cabalist who counted among his friends Adam Weishaupt (1748–1830), the founder of the Illuminati—the eighteenth-century secret society that virtually every NWO discussion cites as direct precursor of the modern one-world government movement (see Chapter 13). Thus Cabala is linked quite directly to the NWO conspiracy, and the NWO is thereby connected, through Cabala, to a secret society tradition that reaches back to Sumer and the very beginning of civilization.

INTEL

Critics of those who claim to discern coded messages in the Bible, Cabalistic texts, and other scriptural material argue that virtually any extended text can be decoded to reveal virtually anything. In *Newsweek* (June 9, 1997), *Bible Code* author Michael Drosnin threw out a challenge: "When my critics find a message about the assassination of a prime minister encrypted in *Moby Dick*, I'll believe them."

Computer scientist Brendan McKay (b. 1951) did just that. His website, "Assassinations Foretold in Moby Dick!" (http://cs.anu.edu.au/~bdm/dilugim/moby.html), "reveals" coded predictions of multiple assassinations (including Indira Gandhi, Dr. Martin Luther King Jr., John F. Kennedy, and others) in the text of Herman Melville's 1851 novel.

Ultimate Secret? Ultimate Truth

Students of secret societies in general and the NWO conspiracy in particular endlessly pursue precursors and links to the past. The point of such exercises is not always clear. It may be possible to trace the lineage of, say, the CFR or even the Federal Reserve to the Illuminati and the Illuminati in turn to Cabala and Cabala to the very dawn of civilization. But does anyone seriously propose that Woodrow Wilson's adviser Colonel House or U.S. magnate J. P. Morgan had the Sumerians on their minds when the CFR and the Federal Reserve came into being?

There is a more plausible and relevant connection. Although some NWO conspiracy theorists really do attempt to draw direct causal links between the ancient secret societies and the agencies they identify today with the one-world government movement, the majority are more concerned with identifying *similarity* of motive. The Rothschilds, Rockefellers, and Morgans, they argue, like Constantine I and the fourth-century church leaders at Nicaea, were interested in possessing secret knowledge while withholding it from the masses.

Knowledge is power runs the cliché, and, like most clichés, it conveys more than a little truth. Those who possess the knowledge wield the power over those who are left in darkness. But just what is the final knowledge, the ultimate truth? For most students of the NWO conspiracy, it is simply the fact of deception on an enormous scale—the proposition that a number of public or quasi-public organizations and agencies actually operate as secret societies and, behind the veil of democracy, ensure that real authority and control of government are concentrated in the hands of the super-select power elite.

That would seem to be secret enough. Yet a few theorists, most notably Jim Marrs, discern an even more spectacular secret. Archaeologists identify the Anunnaki as the collective name for the Sumerian deities who appear in the *Enuma Elish*, the Sumerian creation myth. Marrs and a number of other authors interpret the Anunnaki as humanoid extraterrestrials who visited the earth some 450,000 years ago from a world the Sumerians called Nibiru. A Sumerian text depicts it as the twelfth planet of our solar system (a planet yet to be discovered).

Thus, the final secret—the ultimate truth that has been kept from us—is *not* the covert existence of real power in the hidden hands of a very few who will not rest until they control the world, but the existence of a body of infinitely advanced knowledge of extraterrestrial origin that is embedded in the most ancient texts of the earth's earliest civilization.

The Least You Need to Know

- The most thorough NWO conspiracy theorists trace the modern one-world government movement to remote historical origins, potentially leading back to the origin of civilization in Sumer.

- Constantine I and his efforts to establish the Christian Church throughout the fourth-century Roman world constitutes the historical prototype of the one-world government.

- At the heart of all large conspiracies, including the NWO conspiracy, is control of knowledge. Secret societies exist to obtain, preserve, and guard the kind of knowledge believed to confer power on those who possess it.

- The Gnostics and Essenes are the "original" secret societies, which preserve and protect true religion, in contrast to the religion transmitted to the masses by the wealthy and powerful. Some of the truth is also preserved, in coded form, in the Bible, Cabalistic texts, and other sacred scripture.

The Templars and Others

Chapter

12

In This Chapter

- The Crusades as a search for suppressed religious truths
- Historical and conspiracist interpretations of the Knights Templar
- Templars and Assassins—roles in the NWO conspiracy
- The Templars' influence on modern secret societies
- Templars, Hospitallers, and the NWO conspiracy

Those New World Order (NWO) conspiracy theorists who believe the Council on Foreign Relations (CFR), the Bilderberg Group, the Trilateral Commission (TC), and other modern globalist organizations are rooted in the so-called "elder secret societies" of the pre-Christian past also typically assert that the connection between the current "secret" societies and the very ancient ones runs back through the Illuminati of the eighteenth century (see Chapter 13), the Rosicrucians of the seventeenth century (see Chapter 14), and the Freemasons, who began in the sixteenth and seventeenth centuries (see Chapter 15). From here, conspiracy writers take the story back to and through certain secret orders of the Middle Ages, most notably the Knights Templar and the Assassins (Hashashins) of the Islamic world.

Some writers insist that the inner circles of the modern groups—even such ostensibly public and governmental institutions as the Federal Reserve and the United Nations—consciously and deliberately derive their traditions, values, and even practices from the earlier secret societies. Others hold that the modern groups merely operate in the tradition created by the earlier ones, much as, for example, modern democracies and republics claim to be inspired by the tradition of ancient Greece and Rome.

Out of the Crusades

The Crusades, as commonly understood, were a series of military campaigns fought between 1095 and 1291, sanctioned by the pope, and carried out by Christian Europeans chiefly from France and the Holy Roman Empire. Their original objective was to recapture Jerusalem and the Holy Land, freeing it from Muslim rule. The immediate practical motivation was the threat posed to the Christian Byzantine Empire by the Muslim Seljuk Turks at the doorstep of Anatolia (a region mainly encompassing modern Turkey).

The reason the Crusades spanned such a long period was that they were inspired by the concept of holy pilgrimage and were considered "the expedition of God" and "the business of Christ." But the Crusades were also massive and costly military expeditions seeking by the might of the sword to expand the dominion of the Catholic Church and to bring an outpost in the east under the authority of the pope in Rome. Yet, on a more enduring and broader scale, the Crusades were the first undertakings in which the European nations cooperated together. The idea of rendering service to God by conquering the Holy Land took hold of the imagination of generations of Europeans and fired the energies of the continent's warriors. Moreover, the Crusades were a substantial economic boon for Europe and were especially stimulating for the commercial trading cities of Italy, foremost among them Venice. Because the ports of Byzantium and the Levant already served as key ports in the trade between Europe and Asia, the arrival of Christian powers in the east would also help spark worldwide commerce. As the financing grew to fund new trade, not only would exotic goods travel the world, but also new diseases and strange ideas.

As a result of the Crusades, the world became a smaller but richer, better informed, less rigid, and less religious place. In a sense, these wars were an early and tangible step in what conspiracy theorists see as the long march toward globalism. But NWO writers do not condemn the Crusades for this particular globalist outcome. Instead, they question the generally understood rationale for the Crusades. NWO conspiracy theorists argue that the *true* motive for the original Crusades was very different. It was to search for the very knowledge suppressed by the church since the fourth century (see Chapter 11).

INTEL

Although the original Crusades were fought between 1095 and 1291 to regain the Holy Land from the Muslims, a number of other military campaigns, also designated as Crusades, were fought in Eastern Europe and Spain well into the fifteenth century. Most of these campaigns pitted Christians against Muslims, though other groups deemed threatening to the Catholic Church were also sometimes targeted, including Russian and Greek Orthodox Christians, Jews, pagan Slavs, Mongols, and such Christian sects or orders as the Cathars, Hussites, and Waldensians. Sometimes, a pope would call for a Crusade against any group that opposed him.

A few sixteenth-century conflicts called "Crusades" by contemporaries were campaigns against groups deemed heretical.

The World Order, Eleventh Century

The Christian Church began its rise to supremacy in governing the Western World in the fourth century, when Constantine I identified himself—and the Roman Empire—with it. By the fall of that empire in the fifth century, Christianity had become *the* world order, at least in the West. The church evolved into "catholic," or universal Christianity and, throughout the Middle Ages, controlled virtually all secular kings and queens.

It is an axiom of power that the powerful always crave more power. Thus the Catholic Church sought to extend its hegemony into the East and therefore called upon the western kings and queens it controlled to mount a Crusade and retake the eastern heart of Christianity: Jerusalem and the Holy Land.

The Subversive Truth

Rewards both secular (political power, augmented wealth) and spiritual (an eternity in paradise) enticed the kings and queens to sponsor and sometimes even lead Crusades. According to some conspiracy writers, however, a few who undertook them did so with the ulterior motive of searching for the core truths of Christianity, which the church had suppressed. This motive was especially prevalent in the Languedoc region of France, which (some believed) was home to the descendents of a marriage between Mary Magdalene and Jesus Christ. Knowledge of this union was said to have been purged from the official Bible and suppressed by the official church.

In effect, therefore, the Crusades were publicly an attempt by the existing world order to protect itself and to expand; covertly, however, the Crusades were an effort by some to verify certain "heretical" propositions as the truths of genuine Christianity.

The Magdalene Theory

At the heart of the Christian truth allegedly suppressed is Mary Magdalene (Mary of Magdala—a location in ancient Palestine). Her identity and role in the life of Jesus Christ have long been subjects of controversy in Christianity. The New Testament and the Apocrypha both mention her as a woman who accompanied Jesus on his travels; all four Gospels agree that she was the first person to witness the resurrection of Christ.

Traditionally, Mary Magdalene has been portrayed as a "fallen woman" or prostitute, albeit repentant. This view has its origin in a speech Pope Gregory the Great made in 591 and was quietly retracted by the Catholic Church in 1969—although relatively few of the faithful seem to have taken note of the retraction. In fact, not only does the New Testament make no reference to her as a prostitute, but the earliest Christian writings refer to her as "the apostle to the apostles," and in the Apocrypha she appears as an early Christian leader greatly loved by Jesus—indeed, loved by him above all other disciples.

Whereas Christ's "love" for Mary Magdalene has usually been interpreted as spiritual, some writers cite Gnostic texts to support their claim that she was the wife of Jesus and that she even bore him children. The apocryphal Gospel of Philip depicts Mary as his close companion, whom Jesus often kissed. Whereas some have interpreted this as suggesting a carnal relationship, others insist that it describes a customary greeting.

Recently, the modern revisionist interpretation of Mary Magdalene has gained great popularity as a result of *The Da Vinci Code* (2003), Dan Brown's bestselling novel. It depicts a bloody struggle between Opus Dei (an organization dedicated to Catholic "fundamental" tradition) and The Priory of Sion—a supposed secret society possessed of proof that Christ and Mary Magdalene produced a child or children whose descendents live in southern France, near Marseilles.

Opus Dei is a very real organization, whereas the Priory of Sion has a more questionable authenticity. It was founded by Pierre Plantard (1920–2000), a right-wing French nationalist, anti-Semite, and anti-Mason, who favored the Vichy French (Nazi collaborationist) government during World War II. In 1956, he founded the Priory of Sion, which he claimed had its origin in Crusader Jerusalem, having been originally established there in 1099. Plantard further claimed that the Priory possessed proof that the French Merovingian dynasty and its bloodlines are all traceable to the offspring of Jesus and Mary Magdalene.

By the 1980s, the Priory of Sion had been exposed as Plantard's fictitious creation; however, some conspiracy theorists and others continue to believe that it is authentic and was founded to protect the secret of Mary Magdalene as the wife of Jesus.

The "Poor" Knights

In 1118, nine French Crusaders secured an audience with Baldwin II of Bourcq (d. 1131), successor to Baldwin I (1058?–1118), the first crowned European king of Jerusalem. They humbly requested that they be allowed to protect pilgrims en route to the Holy Land, and they additionally asked permission to establish themselves in the ruins of Jerusalem's Temple of Solomon. Baldwin agreed, pronouncing the nine men the Order of the Poor Knights of Christ and of the Temple of Solomon. Because this was rather a mouthful, they became known simply as the Knights of the Temple, which was shortened even further to Knights Templar.

"Mainstream" history depicts the Knights Templar at their founding as selfless and pious—knightly and militant monks sworn to poverty and dedicated to protecting pilgrims. Others, however, argue that no one could have reasonably believed that nine knights constituted a sufficient force to protect the numerous pilgrims who routinely made the Holy Land trek. Their true motive—and quite possibly the motive of Baldwin II in sanctioning them—must therefore lie elsewhere.

Sacred Ancestry?

Hugues de Payens (ca. 1070–1136) was born, it is believed, at Château Payns in Champagne, but most of the other eight knights who became the first Templars hailed from southern France, Provence and Languedoc, the region (according to some) to which Mary Magdalene journeyed and settled after the crucifixion of her husband, Jesus Christ. The eight—Godfrey de Saint-Omer, Payen de Montdidier, Archambaud de St. Agnan, Andre de Montbard, Geoffrey Bison, two men known only as Rossal and Gondamer, and an eighth whose name is unknown—were related to Hugues either by blood or marriage.

For the first nine years of their existence, the Templars remained a closed order. That they attempted to attract not a single new recruit during this period argues against their official mission of protecting pilgrims. An even stronger argument against this is the fact that the so-called Knights Hospitallers (later called the Knights of Malta) soon assumed this role, which, therefore, must have been left unfulfilled by the Templars.

It is a fact that Hugues and his men spent their time excavating Solomon's Temple. Most have assumed that they were in search of treasure, but some, certain NWO conspiracy theorists among them, believe that they were far more interested in finding scrolls secreted there. The scrolls supposedly contained revelations concerning Christ, including his connection to the Essenes and the Gnostics (see Chapter 11) and information relating to his marriage to Mary Magdalene. Some also believe that they searched for the Ark of the Covenant (which supposedly contained the Ten Commandments) and the Holy Lance, or Spear of Longinus—the spear that pierced Jesus' side while he hung on the cross.

Any of these relics would have been invaluable for establishing a claim to a religious truth that posed a challenge to the Catholic Church. Moreover, if proof of Jesus' marriage to Mary Magdalene could be found, it would also be possible to establish the claim some writers believe Hugues and his fellow knights secretly made: that they were all directly descended from Jesus, the ultimate source of the one true faith. This would mean that they were by right the most powerful men in the world.

PASSWORDS

"It is not easy for anyone to gain an idea of the power and wealth of the Templars—for they and the Hospitallers have taken possession of almost all the cities and villages with which Judea was once enriched … and have built castles everywhere and filled them with garrisons, besides the very many, and indeed numberless, estates which they are known to possess."

—Theoderich (a Christian pilgrim), *Description of the Holy Places* (ca. 1172)

The Templars Rise

Sworn to poverty and having dwelled in isolation at Solomon's Temple for nearly a decade, the Templars suddenly returned to the wider world in 1128. They were now possessed of great wealth. Some believe this flowed from the treasure, especially the gold, they had excavated, whereas others hold that the Templars exploited their discovery of scrolls containing knowledge that threatened the authority of the established church to extort a fortune in hush money from church leaders.

In any event, Payens and Andre de Montbard journeyed to Troyes, southeast of Paris, where they argued before the Council of Troyes their right to official church recognition. In response, Pope Honarius II sanctioned the Knights Templar and, most important, authorized contributions to what was now an official religious order. In this way, the Templars' wealth and power quickly multiplied.

Armed with the papal blessing, the Templars finally recruited new members into the *Order*, founding "Houses" in and near Edinburgh, Scotland, and elsewhere. The Rule of the Order obliged all members to make vows of chastity and to turn all of their property over to the Order. Thus, there were no wives or children to make claims against the growing wealth that now belonged to the Templars.

> **DEFINITION**
>
> The word **order,** which is often used as a synonym for a secret society, is derived from the use of "order" in a religious context, designating a group or lineage of organizations of people who live and work apart from the common run of society in observance of and obedient to a specific religious belief.

Before Payens died in 1136 and was succeeded as Grand Master by Robert de Craon, the Knights Templar are said to have numbered more than 20,000. They were men who had taken holy vows, but they were also soldiers, whose military vows included a pledge never to retreat unless they were outnumbered more than three to one or unless the Grand Master (to whom they pledged absolute obedience) or his appointed commander gave the order. They soon acquired a reputation as an elite fighting force, a vivid red cross emblazoned on their snow-white surtouts always conspicuous in any battle of the Crusades.

Yet their organization was not purely military. Membership was divided into four hierarchical ranks, descending from knights to sergeants to chaplains to servants. Suggestive of the structure of other secret societies, especially the Freemasons, this arrangement ensured that the Templars were divided into a very select all-knowing, all-powerful inner circle and a larger subordinate outer circle, which was not privy to all the Order's secrets.

Templars as Global Bankers

Thanks to the combination of riches, power, and church sanction (perhaps under duress), the wealth and influence of the Knights Templar continued to grow. Although its fortunes were directly related to the ongoing Crusades, the military importance of the Order waned as its financial importance grew.

By 1150, the Templars were so wealthy that they began lending money to pilgrims to finance their journeys to the Holy Land. For a fee, pilgrims could also deposit their valuables with a local Templar "office" (for lack of a better word) before leaving, take possession of a receipt for the deposit, then, upon arrival in the Holy Land, present the receipt to another Templar office to claim their funds. Economic historians believe this was history's first use of checks.

Like modern global bankers, the Templars created a multinational financial network of the equivalent of branch banks. This gave them a global reach unknown to secular political leaders in the Middle Ages. Additionally, it provided the finance for the acquisition of vast real estate holdings in Europe as well as the Middle East, and such enterprises as farms and vineyards and manufacturing and mercantile concerns. Some think of the Templars as medieval precursors to the magnates of the nineteenth, twentieth, and twenty-first centuries: the Rothschilds, Morgans, and Rockefellers.

The Templars Fall

Most historians see the decline of the Knights Templar as chiefly military in nature. As the tide of the Crusades turned against Christian forces generally—the Muslims became increasingly better organized, their fighting forces more effective—the usefulness of the Knights Templar declined and, with this, so did the support of the church. Those who favor a more conspiratorial view believe that, irrespective of the Order's declining role in the Crusades, the church seized on Templar certain vulnerabilities that would forever end the threat it posed to its own world dominance.

In 1305, Pope Clement V, seeking to bring an end to persistent conflict between the two main Crusading orders, the Knights Hospitallers and the Templars, attempted to broker a merger between the orders. He summoned the current Templar Grand Master, Jacques de Molay (ca. 1244/5–1249/50), and the Hospitaller's Fulk de Villaret (d. 1327) to France. De Molay arrived first, early in 1307, whereupon Clement brought up charges of immorality, sodomy, corruption, and general apostasy that had been leveled against the Templars.

Although the pope was apparently inclined to believe the charges false, he asked King Philip IV of France to assist in investigating the Order. Philip, deeply in debt to Templar banks, seized on a golden opportunity to discredit and dismantle them and thereby eliminate his creditor. Ostensibly acting to assist the pope, Philip ordered the arrest of de Molay and many other French Templars. They were forthwith brutally tortured. Many confessed, whereupon Pope Clement issued the *papal bull Pastoralis Praeeminentiae* (November 22, 1307), ordering all Christian monarchs to arrest every Templar in their realm, seizing their assets.

> **DEFINITION**
>
> A **papal bull** is an official charter or authoritative communication issued by the Pope. Originally, these documents bore a metal seal, called a *bulla,* which authenticated it.

Over the next few years, Templars were arrested and many were executed by burning at the stake. In 1312, Clement issued bulls dissolving the Order and turning over Templar assets to the Hospitallers. De Molay was burned at the stake in Paris on March 18, 1314.

Strange Bedfellows

Whereas the Christian Templars and Christian Hospitallers were in conflict, the Templars seemed to have forged a bold alliance with, of all groups, the most extreme *Muslim* sect (or secret society) of its time. This sect's reputation for ruthless violence was so pervasive that the group bequeathed to the English language another word for murderer. The members were called Assassins.

In 1094, the eighth caliph of the Fatimid dynasty, the Isma'ili Muslim imam (leader) Ma'ad al-Mustansir Billah fell ill in Cairo. Al-Afdal, his vizier (equivalent to a prime minister or chief adviser), led a coup d'etat, which placed his brother-in-law, the caliph's younger son, Al-Musta'li, on the throne, squeezing out the older son, Nizar, who was the legitimate heir apparent.

Nizar withdrew to Alexandria, where he recruited supporters—called Nizaris—to stage a counter-coup. It failed, and Nizar was executed by his brother. This created a schism among the Isma'ilis and the Nizaris, under the leadership of a Persian named Hassan-i Sabbah (1050s–1124). The Nizari schismatics dedicated themselves to the overthrow of the prevailing rulers of the Fatimid dynasty.

PASSWORDS

"So when the Old Man [of the Mountain—the Assassin leader] would have a prince slain, he would say to such a youth: 'Go thou and slay so-and-so; and when thou returnest, my angels will bear thee into paradise. And shouldst thou die, nevertheless even so will I send my angels to carry thee back into paradise.'"

—Marco Polo, *Travels* (1298), on the Assassins

Hassan was able to recruit many followers in the Levant, Persia, and Iraq, but the Nizaris remained an underground minority within Egypt itself, the core of the Fatimid Empire. Hassan drew on ancient Greek philosophy and various mystical and esoteric sources, perhaps including Cabala, to lay out a new order, a utopian version of the Fatimid Empire, which would span the Mediterranean and the Levant. Toward this end, in 1090, Hassan built a stronghold in Daylam at the fortress of Alamut (Persian for "Eagle's Nest"), south of the Caspian Sea. This was the first of many fortified enclaves set up throughout the current region of Iran, Iraq, Syria, and Lebanon, and the beginning of the Assassins, or Federation of the Assassins, who called themselves the Lords of Alamut.

Outnumbered, the Assassins used what today would be called terror tactics to infiltrate and undermine the centers of Fatimid power. Chief among these was assassination—actual as well as threatened. In some cases, powerful Fatimid officials were murdered, but, often, the Assassins merely intimidated an official into taking whatever course of action they desired. This was done by stealing into the official's home or palace, no matter how well guarded, and placing a characteristic Assassin dagger on the man's pillow. In this way, he was made aware that he was vulnerable and could find safety nowhere.

The Assassins as a Secret Society

Whereas most historians regard the Assassins as a state within a state—or, really, within several states around the Mediterranean—students of secret societies regard the group as a very powerful secret society or cult whose leaders were dedicated to achieving power over a vast empire. Toward this end, they deceived their followers into believing they were working toward a kind of religious utopia so absolutely desirable that the use of any means—treachery, murder, terror—was justified in attaining the goal.

INTEL

Some believe the English name, *Assassins,* for the secret society Hassan founded is a corruption of *Hashshashins,* designating one who smokes hashish. Some believe that this drug was consumed to embolden a member to commit the ordered assassination.

Marco Polo wrote in his *Travels* that the Assassins recruited members by subjecting them to an initiation rite in which they were drugged in a way that mimicked death. They were then revived in a lovely garden and treated to a sumptuous feast served up by delectable virgins. In this way, the recruit was persuaded that he had visited Paradise and discovered there the leader—the Old Man of the Mountain—as a kind of god, whose orders must be obeyed as divine.

Outside Religion and Beyond Loyalty

The Assassins endured as a powerful political force from 1090 until the Mongol warlord Hulagu Khan (ca. 1217–1265) successfully besieged Alamut on December 15, 1256. In this culminating battle, the Assassin library, reportedly a repository of mystical and esoteric writings, was destroyed, and with it was lost anything approaching a reliable, firsthand record of the Assassins. Much of the material that survived is more in the way of legend and lore than history and includes an elaborate account in Marco Polo's celebrated *Travels.* That Polo claimed to have visited Alamut in 1273, however, strongly suggests that his account is fiction; Hulagu Khan had destroyed Alamut 17 years earlier.

But there is strong historical evidence that the Assassins, often called a "fanatical" Muslim sect, collaborated freely with *Christian* Crusaders, including the Knights Templar. Baldwin attempted to take Damascus in 1129, for example, with the aid of Assassin agents operating in the city. Some historians believe that the alliance between the Templars and the Assassins both predated and outlasted this attack.

Most historians interpret the collaboration between the Muslim Assassins and Christian Crusader groups not as long-term alliances so much as short-term contracts. For example, they believe that the English Crusader King Richard the Lionheart (1157–1199) may have hired Assassins to *assassinate* his Italian rival for power in Jerusalem, Conrad de Montferrat (1140s–1192). In effect, the Assassins operated as the medieval equivalent of organized crime's infamous Murder Incorporated, professional assassins willing to kill anyone, anytime—for a price.

Conspiracy theorists, however, see in the relationship between the Templars and the Assassins more than a business transaction. In the coming together of these Christians and Muslims, they see the medieval equivalent of one-world government—and its purpose, then as now, is not to bring peace or to create a better world, but to concentrate in the hands of a few the power over many.

Templar Diaspora

France's Philip IV and Pope Clement did their best to wipe the Knights Templar from the face of the earth, but many managed to survive nevertheless. Some shaved their long beards, symbolic of the Order, and simply blended in with the general population. Others found other knightly orders to join, the most important of which was the Templars' former rivals, the Knights Hospitaller.

Coming to America?

Before pursuing the implications of the Templar-Hospitaller connection further, you need first to take note of a theory proposed by Robert Lomas and Christopher Knight, popular writers on Freemasonry and on the Knights Templars. Some Templars, they believe, voyaged to and settled in New England in 1308—184 years before Columbus reached the Caribbean and 312 years before the Pilgrims set foot on Plymouth Rock.

Lomas and Knight theorize that the Templars first learned of a far-off place called "Merica" from the Mandaeans, members of a sect centered on the lower Euphrates who revered a number of Old Testament prophets and, in the New Testament, John the Baptist. The authors also cite evidence that the Templars sought—and found—Merica. There is, the authors write, a rock in Westford, Massachusetts, which bears an engraving of a fourteenth-century knight; they also note that the Italian navigator Giovanni da Verrazano (1485–1528) recorded on a sixteenth-century map of the New England coast the existence of a "Norman villa." Scotland's Rosslyn Chapel, which some claim was built by the Templars (even though the Order had been dissolved some 150 years earlier), is decorated in places with what Lomas and Knight believe are ears of corn—maize—a New World crop that should have been unknown to Europeans before the voyages of Columbus. (More conventional historians believe the carvings to be somewhat stylized depictions of wheat or, perhaps, lilies or strawberries.)

As for the long-accepted belief that the name *America* was coined by the mapmaker Martin Waldseemüller in 1507 to honor the Italian explorer Amerigo Vespucci, Lomas and Knight contend that Waldseemüller erroneously connected the name *Merica* or *la Merica* with *Amerigo* Vespucci.

The point of the attempt to establish for the Templars an American connection is to suggest that this order—an early secret society that produced a powerful international banking network and attempted to undermine and replace conventional Catholic Christian doctrine—is directly related to later secret societies that emerged in the United States with analogous NWO ambitions. The Freemasons (see Chapter 15) are most closely identified with Scotland and the United States. Could it be, the authors ask, that the Templars, who (they and others claim) built an important chapel in Scotland and came to America long before Columbus, are the reason the presence of the Freemasons was so powerful in Scotland and America?

Heritage of the Hospitallers

Even those who are inclined to accept the theory of Lomas and Knight admit that the evidence for the Templars' discovery of America is far from conclusive; however, a number of NWO conspiracy theorists find another direct link between the Knights Templar and modern American globalist secret societies.

The Knights Hospitaller came into being about 1080 as the caretakers of a hospital established in Jerusalem to care for sick and injured Christian pilgrims. After Jerusalem fell to the Christians in 1099, the knights became a military order. Along with the Knights Templar, they were the most powerful and influential Christian group in the Holy Land. When the Holy Land was lost to the Christians, the Muslims expelled the Hospitallers, who settled first in Cyprus and then in Rhodes before Charles V, king of Spain and Sicily, gave them Malta in 1530. Operating from this island, the Hospitallers (now called the Knights of Malta) fought Muslim pirates who preyed upon the shipping of European nations. They endured as an important force on Malta until the island was captured by Napoleon Bonaparte in 1798.

The Knights Hospitaller absorbed a significant number of Templars after the dissolution of that order. Through the Hospitallers, therefore, the influence of the Knights Templar continued long after the Order itself had been crushed. After Napoleon evicted the Hospitallers—or Knights of Malta—they established a new headquarters in Rome in 1834 and officially became the Sovereign Military Order of Malta. This entity still enjoys unique status as a "sovereign subject of international law"; in other words, to this day, it is a religious (Roman Catholic) order that exists in political independence from the church as well as from any nation. Some nations even recognize it as a sovereign state, and it has been accorded permanent observer status by the United Nations.

NWO conspiracy writers regard the Military Order of Malta as a legally sanctioned secret society whose status transcends any ordinary definition of nationality or national sovereignty. Moreover, through a related British offshoot, the Knights of Saint John of Jerusalem, the ostensibly Catholic Military Order of Malta has spawned an ostensibly Protestant counterpart, headed by (though not controlled by) the British monarch.

Today, the Military Order of Malta operates as a paramilitary force for the purposes of carrying out international medical missions, humanitarian actions, and disaster relief. Conspiracy writers point out that it is also heavily involved in international banking, as were the Knights Templar of old. Beyond this, these writers assert, a roster of powerful statesmen, industrialists, financiers, politicians, and government officials are in various ways associated with the Military Order of Malta.

According to Jim Marrs, former CIA directors William Casey and John McCone were associated with the Order, as were conservative pundit and publisher William F. Buckley, Chrysler Corporation chairman Lee Iacocca, Kennedy family patriarch and U.S. ambassador to Britain Joseph P. Kennedy Sr., and the late former Secretary of State Alexander Haig. Some NWO conspiracy writers believe that the Military Order of Malta functions today as a back channel of communication between the CIA and the Vatican. These same writers also assert that the Military Order is a kind of modern melting pot in which strains of the Freemasons, Rosicrucians, and Knights Templar are blended to link this influential, independent, transnational, multi-religious organization with the most ancient of secret societies and esoteric knowledge.

Thus the Military Order of Malta connects powerful elite with ancient sources of authority and secret knowledge for the purpose of accumulating and exercising power outside of the ordinary channels of national governments.

The Least You Need to Know

- Conspiracy theorists believe that secret societies such as the Knights Templar used the Crusades as cover for expeditions to unearth religious secrets they could use to extort money and political cooperation from the Catholic Church.

- The most important religious secret the Knights Templar possessed (according to conspiracy theorists) was the marital relationship between Mary Magdalene and Jesus Christ, which produced offspring whose descendents were the Merovingian dynasty in France.

- The Knights Templar, ostensibly crusading on behalf of Christianity, and the Assassins, characterized as a "fanatical" Muslim secret society, collaborated on extensive schemes for mutual enrichment and acquisition of power.

- Many survivors of the suppression of the Knights Templar joined the Knights Hospitaller, which became the Knights of Malta and the Military Order of Malta—today a uniquely autonomous sovereign secret society protected by international law, affiliated with the Catholic Church, and (according to NWO conspiracy writers) serving as a conduit between the CIA and the Vatican as well as the nexus for global banking.

Illumination

In This Chapter

- Illuminati conspiracy theories
- Illuminati as a Satanic/New Age world-domination conspiracy
- Purported Illuminati/Jewish/Zionist connection
- History of the original Bavarian Illuminati
- Connections between the Illuminati and Freemasonry

John Robison possessed one of those remarkably curious, not to say scattershot, intellects of the eighteenth century. Born in Boghall, West Lothian, Scotland, in 1739, he was educated at the Glasgow Grammar School and the University of Glasgow. As a navigator and surveyor, he accompanied British general Thomas Wolfe to Quebec when he defeated his French counterpart, General Louis-Joseph de Montcalm, at the decisive Battle of Quebec during the French and Indian War in 1758. In 1762, he headed a team of scientists who tested, in a voyage to Jamaica, master clockmaker John Harrison's celebrated "marine chronometer" as a means of accurately navigating by longitude. He taught chemistry at the University of Glasgow in 1766; taught mathematics to Russian naval cadets in St. Petersburg in 1770; was appointed professor of natural philosophy at the University of Edinburgh in 1773; and became general secretary of the Royal Society of Edinburgh in 1783. And at some point during all this found the time to work with steam-engine pioneer James Watt on a steam car (unsuccessfully) and, independently, invent a steam-driven siren (successful but impractical).

In 1797, he published two major pieces of writing. One was a comprehensive set of articles on modern science and mathematics for *Encyclopædia Britannica*, the other was *Proofs of a Conspiracy against all the Religions and Governments of Europe, carried on in the secret meetings of Freemasons, Illuminati, and Reading Societies.*

Whereas Robison's *Britannica* articles did much to cement his minor historical reputation as a solid if unspectacular scientist, *Proofs of a Conspiracy* sent shock waves throughout Europe that reached all the way to America. Robison argued that members of an obscure Bavarian secret society founded by an obscure Bavarian professor named Adam Weishaupt infiltrated any number of seemingly benign organizations, including the Freemasons, and, through them, fomented the French Revolution and the Reign of Terror that followed it. This society intended to radicalize the newly established republic of the United States. They called themselves the Illuminati.

The SCP Theory

In the 1970s, a Christian evangelical organization calling itself the Spiritual Counterfeits Project (SCP) was launched in Berkeley, California. Its purpose was to expose and counteract a variety of emerging religious movements, New Age activities, and so-called "cults," which ran counter to mainstream Christian belief. The organization's most widely publicized fight was against Transcendental Meditation (TM) during the 1970s. Under the leadership of Tal Brooke beginning in the late 1980s, however, SCP began specifically targeting certain New Age initiatives as aspects of a Satanic conspiracy to bring about an anti-Christian, one-world government.

Citing the work of the respected if controversial Harvard and Princeton historian Carroll Quigley (1910–1977), who believed that secret societies played a major role in history, Brooke asserted that the New World Order (NWO) conspiracy was all about "completing" the work of the eighteenth-century Bavarian Illuminati. As Adam Weishaupt and his followers had infiltrated the Freemasons and other organizations to foment revolution, so their spiritual and intellectual heirs were currently infiltrating the international banking system through the Federal Reserve (see Chapter 9), the United Nations (World Bank and International Monetary Funds; see Chapter 6), and banks controlled by the Rothschilds (see Chapter 8) with the ultimate goal of creating and controlling a one-world government.

Brooke is not unique in proposing the modern survival of the Illuminati as an agency of the NWO conspiracy, but his presentation is the most often cited by others with similar beliefs. His own most important predecessors are Nesta Webster and William Guy Carr.

The Revival Begins

Born into an upper-crust London family, Nesta Helen Webster (1876–1960) believed she was the reincarnation of a countess guillotined by French revolutionaries. She drew attention to herself before World War I with a series of articles arguing that the French Revolution had been the product of a Judeo-Masonic conspiracy. After the war, she wrote *World Revolution: The Plot against Civilisation*; *The French Revolution: A Study in Democracy* (which distilled her earlier writing on the subject); and *Secret Societies and Subversive Movements*. Seizing on *The Protocols of the Elders of Zion*, a book that appeared after the abortive 1905 Russian Revolution and achieved international popularity after the Bolshevik Revolution of 1917, Webster contributed to a series of *London Morning Post* articles in 1920 entitled "The Jewish Peril," in which she posited the existence of a Jewish-Illuminist plot behind both the French and the Bolshevik revolutions. The purpose of the plot was Jewish domination of the world.

PASSWORDS

"This movement among the Jews is not new. From the days of … [Illuminati founder Adam] Weishaupt to those of Karl Marx, and down to Trotsky (Russia), Bela Kun (Hungary), Rosa Luxembourg (Germany), and Emma Goldman (United States), this world-wide conspiracy for the overthrow of civilization and for the reconstitution of society on the basis of arrested development, of envious malevolence, and impossible equality, has been steadily growing. It played, as a modern writer, Mrs. Webster, has so ably shown, a definitely recognizable part in the tragedy of the French Revolution. It has been the mainspring of every subversive movement during the Nineteenth Century; and now at last this band of extraordinary personalities from the underworld of the great cities of Europe and America have gripped the Russian people by the hair of their heads and have become practically the undisputed masters of that enormous empire."

—Winston Churchill, quoted in the *Illustrated Sunday Herald,* February 8, 1920

Although Webster acknowledged that the authenticity of the *Protocols* was an "open question" (most historians believe it the pure fabrication of Russian journalist Matvei Golovinski), she was nevertheless confident that the conspiracy it identified did exist and continued to exist. To counter the conspiracy, Webster proposed importing fascism into Britain, and, in the run-up to World War II, she wrote articles supporting the Nazi persecution of the Jews. Even after the war, in *Germany and England*, she wrote that Adolf Hitler, far from attempting to conquer the world, had sought to save it from domination by the Jews—and, despite his military defeat, had succeeded in doing so.

Secret Life: Matvei Vasilyevich Golovinski

Matvei Vasilyevich Golovinski (1865–1920) was a Russian journalist who has been widely identified as the true author of *The Protocols of the Elders of Zion*, a sensational text which many see as the foundation of most modern NWO conspiracy theories, purporting to be the plan of early twentieth-century *Zionists* to achieve world domination.

> **DEFINITION**
>
> **Zionism** is the historical label for an international political movement that supported and promoted the reestablishment of a homeland for the Jewish people in the land of Israel. Today, the term is used to describe a movement that supports the continued existence and welfare of the state of Israel. Zionism is a political, not a religious term. Not all Jews are Zionists, and not all Zionists are Jews.

Born into an aristocratic Russian family, Golovinski studied law and, while a student, joined the Holy Brotherhood, a pro-czarist, right-wing, anti-Semitic group that sought to counter the Russian revolutionary movements of the early twentieth century. Golovinski apparently worked undercover for the czar's secret police, arranging pro-government press coverage; however, after the success of the Bolshevik Revolution in 1917, he switched allegiances and put himself at the service of the Bolsheviks until his death.

He is believed to have fabricated the *Protocols* around 1903, while he was associated with the Holy Brotherhood, as a means of amplifying the anti-Semitism that was long a feature of Russian life. His object was to link Jewish political activity—Zionism—with the work of Communist revolutionaries. Zionism, in the guise of communism, was portrayed as a conspiracy to topple Christianity and Christian governments and to bring the world under Jewish domination, in large part to satisfy the rapacious greed of international Jewish bankers.

Three World Wars and SOS

The work of Nesta Helen Webster inspired William Guy Carr (1895–1959), a British-born Canadian, to write his bestselling *Pawns in the Game* and *Red Fog over America*, both published in 1955. These books linked the international Communist conspiracy to dominate the world with the idea of a Jewish-controlled Illuminati-run international banking conspiracy that employed various means of mind control and brainwashing. In Carr's view, the Bilderberg Group (see Chapter 3) was a modern incarnation of the Illuminati in which Jewish bankers met to decide global banking policy toward the end of world domination.

Carr's conspiracy theory focuses on two major ideas:

- That the Illuminati (working through the Freemasons) have planned three world wars as a means of achieving world domination.

- That the "Synagogue of Satan" (SOS) has created a "World Revolutionary Movement," a "Luciferian conspiracy" through which Satan will wrest control of humankind.

World War I, Carr argued, was fomented by the modern Illuminati to enable them to overthrow the Russian czar and thereby transform Russia into the vast fortress of atheism that (in his view) was the Soviet Union. World War II was fomented to destroy fascism and Nazism and thereby enable "political Zionism" to take hold over Israel. Simultaneously, with the fall of fascism, communism would rise to equal power with Christianity. Finally, the Illuminati, in part via the United Nations, would foment World War III between the political Zionists and the leaders of the Islamic world. The purpose of this war would be the mutual destruction of both the political Zionists and Islam, leaving the rest of the nations to fight among themselves to the point of total depletion. The atheistic forces of communism could then assume ultimate control over the exhausted combatants. (See Chapter 17 for a more complete discussion of the "three world war" conspiracy theory.)

Even the most objective analyst must see Carr, like Webster, as anti-Semitic; yet whereas Webster made no apologies for her comments on the Jews, Carr took pains to deny that he meant to link the Jews with the devil via what he called the SOS, the "Synagogue of Satan." This point made, he declared that the SOS was nevertheless comprised of people who "called themselves Jews." In fact, he argued, they were Zionist members of a modern Illuminati that was driven by a Satanic force to bring about one-world government.

The Role of "Lucifer"

"Lucifer" is commonly used as a synonym for Satan or the devil. In fact, Lucifer does not appear in the New Testament. It is a Latin name meaning "light-bearer" and has sometimes been used as a synonym for the planet Venus as the harbinger of the dawn, the so-called Morning Star. The use (or misuse) of Lucifer as a simple alias for Satan comes from the King James translation of Isaiah 14:13, in which a Babylonian king is referred to as "Lucifer, son of the morning," now "fallen from heaven." The authors of the King James version simply imported the Latin Lucifer, whereas the New Standard Version does not use the name Lucifer but its English translation, referring to the king as "Day Star, son of Dawn."

Since the eighteenth century, conspiracy theorists have drawn a parallel between the Illuminati, which means "enlightened ones," and Lucifer, which literally means "light-bearer," but has long been associated with Satan. In this tradition, William Guy Carr wrote of a "Luciferian conspiracy," thereby conflating the Illuminati ("enlightened ones") with Satan via the "light-bearer" Lucifer.

Trouble in Bavaria

Colored as it is by generations of conspiracy theorists, and more than tinged by an association with Satanism and an anti-Semitic vision of a world Jewish conspiracy, the modern image of the Illuminati is both obscure and magnified. It is a cross between a collection of the boogeyman and demons. Little wonder, then, that it is difficult to unearth a true likeness of the historical Illuminati. Indeed, perhaps there is little to unearth.

The Founding

Adam Weishaupt was born in 1748 in the Bavarian university town of Ingolstadt. He was educated by the local Jesuits, who dominated the church as well as the schools. When Weishaupt was appointed to the professorship of natural and canon law at the University of Ingolstadt in 1775, he was the first layman, let alone non-Jesuit, to hold the post. This was sufficient to outrage the local clergy.

Even worse, however, Weishaupt rebelled against his own early Jesuit education and embraced the wave of rationality sweeping over Europe, known as the Age of Enlightenment. He not only accepted the professorship, but also founded a liberal, free-thinking faction or party within the university that opposed what it considered the bigotry and superstition of the priests. On May 1, 1776, this became the Perfectabilists, a secret society that became known to the world as the Illuminati.

INTEL

Unlike many other secret societies, the founding date of the Illuminati (May 1, 1776) is a matter of historical record. However, many conspiracy theorists believe the Illuminati are linked to an ancient body of esoteric knowledge and have an ancestry that extends back to the beginning of civilization in Sumer (see Chapter 11). The term *Illuminati* goes back to an early sixteenth-century Spanish religious group, the *aluminados* ("illuminati") or *alumibrados* ("out of the shadows"). The adherents claimed to have had direct contact with the Virgin Mary or even God Himself. By the seventeenth century, the *aluminados* movement spread to France, where it was officially suppressed in 1635. There is no evidence that Weishaupt's Perfectabilists—which others called the Illuminati—bore any tangible relation to the earlier Spanish or French groups.

Historical Connection to the Freemasons

Most conspiracy theorists believe there was a strong linkage between the Illuminati and the Freemasons. Many believe that the Illuminati deliberately infiltrated the Freemasons, creating so-called "Illuminized Lodges" to serve as organized "cells" or centers of subversion.

All that is known historically is that Adam Weishaupt was not a Freemason when he founded the Illuminati, but a year later, in 1777, he was inducted into the Lodge Theodore of Good Council (*Theodor zum guten Rath*) at Munich. Most authorities believe that Weishaupt modeled the organization of the Illuminati on the Freemasons and divided membership into three main classes (each with several degrees), thereby creating the equivalent of outer and inner circles.

Reverend G. W. Snyder, pastor of the Reformed Church of Fredericktown, Maryland, had read John Robison's *Proofs of a Conspiracy*. In August 1798, he sent former president George Washington a letter to alert him to "a Society of Free Masons that distinguished itself by the name of 'Illuminati,' whose Plan is to over throw all Government and all Religion." He continued: "it might be within your power to prevent the Horrid plan from corrupting the brethren of the English Lodges over which you preside."

Washington replied "to correct an error … of my presiding over English Lodges in this country. The fact is I preside over none, nor have I been in one more than once or twice within the last thirty years," but when Snyder persisted in a second letter, Washington replied on October 24, 1798:

It was not my intention to doubt that, the Doctrines of the Illuminati, and principles of Jacobinism had not spread in the United States. On the contrary, no one is more truly satisfied of this fact than I am.

The idea that I meant to convey, was, that I did not believe that the Lodges of Free Masons in this Country had, as Societies, endeavoured to propagate the diabolical tenets of the first, or pernicious principles of the latter (if they are susceptible of seperation [sic]). That Individuals of them may have done it, or that the founder, or instrument employed to found, the Democratic Societies in the United States, may have had these objects; and actually had a seperation [sic] of the People from their Government in view, is too evident to be questioned.

Thus, although Washington denied that Freemasonry as an institution supported the Illuminati, he apparently did not doubt the existence of the Illuminati. He didn't doubt the probability that it influenced individual Freemasons, and that the Illuminati's intention was to separate "the People from their Government."

Membership

Most historians believe that there were never any more than 2,000 Illuminati in Europe and America. The names of few members survive. The Abbé Austin Barruel (1741–1820), a French Jesuit priest whose *Memoirs Illustrating the History of Jacobinism* (1797) inspired Robison's *Proofs of a Conspiracy* and was the first book to attribute the French Revolution to the Illuminati, listed 67 members of the organization. These included 13 noblemen, 10 professors, and 7 church officials among others. By far the most famous member was the polymath author of *Faust*, Johann Wolfgang von Goethe (1749–1832).

PASSWORDS

"Weishaupt believes that to promote this perfection of the human character was the object of Jesus Christ. That his intention was simply to reinstate natural religion, & by diffusing the light of his morality, to teach us to govern ourselves. His precepts are the love of god & love of our neighbor. And by teaching innocence of conduct, he expected to place men in their natural state of liberty & equality. … He proposed to initiate new members into his body by gradations proportioned to his fears of the thunderbolts of tyranny. This has given an air of mystery to his views, was the foundation of his banishment, the subversion of the masonic order, & is the colour for the ravings against him …."

—Thomas Jefferson, letter to Reverend James Madison, January 31, 1800

Opposition

There is no hard evidence that the Illuminati conspired in a practical way to overthrow governments, unless one believes that any forum in which highly educated—and, in some cases, highly placed—people gather for free and frank discussion in confidence is by definition subversive. (In the context of an oppressive society, such a belief is probably well founded.) In any event, from the beginning, some condemned the Illuminati as atheists, radicals, and anarchists. Certainly, the Jesuits had an axe to grind against Weishaupt personally and against the Illuminati on principle. However, the far more potent opposition came from Karl Theodor (1724–1799), who became elector of Bavaria in 1777. A strict conservative whom historians label a benevolent dictator, he decreed a ban on *all* secret societies in 1784.

Under the aegis of this ban, the home of Xavier von Zwack, a Bavarian diplomat who was Weishaupt's second in command, was searched. Documents obtained from his home (according to Karl Theodor's officers) revealed that the aim of the Illuminati was to create a new religion of reason and to establish a single universal democratic republic—that is, one-world government. By means of universal "enlightenment," humankind would be liberated from all prejudices, which meant that they would be cut loose from both "priest and prince."

Proud to Be the Founder of the Illuminati

The documents seized from Zwack's house sealed the ban on the Illuminati in Bavaria. Dismissed from the University of Ingolstadt, Weishaupt fled the country and found refuge in Gotha under the protection of the liberal Duke Ernest II of Saxe-Gotha-Altenburg (1745–1804).

His exile prompted him to write a series of works on Illuminism and therefore certainly did more to spread the doctrine of the Illuminati and give it historical longevity than if Karl Theodor had simply left him and his associates alone. Between 1785 and 1787, he wrote *A Complete History of the Persecutions of the Illuminati in Bavaria*, *A Picture of Illuminism*, *An Apology for the Illuminati*, and *An Improved System of Illuminism*. Although he wrote about Illuminism, Weishaupt denied that he had created anything radically new, but had merely reaped a crop of rational enlightenment that had already taken root throughout Germany.

"I did not bring Deism into Bavaria more than into Rome. I found it here, in great vigour, more abounding than in any of the neighboring Protestant States. I am proud to be known to the world as the founder of the Illuminati."

—Adam Weishaupt

The Illuminist Lens

Many of the most prominent NWO conspiracy writers insist that Illuminism survives, either as an actual, active secret society or as a paradigm and inspiration for a panoply of globalist secret societies, including the Council on Foreign Relations (CFR), the Bilderberg Group, and the Trilateral Commission (TC). In the end, this latter proposition can neither be proved nor disproved. What *can* be definitively demonstrated is that reaction against the Illuminati has survived and almost certainly possesses more potent substance than the Illuminati itself.

From the eighteenth century on, beginning with Barruel and Robison, the conspiracy theories woven around the Illuminati have been far more vivid than the organization itself. The label *Illuminati* was attached to the French Revolution and the Terror. From this, it was extrapolated to describe a secret conspiracy to bring about a world revolution intended to globally institutionalize the most radical Enlightenment ideas, including an end to clergy-dominated religion and the overthrow of all autocratic and monarchical governments.

Whatever it may have been or may have failed to be to its members, Illuminism has long been a powerful lens through which the ruling classes of the world have viewed political, religious, and social reform. To the degree that fear of the Illuminati prompted increased autocratic oppression throughout Europe, it may indeed have prompted rebellion and revolution—less because of anything they actually advocated or did than because the masses reacted against the oppression that had been intended to destroy the Illuminati. In other words, attempts to suppress the Illuminati brought about the very revolutions the ruling classes feared from the Illuminati.

As a way of viewing political movements, economic actions, popular spiritual movements, and the initiatives of statesmen and diplomats, the lens of Illuminism has continued to prove durable through the twentieth century and into the twenty-first. That much is certain. Far more doubtful is whether that lens is transparent or opaque, revealing anything beyond itself or nothing but itself.

The Least You Need to Know

- The historical Illuminati was founded in Bavaria by Professor Adam Weishaupt on May 1, 1776, as a gathering of well-educated, liberal thinkers. It almost immediately provoked a strong reaction from religious conservatives and the ruling class.

- Many NWO conspiracy theorists believe the Illuminati survived its suppression by Karl Theodor, elector of Bavaria, in 1784, and is today behind globalist organizations such as the CFR, the Bilderberg Group, the TC, the Federal Reserve, and the United Nations intent on creating and controlling a one-world government.

- Conspiracy theorists such as Nesta Helen Webster and William Guy Carr linked the Illuminati to a global Jewish—or Zionist—conspiracy aimed at fomenting revolution (including the French Revolution and the Bolshevik Revolution) to replace established national governments with a one-world government controlled by Jewish bankers.

- Whatever the truth of the actual influence of the Illuminati, the fear of conspiracy the Illuminati inspired has proven far more powerful and pervasive than the historical organization itself.

The Rose Cross

In This Chapter

- The historical development of the Rosicrucians
- AMORC and other modern incarnations of the Rosicrucian tradition
- The Rosicrucian-Freemasonry connection
- The Rosicrucian tradition as a link between ancient mysteries and modern secret societies
- Rosicrucian-centered conspiracy theories

Most secret societies are thickly enshrouded in lore, legend, myth, and outright fiction. This is to be expected. What is surprising is that the single most pervasive fiction about secret societies is that they are secret.

Most so-called secret societies are very well publicized, especially those usually cited in connection with the New World Order (NWO) conspiracy. For example, most sizable American towns have at least one Masonic lodge, often a conspicuous Main Street building, and it's always listed in the phonebook. As for the Rosicrucians, which commentators often call the most mysterious of all secret societies, the biggest modern version of it, the Ancient and Mystical Order Rosae Crucis (AMORC), is a worldwide organization that maintains an elaborate website (www.rosicrucian.org); is on Facebook; publishes books, videos, and podcasts; and has advertised widely in magazines and even comic books.

AMORC claims participation in the Rosicrucian tradition, a tradition that appears in much NWO conspiracy literature as a link between ancient mysteries ("esoteric truths" concealed from ordinary people) and modern globalist conspiracies. Is this sufficient to brand AMORC and other modern Rosicrucian groups as part of a covert one-world government movement? Many NWO conspiracy writers raise the question, though none has answered it.

Rosicrucians: The Historical View

Perhaps the most that can be said about NWO conspiracy theory views of the Rosicrucian Order in an age-old conspiratorial movement toward one-world government is that it plays a linking role. Certainly, the currently active Rosicrucian organizations define themselves as links with the ancient truths of the ancient past.

Origin

Of all Rosicrucian mysteries, the most mysterious is the origin of the order. It first came to public notice in Germany through publication of *Fama Fraternatis of the Meritorious Order of the Rosy Cross* in 1614. Even so, a number of the most celebrated intellectuals of the day, Renè Descartes among them, came to the conclusion that the *Fama Fraternatis* was either a kind of allegorical philosophical manifesto or an outright hoax and not the history of an actual secret society.

Fama Fraternatis presents the biography of a mystic called Frater C. R. C.—whom a subsequent publication identifies as one Christian Rosenkreuz (literally "Rose-cross"), who was born in 1378 and lived 106 years. He studied the *Sufi* and *Zoroastrian* faiths in the Middle East, and then returned to Europe, where he founded the Rosicrucian Order in 1407 with just eight members.

DEFINITION

Sufi is the mystical aspect of conventional Islam. Adherents—called Sufis or Dervishes—strive for the acquisition of wisdom to enable them to turn away from all worldly things and toward God and God alone. **Zoroastrianism** is a Persian-based religion based on the teachings of the prophet Zoroaster, who wrote about the universe as a continual contention between the forces of light and dark.

Many historians believe that Rosicrucianism may well have originated in the early Renaissance as part of the general reawakening of interest in ancient knowledge. However, instead of drawing on Greek and Roman sources, as the Renaissance mainstream did, the Rosicrucians turned to the Middle East, the Jewish Cabala, Sufi, and Zoroastrian sources, and especially the body of wisdom called "Hermetic" after the legendary philosopher-magician-alchemist Hermes Trismegistus. Much of this material was likely brought back to Europe by Crusaders returning from the Holy Land.

Symbolism

At the heart of the Rosicrucian Order is the Rose Cross, which symbolizes the culturally and intellectually hybrid nature of the movement. Most obviously, the cross is the central symbol of Christianity, but it is also an important alchemical symbol, signifying the four elements—air, water, earth, and fire. The cross is often used in alchemical texts as a shorthand symbol for light, readily interpreted as enlightenment. For Hindus, the cross is a symbol of the creation; for ancient Egyptians, it is a symbol of rebirth (the Ankh). The pre-Christian Greeks associated it with Dionysus, who was among other things a patron of the Eleusinian Mysteries, a set of secret rites and beliefs said to unite the initiate with the gods.

The rose is a symbol of love, passion, and purity; however, the "rose" in the word *Rosicrucian* may be either a deliberate pun on or a mistranslation of the Latin word *ros*, which means "dew"—a substance alchemists believed to be a solvent more powerful than ordinary water. Symbolically, *ros* may therefore have signified the search for or discovery of the universal solution ("solvent") to life's deepest mysteries.

Seventeenth and Eighteenth Centuries

Although the Rosicrucian Order may have been born in the late Middle Ages or early Renaissance, and while its modern adherents believe it embodies even more ancient wisdom, its heyday came during the Reformation and the Enlightenment of the sixteenth and seventeenth centuries. Its teachings and its teachers—including Robert Fludd (*A Compendious Apology for the Fraternity of the Rosy Cross, Pelted with the Mire of Suspicion and Infamy, but now Cleansed and Purged as by the Waters of Truth*, ca. 1617); Michael Maier (*Themis Aurea*, 1618); and Irenaeus Agnostus (*Epitimia Fraternis Rosae Crucis*, 1619)—were Protestants and critical of what they believed were the prejudices of the Catholic Church.

During the eighteenth century, the Rosicrucian Brotherhood (as it was usually called) came to resemble the Freemasons, and, like the Masons, its members produced a number of constitutions and sets of bylaws. Some monarchs, such as Catherine the Great (1729–1796) of Russia, regarded the Brotherhood as a sufficient threat to merit official suppression. She may have identified it with the Illuminati, and, in fact, many students of secret societies—and virtually all conspiracy theorists—believe that the two orders are closely connected with one another. In most places, however, the Rosicrucians were regarded as relatively harmless.

Decline and Rebirth

Perhaps it was because relatively few powerful people took the Rosicrucian Brotherhood seriously in the seventeenth and eighteenth centuries that the order began to diminish. Its members seem to have turned from serious study of the ancient mysteries to absorption in ritual and regalia. The "furniture" of the typical lodge included a glass globe standing on a pedestal of seven steps and divided into two parts, representing light and darkness; three candelabra, placed triangularly; nine glasses, symbolizing male and female properties and other things; a brazier; a circle; and a napkin. All these played a part in elaborate initiation rituals.

During the nineteenth century, more serious interest in the brotherhood revived and served to stimulate such quasi-Hermetic movements as theosophy. AMORC and the other Rosicrucian bodies that are active today are rooted in the organizations of the late nineteenth century.

AMORC and Others

From the AMORC website you learn that the "word *rosicrucian* is so old it cannot be trademarked, so other groups cannot be prevented from using it." There are at least 30 such groups currently active—and probably even more. The AMORC is by far the largest and most public, classified by the Internal Revenue Service as a nonprofit, educational charitable organization. It disavows any religious intention, content, affiliation, or membership requirement and claims to provide "a foundation that ties together all of the different aspects of metaphysical study, and demonstrates their interconnectedness." In short, its declared purpose may be described as enlightenment.

AMORC has been operating since 1915 and today has hundreds, perhaps thousands of affiliated "lodges and chapters" worldwide. Prospective members are invited either to join an established local group or start their own. Although members receive various "monographs" from AMORC, each group is encouraged to conduct an independent discussion of "esoteric principles passed down through time as the various manifestations of the Western Esoteric Tradition." All groups are asked to e-mail the names of their members and a list of the topics that interest them to a designated central contact. The AMORC website explains that, as a group grows and develops, members may be invited to "confer rituals as part of [their] group experience." This is referred to as AMORC's *Initiatic Tradition*, and is the feature of the order that most closely identifies it with typical secret societies.

DEFINITION

Initiatic Tradition may be a unique AMORC coinage, but its meaning, a tradition of initiation into special ritual, applies to the membership practices of most secret societies. Some conspiracy theorists attach special significance to similarities between Rosicrucian membership rituals and those of Freemasonry, suggesting that these prove a link between the two orders.

Golden Dawn

Late in the nineteenth century, the Hermetic Order of the Golden Dawn was founded in Great Britain by three Freemasons, William Robert Woodman, William Wynn Westcott, and Samuel Liddell MacGregor Mathers. They were also members of Societas Rosicruciana in Anglia (S.R.I.A.), a Masonic Christian esoteric order.

Not surprisingly, the Golden Dawn lodges were modeled on Masonic initiation and ritual practices, but the emphasis was on Hermetic material attributed to Hermes Trismegistus ("Thrice-Great Hermes"), which blends pantheism and monotheism and teaches that all beings are aspects of "The All," an ultimate universal unity. Insight into The All can be achieved through certain mystical and magical practices, many of which (such as *alchemy*) may yield practical and potent results.

DEFINITION

Alchemy has long been dismissed as a medieval pseudoscience superseded by the "genuine" sciences introduced during the Renaissance. More properly, alchemy should be viewed as a philosophy related to Hermeticism—the discovery of ancient wisdom relating to ultimate truths. Some of its practical aspects laid the foundation for modern inorganic chemistry.

In 1977, the Hermetic Order of the Golden Dawn, Inc., was established by esoteric author and ceremonial magician Chic Cicero in Columbus, Georgia, for the purpose of "the continued preservation of that body of knowledge known as Hermeticism or the Western Esoteric Tradition." In 2002, Sam Webster—author and Wiccan adherent of the Golden Dawn tradition—among others, founded the Open Source Order of the Golden Dawn as an esoteric community of magical practitioners and as an initiatory order dedicated to teaching Hermetic wisdom. Temples are located in San Francisco; Seattle; and Manchester, United Kingdom. The Order offers "a progressively tiered system of spiritual development designed to invoke the Higher or Divine Genius latent in every human being."

SECRET LIVES

Hermes Trismegistus is a god or demigod to whom the Hermetic writings (called the "Corpus Hermeticum") are attributed. Some mythologists view him as a hybrid of Thoth, the scribe of the Egyptian gods, and the Greek god Hermes, guide to the underworld. Others distinguish him from the Greek Hermes and identify him with both Thoth and Anubis, the jackal-headed Egyptian deity associated with mummification and the afterlife.

Modern Rosicrucians and others believe Hermes Trismegistus was an incarnate source of divine wisdom. Others, however, regard him as nothing more than a conveniently sonorous name to attach to an eclectic compilation of writings that would otherwise seem entirely miscellaneous.

Societas Rosicruciana

Like AMORC, the Hermetic Order of the Golden Dawn, Inc., and the Open Source Order of the Golden Dawn are initiatory groups but not secret societies, because membership is ostensibly open to all who are interested.

Those who identify the Freemasons as a long-established vehicle of conspiracy argue that the Illuminati infiltrated—and effectively hijacked—certain lodges as a means of propagating their one-world aspirations. They co-opted the Freemasons who held important positions in commerce, the community, the military, and government (see Chapters 13 and 15). Many of these same conspiracy theorists believe that certain Freemasons used the Rosicrucian forum as a means of connecting Freemasonry more intimately with ancient wisdom (namely, the Hermetic tradition) and of extending the influence of Freemasonry through yet another secret society network.

To bolster this assertion, they point to the origin of the nineteenth-century Golden Dawn, founded by Freemasons, and to the existence of the modern Societas Rosicruciana. This is a Rosicrucian order that limits membership exclusively to Master Masons (third-degree Freemasons) who also profess to be Christian. Founded in Scotland, the order currently operates there as well as the United States, Canada, England, Ireland, France, and Portugal. In some lodges, moreover, membership is by invitation only. Interestingly, although one must be a Master Mason to qualify for membership, the Societas Rosicruciana is not officially recognized by the Freemasons.

> **INTEL**
>
> The Scottish Rite of Modern Freemasonry includes an eighteenth degree specifically identified with the Rosicrucian tradition and known as the Knight Rose Croix or Knight of the Rose Croix de Heredom Council of Kadosh. Whereas some students of secret societies cite this as demonstrating a deep-rooted relationship between the Rosicrucians and Freemasonry (some have claimed that Freemasonry was an offshoot of the Rosicrucian Order), it is also the case that secret societies and fraternal orders frequently borrow extensively from one another. Members of one order are more likely to belong to others as well—joiners tend to be joiners.

Like other Rosicrucian organizations, the Societas Rosicruciana defines its mission as the preservation and transmission of the Hermetic-based wisdom taught by the "original" Rosicrucian Order (which is addressed shortly).

The One-World Conspiracy Connection

Most of the NWO conspiracy literature that mentions the Rosicrucians cites the "order" or "movement" without specifying any particular modern group such as AMORC or the Hermetic Order of the Golden Dawn, Inc. The role of the Rosicrucians in the NWO conspiracy seems to be defined as simply one more link between ancient secret societies as convocations of a power elite—the few who aspire to rule the many—and contemporary globalist or one-world organizations and institutions.

Some assert that the most influential and powerful people of today—the individuals who pull all the strings and the constituents of shadow government—have access to ancient wisdom, possession of which potentially undermines officially constituted government and established religion. Others make less specific assertions, arguing that the importance of the Rosicrucians and other historical or historically based secret societies is found in the ways in which these groups perpetuate the traditions of secrecy and exclusive knowledge. These traditions serve as archetypes, patterns, and models for contemporary secret societies ranging from the Council on Foreign Relations (CFR) to the Federal Reserve to the United Nations.

The Gladio Affair

There is one striking exception to the typically vague and general nature of conspiracy theorist claims concerning the Rosicrucians. Yet even this is inconclusive.

Gladio is an Italian word from the Latin *gladius,* the short sword of the Roman legionnaire. "Operation Gladio" was a secret program established by NATO early in the Cold War to create so-called "stay-behind" underground paramilitary groups that would resist communist rule in case the Warsaw Pact (the military alliance of the Soviet Union and its satellites) defeated conventional NATO forces and succeeded in occupying Western Europe. The name originally applied specifically to the Italian stay-behind units; however, its use was broadened to take in all NATO-created, stay-behind paramilitary units in other NATO nations and, eventually, in some non-NATO nations as well. Many believe that the U.S. Central Intelligence Agency (CIA) played an important role in sponsoring Operation Gladio.

Gladio came to public notice in 1990 when the European Parliament voted a resolution condemning it and ordering investigations (which, as of 2010, have yet to be conducted). Although Operation Gladio units were created to oppose Soviet aggression, many of the units continued to exist after the fall of the Soviet Union in 1990 and 1991. They have been suspected of operating in various ways outside official government control, and in violation of the sovereignty of individual nations—perhaps for the purpose of creating a one-Europe government.

The Solar Temple Deaths

In 1984, the Ordre du Temple Solaire (OTS)—the Order of the Solar Temple—was founded in Geneva, Switzerland. The OTS may have been modeled on two earlier groups, the Sovereign Order of the Solar Temple (founded in 1952) and the Renewed Order of the Solar Temple (which split off from the 1952 group in 1968). All the groups were based on a belief in the continued existence of the Knights Templar (see Chapter 12), and the 1968 group also identified its purpose as defining and establishing the "correct notions of authority and power in the world" and preparing its members for the Second Coming of Christ.

The cofounder of the 1984 group, Luc Jouret, was also cofounder of Parti Communautaire Européen (PCE), a Belgian-based political party advocating pan-Europeanism, the creation of a single European government. Some conspiracy theorists claim that PCE was controlled by those associated with Operation Gladio. At its height, OTS had lodges in Quebec, Canada; Switzerland; Australia; and

Martinique, as well as in other countries. Despite its international presence, OTS never had a great many members, but those who did belong contributed hefty dues and spent big money on costumes and regalia, including Crusader-style robes, which they wore in elaborate rituals.

Like most other organizations identified as fringe groups, the OTS attracted little notice. Then, in October 1994, it turned bloody. The three-month-old son of a member of the Morin Heights, Quebec, lodge was stabbed to death with a wooden stake. The story was that Joseph Di Mambro, OTS cofounder with Jouret, had ordered the ritual murder because he believed the baby was the Antichrist. Shortly after this horror, Di Mambro and 12 followers reportedly held a ritual Last Supper. This was followed days later by what were apparently mass suicides and murders at Morin Heights. In all, 15 OTS members poisoned themselves, and another 30 were either shot or smothered. Eight others were found dead, killed by unspecified means. Autopsies revealed the presence of drugs in many of the victims, suggesting that even the "suicides" were not voluntary. The lodge buildings in which many of the killings had occurred had been set ablaze by timer-operated incendiary devices.

And it got even bloodier. OTS members were found dead in an "underground chapel" in western Switzerland. Most were arrayed in their Crusader-style robes and arranged in a circle, feet together and heads pointing outward. Many had been asphyxiated by plastic bags fastened over their heads, and all had each been shot, execution-style, in the head. More victims, including children, were discovered in three nearby ski chalets. A total of 48 persons associated with OTS were found dead in western Switzerland. Three years after these deaths, on March 23, 1997, five OTS members killed themselves in Saint-Casimir, Quebec, having set timers to ignite the building they occupied.

Dr. Abgrall's Accusations

Dr. Jean-Marie Abgrall (b. 1950), a French forensic psychiatrist, expert witness, and authority on cults, asserted ties between OTS and Operation Gladio as well as with persons associated with or at one time associated with AMORC. Abgrall, himself a former member of AMORC, also asserted that AMORC had ties to the clandestine right-wing networks of Jacques Foccart (1913–1997), a one-time adviser to French presidents Charles de Gaulle and Georges Pompidou.

Although Abgrall is a highly respected criminal investigator, the accusations, vague at best, remain controversial.

What Does It All Mean?

The Solar Temple tragedies contain many elements found in abundance throughout the NWO conspiracy literature: a secret society associated with ancient mysticism and involving at least some leaders who have extreme political agendas, including possible one-world aspirations. Moreover, it is possible to draw connections between the secret society at the center of the murder-suicides, the OTS, and clandestine multi-government activities (Operation Gladio). Through some individuals, it implies a further connection with an apparently open and benign organization, AMORC.

Yet it is impossible to determine whether the connections are mere conjecture or something more substantive. And even if one believes that they have real substance, what do the connections finally mean? No definitive evidence has come to light demonstrating that Operation Gladio or AMORC had anything to do with the Solar Temple, let alone the atrocities associated with it. Nevertheless, the members of the Order of the Solar Temple were clearly interested in ancient mysteries, including those of a specifically Hermetic nature, and how these mysteries might bear upon the "true" meaning of life. Likewise, the members of AMORC and other Rosicrucian groups have similar interests. To some people, this commonality of interests may be sufficient to suggest conspiracy, yet it cannot be denied that a lot of people are interested in mysticism, ancient wisdom, and the meaning of life.

Guilt by Association?

Many conspiracy theories identify intellectual, political, and spiritual movements in the past, find surviving remnants of them in the present, and therefore conclude that an active modern conspiracy, founded in the distant past, *must* be active now. The theories, intriguing as they may be, typically stumble over the speculative word *must*, which is no substitute for the definitive word *does*.

The fact is that the Rosicrucian movement came into prominence during an era that questioned religious dogma and especially challenged the Catholic Church. The Enlightenment also saw the birth of modern scientific inquiry and the scientific method. Thus Rosicrucianism was more a symbol and symptom of truth-seeking and rebellion than it was a secret cause of either.

In the twentieth century, the Rosicrucian movement was one of many gatherings of spiritually minded intellectuals who hoped to find a new meaning for life in ancient wisdom. This was an era marked by catastrophic global war and dehumanizing industrial mechanization—two forces that prompted many to doubt that life had any meaning at all. As such, it is easy to identify the Rosicrucian movement with the New Age beliefs that many NWO conspiracy theorists see as part and parcel of an effort to undermine both traditional religious (mainly Christian) faiths as well as patriotic allegiance to one's country. They believe in replacing these with one-world values that make the many ripe for rule by the few.

The Least You Need to Know

- The Rosicrucian Order may have come into being during the late Middle Ages or early Renaissance, and rose to its height during the Protestant Reformation and the Enlightenment as one of many groups and "secret societies" that questioned dogmatic religion and other aspects of the cultural, political, and spiritual status quo.

- AMORC and other modern incarnations of the Rosicrucian tradition claim an interest in preserving, perpetuating, and exploring the ancient wisdom chiefly of the Hermetic tradition to achieve an enlightenment that enhances one's life.

- Some NWO conspiracy theorists have attempted to link a Rosicrucian group (AMORC) with both a specific pan-European underground organization (Operation Gladio) and with a now-defunct secret society (the Order of the Solar Temple) that is associated with mass murder-suicides.

- The Rosicrucian Order figures in most NWO conspiracy literature as a link between ancient secret societies and modern globalist groups said to be aspiring to one-world government.

Men in Aprons

In This Chapter

- The Morgan Affair and the American anti-Masonic movement
- International persecution of Freemasons
- Alleged Masonic conspiracies
- Origin and early history of Freemasonry
- Alleged role of Freemasonry in the NWO

William Morgan was a brewer, a gambler, a drunk, and a bankrupt. He claimed to have been a captain in the War of 1812, but that was almost certainly a lie. Although he had been admitted to the Freemasons lodge at Leroy, New York, in 1825, the Masons in Batavia, New York (where he lighted after losing his money), refused to admit him. By way of retaliation, he announced that he had secured a cash advance from local newspaper owner David Cade Miller (who had his own beef with the Batavia lodge) to publish a book that would reveal every secret of the Freemasons. The Batavia lodge responded by taking out an ad in a rival paper denouncing Morgan. Then persons unknown tried several times to burn down Miller's office.

On September 11, 1826, William Morgan was arrested for debt. Predictably, the complainants were Freemasons who said he owed them money. Miller stepped in and paid them off. Morgan was released, but before sunset was jailed in another town, Canandaigua, for another unpaid loan and for the theft of some clothing. That night, an unidentified man stopped by the jail, paid Morgan's debt, and took him away in a carriage. The vehicle showed up at Fort Niagara. Morgan did not.

So began the "Morgan Affair" and, with it, a short-lived but well-organized anti-Masonic movement in the United States.

Conspiracy Theories

Almost everyone seems to have assumed that the stranger who bailed Morgan out of the Canandaigua jail was a Freemason and that he and other Masons murdered him, probably by drowning him in the Niagara River. Barely a month after Morgan was last seen alive, a rotten body washed up on the Lake Ontario shore. The corpse was no longer identifiable, but the clothing belonged to a missing Canadian named Tim Monroe. This notwithstanding, most people wanted to believe that the body was Morgan's, and three Freemasons—Loton Lawon, Nicholas Chesebro, and Edward Sawyer—were arrested, tried, and convicted of kidnapping. That pleased the growing numbers of local anti-Masons, but when the defendants were given nothing more than token sentences, anti-Masonic protests erupted in New York, Connecticut, and New Jersey.

In the meantime, Miller published what was reputedly Morgan's book and made a small fortune from it—leading some to conclude that the Morgan Affair was a publicity stunt designed to sell the book. No matter. New York political boss Thurlow Weed, a prominent political enemy of Andrew Jackson—who was a Freemason—organized the Anti-Masonic Party, which won five seats in the House of Representatives in 1828. It was the nation's first third party to win *any* congressional election. The party fielded Virginia politician William Wirt for president in 1832, garnering for him a mere seven electoral votes, and then vanishing into extinction by the early 1850s.

INTEL

In 1819, 44-year-old William Morgan married Lucinda Pendleton, age 16. After Morgan's disappearance and presumed death, she became one of the multiple wives of Joseph Smith Jr. (1805–1844), founder of the Mormon Church. This has bolstered accusations over the years that Mormon ritual was lifted wholesale from Masonic ritual and that Mormonism is really a form of Freemasonry. The Church of Jesus Christ of Latter-day Saints denies this, of course; still, for some, the controversy has been kept alive by the fact that William Morgan was accorded one of the church's first baptisms for the dead.

The Anti-Masonic Background

In the United States, organized political opposition to Freemasonry was spectacular but short-lived, and owed as much to Thurlow Weed's ambition to topple the popular and powerful Andrew Jackson as it did to any actual objections Weed may have had to the Freemasons. Nevertheless, the political movement reflected a long tradition of anti-Masonic sentiment.

From as early as the end of the seventeenth century, clergymen and others warned of Masonic treachery, accusing Freemasons of everything from treason to atheism and even sometimes identifying *the Craft* as, collectively, the Antichrist. Even to the present day, some British politicians (including former Home Secretary Jack Straw) have agitated for passage of laws requiring Freemasons to declare themselves publicly before seeking appointment to law-enforcement agencies or the judiciary. The fear is that Masons in these positions will trade favors with other Masons.

DEFINITION

The Craft is the term Freemasons themselves often use as a synonym for Freemasonry. A direct reference to the order's origins in the actual craft of the stonemason, the word also resonates for some non-Masons with the likes of *witchcraft, priestcraft,* and so on.

Historically, fear of the Freemasons is based on secular suspicions of treason and ecclesiastical suspicions of heresy and agendas geared to destroying religion. In 1799, for example, the British Parliament passed an Unlawful Societies Act, which defined as "unlawful combinations" all societies whose members were required to swear an oath not authorized by law. The official reason was to suppress "societies established for seditious and treasonable purposes," and it applied to the Freemasons along with all other oath-taking secret societies.

Over the years, several totalitarian regimes have banned Freemasonry. Under Communist dictator Béla Kun, Freemasonry was outlawed in Hungary in 1920. Elsewhere in Eastern Europe, including the Soviet Union, it was also suppressed, often brutally.

In Mussolini's Italy, the Craft was banned in 1925. However, as shown later in this chapter, some former highly placed fascists became members of the so-called P2 Lodge, which figures prominently in the New World Order (NWO) conspiracy literature. The proto-fascist Spanish dictator, Miguel Primo de Rivera, decreed the abolition of Freemasonry in Spain in 1928, and Freemasons were aggressively persecuted—arrested, imprisoned, and even killed—during the Spanish Civil War beginning in 1936. Freemasonry was suppressed in Spain until 1975, when long-time fascist dictator Francisco Franco died.

In both Nazi Germany and militarized Japan during the 1930s, Freemasonry was identified with an international Jewish conspiracy. Adolf Hitler presented this thesis in his autobiographical political manifesto *Mein Kampf* (1925–1926), and in January 1934, under the Enabling Act by which the Reichstag (German parliament) accorded Hitler dictatorial powers, Freemasonry was abolished and all lodge property was confiscated by the state. Throughout the 1930s, Hitler and his propaganda minister, Josef Goebbels, conducted a campaign linking "international Jewry" to the Freemasons and accusing the combination of conspiring to create a "World Republic"—that is, one-world government. Prominent Freemasons were classed as political criminals, arrested, and confined to concentration camps as political prisoners. As Jews were required to wear a Star of David emblem, Freemasons were identified by an inverted red triangle.

In the meantime, in Japan, there was talk of a "Judeo-Masonic" plot to co-opt the Chinese nationalist leaders Sun Yat-sen and Chiang Kai-shek to wage war against Japan. Some Japanese political leaders went so far as to brand the Sino-Japanese War, which began with the Japanese invasion of Manchuria in 1937, as a war not against China, but against Freemasonry.

INTEL

Jews have been active in many Masonic lodges, a fact that, over the years, has led many anti-Semites to claim that the Craft is controlled by Jews and is a conspiracy to subvert Christian religion and Christian government. By the early 1920s, some claimed that the infamous *Protocols of the Elders of Zion* (see Chapter 13) was a transcript of a meeting of Jewish leaders plotting world domination through or in league with the Freemasons. This idea influenced the anti-Semitic campaigns of Henry Ford in the United States. In Germany, it was used by Hitler and his propaganda minister Josef Goebbels as a rationale for persecuting Jews as well as Freemasons.

As for religious objections to Freemasonry, the Catholic Church has forbidden membership for Catholics since the early 1700s and, until 1983, membership was a cause for excommunication. It remains a cause for interdiction—that is, barring a church member from receiving the Sacraments. Other Christian denominations, including Protestant and Eastern Orthodox, have variously denounced Freemasonry. Sometimes, denunciations have been made not only on religious grounds, but for patriotic reasons. Some Catholic critics in particular have asserted that swearing allegiance to a Masonic lodge is like holding dual citizenship and precludes a full patriotic and loyal commitment to the nation.

Various Islamic religious and political leaders have condemned and continue to condemn Freemasonry as promoting the interests of Zionism. They have even accused the Freemasons of conspiring with Zionist Jews to destroy the Al-Aqsa Mosque in Jerusalem and rebuild on its ruins the Temple of Solomon.

A Catalog of Conspiracy

Masonic conspiracy theories are quite literally too numerous to mention. As conspiracy writer Jim Marrs observes in his *Rule by Secrecy*, "there has been much concern—even outright paranoia as in the anti-Masonic movement—regarding the role of the Masonic orders in world affairs beginning with the American and French revolutions and continuing up to today."

Consider the following sampling of plots frequently associated with the Freemasons:

- The American Revolution *and* the French Revolution were the product of Masonic plots.

- The Kennedy assassination was a Masonic conspiracy.

- Freemasons regularly meet with top business and political leaders at Bohemian Grove, a men's club/camp in Monte Rio, California.

- Freemasons are Satanists who want to ensure the triumph of the Antichrist in the End Time.

- Freemasonry is a religion fundamentally opposed to established religions and worships GAOTU (the "Great Architect of the Universe") in place of God.

- Freemasons insidiously intrude their influence into the general culture through secret signs, symbols, and numerical codes hidden in advertising, national emblems, and corporate logos.

- London's infamous Jack the Ripper was a Freemason; his murders partook of Masonic initiation rites.

- Freemasonry controls a wide array of secret societies, ranging from Skull and Bones (see Chapter 7) to the Ku Klux Klan.

- The *Apollo* moon landings were elaborate frauds staged by the Freemasons.

- The terrorist attacks against New York and Washington, D.C., on September 11, 2001, were actually battles in a secret war between Masonry (as the modern incarnation of the Knights Templar; see Chapter 12) and Islam.

The Craft

The preceding list of plots does not include the alleged Freemason conspiracies that figure most importantly in NWO conspiracy theories, which are examined in detail in the final section of this chapter. First, however, we need to survey the history of Freemasonry—not an easy thing to do, because practically everything about the Craft is shrouded in mystery and, perhaps, deliberate obfuscation.

Scope

Freemasons are found worldwide. Virtually all students of secret societies consider Freemasonry the oldest and largest still-active secret society in the world. Estimates of membership numbers vary from 5 to 10 million globally—with the largest memberships in the United States (about 2 million) and the United Kingdom (just under a half million).

Origins

During the European Middle Ages, few crafts were more important than that of the stonemason, who possessed the arcane knowledge and skill to build the great cathedrals and castles. In high demand and short supply, masons were itinerant and were among the very few groups allowed to travel freely from job to job. Unlike peasants or serfs, they were bound to no master, and unlike nobles, they were vassals to no liege lord. Geographically and politically, they were free: free masons.

Like other craftsmen, they established guilds and, wherever they worked, the guild halls also served as lodges—places to eat and sleep. The guild/lodge was also a kind of union headquarters, which functioned to exclude imposters from the craft. One way to distinguish the master masons from the wannabes was through passwords and "grips" (secret handshakes), both of which remain characteristics of modern Freemasonry as well as other secret societies.

At the heart of all secret societies are, not surprisingly, secrets. The original Masonic secrets were almost certainly those of the mason's craft. Modern Freemasons go beyond this, implying that the order's secrets go back to Euclid, the first geometrician, and to the builders of the Tower of Babel and the Temple of Solomon. Conspiracy theorists believe that the Craft's secrets are far more nefarious and are probably linked to the subversive activities of the Illuminati (see Chapter 13).

Operative and Speculative Masons

The original Freemasons were actual workers in stone—what members of the Craft call *operative masons*. Beginning in the seventeenth century, the guilds or lodges began to confer honorary memberships. These masons, who were not stone workers, are referred to as *speculative*. In 1619, the London Masons' Company established a regular procedure for inducting speculative masons called "Acception." *Accepted masons* were admitted to the lodge on payment of twice an operative mason's dues.

At this point, Masonic lodges began their transition from craft guild to gentlemen's clubs. Why did this happen? Beginning in the period of Enlightenment, there was a great interest in building and architecture. Becoming an accepted mason was a way to learn. Masonic clubs also provided a forum for free-thinking inquiry and discussion. Although none of the speculative or accepted masons had ever wielded a hammer and chisel, their link of origin in the operative (working) masons was commemorated by the ceremonial aprons they wore in homage to the stonemason's work clothes.

DEFINITION

Operative mason is the Freemason's term for a working stonemason, in contrast to a **speculative mason,** the term for a member of a Masonic lodge—that is, an "honorary" mason. Speculative masons are also called **accepted masons.**

Eighteenth-Century Evolution

The eighteenth century saw a codification of Masonic ritual and organization. In 1717, four London lodges merged to form the United Grand Lodge, and their authority rapidly spread throughout England and into the colonies—though Scotland and Ireland retained their own Grand Lodges. From 1722 to 1723, at the request of the United Grand Lodge, Dr. James Anderson, a minister of the Church of Scotland, composed the *Book of Constitutions*, which formalized Masonic ritual.

The founding legend of the Masons—the Craft's reputed origins in the slaying of King Solomon's master mason, Hiram Abif—dates from the early eighteenth century, as does the use of the pyramid symbol with the Grand Master at the apex. An apparent version of this emblem is on the Great Seal of the United States and is reproduced on the U.S. one-dollar bill above the words *Novus Ordo Seculorum*, "A New Order of the Ages"—a fact that has given NWO writers much food for speculation.

In the middle of the eighteenth century, the Freemasons suffered a schism, in which a liberal, free-thinking faction sought to play down the role of traditional Christianity in the Craft, and more conservative members wanted to preserve and perpetuate it. The schism was healed through compromise in 1813.

In the meantime, throughout the eighteenth century, British Freemasonry spread to many Protestant lands, although sometimes with admixtures of Rosicrucian adherents as well as members of other secret societies. Additionally, Masonic lodges became places in which political reform—and even revolution—were discussed.

In Revolutionary America

Nowhere were Masonic lodges more politically active during the eighteenth century than in Britain's American colonies. Prominent Freemasons included Benjamin Franklin, George Washington, Alexander Hamilton, the Marquis de Lafayette, Paul Revere, John Hancock, John Paul Jones, and others associated with the American independence movement.

The first American lodge was founded in April 13, 1733, and was followed by many more. The Boston Tea Party was hatched in the Green Dragon public house, meeting place of the St. Andrew Masonic Lodge in Boston. Although the assertion of secret society historian Charles W. Ferguson (*Fifty Million Brothers: A Panorama of American Lodges and Clubs*, 1937) that Washington's Continental Army was "a Masonic convention" is a gross exaggeration, many patriots and revolutionary officers were Masons, as were many prominent men in any American community.

PASSWORDS

"The religion of Freemasonry is not sectarian. It admits men of every creed within its hospitable bosom, rejecting none and approving none for his particular faith. It is not Judaism … it is not Christianity. It does not meddle with sectarian creeds or doctrines, but teaches fundamental truth. … At its altar, men of all religions may kneel; to its creed, disciples of every faith may subscribe."

—Albert G. Mackey, *Encyclopedia of Freemasonry,* 1873–1878

Revolution Elsewhere

During the eighteenth century, French Freemasons initially supported the French Revolution, only to find the Craft banned during the Reign of Terror that followed. Toward the close of the eighteenth century and into the nineteenth, Masonic lodges were involved in revolutionary activity in Ireland, Greece, Russia, and Italy. Back in America, Masonic radicalism fed the fears that helped spawn the anti-Masonic movement culminating in the founding of the Anti-Masonic Party.

Twentieth Century

We have already mentioned the suppression of Freemasonry and its conflation with Nazi and fascist anti-Semitism in the twentieth century in Europe and Japan. During this same period in the United States, Freemasonry entered the social mainstream and became widely perceived less as a secret society and more as a benign fraternal organization, on par with the Moose, the Elks, or the Rotary Club. For this reason, many Americans to this day tend to dismiss NWO and other Freemason conspiracy theories as paranoid or just plain silly. *Men in aprons conspiring to take over the world? Give me a break!*

Freemasonry and the New World Order

Is contemporary Freemasonry really not much different from any other popular fraternal organization? Even hard-core conspiracy believers admit that, for the great majority of members, Freemasonry is mainly a social club. But, they point out, the majority is the outer circle of Freemasonry. Only the *inner* circle, a small minority, knows the secrets and the secret agenda of the Freemasons.

PASSWORDS

"Freemasonry is a fraternity within a fraternity—an outer organization concealing an inner brotherhood of the elect. Before it is possible to intelligently discuss the origin of the Craft, it is necessary, therefore, to establish the existence of these two separate yet interdependent orders, the one visible and the other invisible. The visible society is a splendid camaraderie of 'free and accepted' men enjoined to devote themselves to ethical, educational, fraternal, patriotic, and humanitarian concerns. The invisible society is a secret and most august fraternity whose members are dedicated to the service of a mysterious *Arcanum Arcanorum* [Secret of Secrets]. Those Brethren who have essayed to write the history of their Craft have not included in their disquisitions the story of that truly secret inner society which is to the body Freemasonic what the heart is to the body human."

—Manly P. Hall, *Lectures on Ancient Philosophy and Introduction to the Study and Application of Rational Procedure,* 1929

Some Basic Assumptions

NWO conspiracy theories involving the Freemasons assume the existence of a super-secret Masonic inner circle, probably the 33rd degree of the Scottish Rite branch of the Craft. Publicly, this is the highest honorary degree conferred by the Craft; secretly (some conspiracy theorists believe) it is a special ruling body of which few Masons are even aware. This inner circle is in contact with a centralized global entity that controls all Grand Lodges, welding Freemasonry into a worldwide secret society.

Many conspiracy theorists believe that the Freemasons of the innermost circle worship a unique god—perhaps a Satanic or a Luciferian deity (see "The Role of 'Lucifer'" in Chapter 13)—which sets the Craft apart from conventional Christianity. Freemasonry may thus be viewed as a secret religion or cult. Some see it as a cover for the Illuminati, or perhaps as a secret society closely related to the Illuminati. So-called Illuminized Freemasons either already control or aspire to control many aspects of society and government. Their ultimate goal is the creation of an NWO based on one-world government.

Although a linkage with the Illuminati is the most common element of modern conspiracy theories involving the Freemasons, some also argue that the Craft is a front for the Knights Templar, a Jewish/Zionist conspiracy, or some combination of the two. The ultimate object of such cabals is world domination.

More on the Illuminati Connection

A number of recent conspiracy theorists regard the Illuminati as essentially a body of anarchists who infiltrated the Freemasons (and other organizations) for the purpose of disseminating political, religious, and social chaos to prepare the ground for revolution. Inspired by the German philosopher Georg Wilhelm Friedrich Hegel (1770–1831) and his "dialectical" paradigm—thought as *thesis* and *antithesis* coming together in *synthesis*—the Illuminati (some assert) sought to create crisis in the clash of ideas, thereby generating fear and frustration in society and rendering it ripe for revolutionary change. With their vast global network of lodges, the Freemasons were an ideal instrument for creating such a chaotic crisis on a large scale—large enough to embrace the entire world and create the global conditions for transnational, trans-cultural government.

Operation Gladio—Again

In Chapter 14, we briefly encountered Operation Gladio, the early Cold War–era plan to create and maintain NATO "stay-behind" paramilitary units to resist the possible occupation of Western Europe by Soviet-led Warsaw Pact forces. Some recent NWO conspiracy theorists believe that former CIA directors John A. McCone (1902–1991) and William J. Casey (1913–1987), and former NATO supreme commander and secretary of state Alexander M. Haig Jr. (1924–2010) were members of the Knights of Malta (see Chapter 12). They conspired during the 1980s to co-opt a rogue Italian Masonic lodge as part of a global fascist conspiracy involving the Vatican Bank, the CIA, and the Mafia with fellow Knight of Malta Licio Gelli (b. 1919). Gelli was an Italian financier who served in the fascist government during World War II.

The Masonic lodge, known as Propaganda Masonica Due (or simply "P2"), dated to 1877, came under Gelli's control by 1966, and was expelled from Grande Oriente d'Italia, the official Italian Masonic organization. A scandal involving a Milan bank, Banco Ambrosiano, whose chairman, Roberto Calvi, was a member of P2, led in 1981 to an Italian government police raid on Gelli's villa in Arezzo, where a list of 962 P2 members was discovered. The list included highly placed Italian military and civil officers; 48 members of the Italian parliament; an assortment of journalists, financiers, and industrialists (including future Italian premier Silvio Berlusconi); and Vittorio Emanuele di Savoia (b. 1937), pretender to the Italian throne, which has been defunct since the creation of the republic in 1946. Also among Gelli's P2 papers was

"Piano di rinascita democratic" ("Plan of democratic rebirth"), a strategy for a coup d'etat aimed at bringing a dictatorship to Italy.

In the course of the scandal that followed the raid and the collapse the following year of Banco Ambrosiano, it was alleged that Gelli had played a role in an Operation Gladio campaign called a "strategy of tension." This was a program of staged "leftist" and "anarchist" acts of terrorism in Italy, allegedly including a 1969 bombing at Piazza Fontana (in Milan) and the 1980 Bologna massacre (a bombing at Bologna's Central Station, which killed 85 people). In 1990, the Italian national television network RAI reported that the CIA had paid Licio Gelli to foment terrorist activities in Italy. (The CIA issued an official denial, and many authorities believe the RAI story was based on fraudulent information.)

Once Feared, Still Dangerous

The entire P2 affair is still very much a subject of controversy and debate, with little or nothing definitively proved. However, NWO conspiracy theorists cite it as a demonstration of the enduring power of the Freemasons (despite the fact that the P2 lodge was ejected from the official Italian Masonic body) and their apparent willingness to collaborate with clandestine forces of industry, finance, military, and government to achieve power. (The Vatican has also been implicated because of its financial ties to Banco Ambrosiano.)

The conspiracy writers point to the P2 episode as the proverbial tip of the iceberg, suggesting that similar plots are underway—or may yet get underway—in any number of nations, including the United States. P2, they say, exposes the Freemasons as still capable of changing or even toppling governments to impose on the many global rule by a select few.

The Least You Need to Know

- Freemasonry is the biggest and oldest "secret society" still operating. It was developed from the stonemasons' guilds of medieval Europe to become gentlemen's clubs and (according to conspiracy theorists) cabals in which revolution and the reform (or overthrow) of religion were hatched.
- Anti-Masonic movements have been active globally, in some places resulting in political opposition (as in the nineteenth-century American Anti-Masonic Party) and in others escalating into outright persecution (as in Nazi Germany).

- Alleged Masonic conspiracies range from Illuminati-controlled attempts to over-throw established religion and government, to Jewish or Zionist conspiracies aimed at world domination, to Luciferian schemes intended to place the fate of humankind in Satan's hands.

- Freemasonry figures into most NWO conspiracy theories as a vast network through which various globalist groups and individuals (often financiers and industrialists) seek to gain influence over governments and institutions to bring about some form of one-world government. An example of this is the abortive P2 conspiracy in Italy.

History as Conspiracy

To look at history through the lens of the New World Order conspiracy is to see it as you have never seen it before. The chapters of Part 3 take the story of the one-world government movement from the American and French revolutions, through the struggle for Italian independence and unity, through the Bolshevik Revolution, and into the two world wars of the twentieth century.

All are viewed here as outgrowths of conspiracy. We look closely at FDR's New Deal and at Adolf Hitler's Third Reich, which globalist conspirators (according to much New World Order literature) have resurrected into a Fourth Reich. The Korean War, the Vietnam War, and the two wars in Iraq are all treated here as aspects of a conspiracy to put an American power elite at the controlling center of global rule.

Revolution: America and France

In This Chapter

- The New Atlantis
- Francis Bacon's vision of a New World utopia
- America's Masonic Founding Fathers
- The American Revolution as a Masonic conspiracy
- The Illuminati work through the Freemasons to create the French Revolution

Manly Palmer Hall (1901–1990), Masonic historian and author of *The Secret Teachings of All Ages: An Encyclopedic Outline of Masonic, Hermetic, Qabbalistic and Rosicrucian Symbolical Philosophy* (1928), claimed that the leaders of the ancient world summoned priest-philosophers from Egypt, Greece, India, and China and assembled in a single sovereign body for the purpose of acting as their advisers. This group constituted the most esoteric of secret societies, because the great knowledge it possessed originated in the fabled lost continent of Atlantis. Its vanished rulers had created a "Great Plan," which they intended to bring into being in the New World (that is, an as-yet-undiscovered America). Here, a *New* Atlantis was to be established—a kind of utopian super-state.

According to Hall, that New Atlantis was no mere dream. It came into being as the United States of America.

Francis Bacon, Founder of America

Sir Francis Bacon (1561–1626) was an English philosopher, essayist, historian, scientist, and statesman. He was, quite literally, a Renaissance man. Lawyer, jurist, statesman, and philosopher, he was also the scientist credited with having developed the "scientific method" by which principles are *derived from* experience—observation and experimentation—rather than *applied to* experience. His father, Sir Nicholas Bacon, was lord keeper of the great seal under Queen Elizabeth I, which facilitated Francis's entry into Trinity College, Cambridge, in 1573 and his admission to Gray's Inn three years later.

For good measure, Sir Francis Bacon was also a writer. By the time he published his first book of celebrated *Essays* in 1597, he had already earned a literary reputation with his political pamphlets. A persistent minority believe he was the true author of William Shakespeare's plays.

Recognized as a genius, young Bacon was soon pressed into service as an English ambassador to France. He returned to England in 1579, was admitted to the bar three years later, and became a member of Parliament in 1584. Under Elizabeth I's successor, King James I, Bacon was a vigorous courtier who quickly secured a knighthood (1603) and was appointed attorney general (1613), lord keeper (1617), and lord chancellor (1618). In 1620, he published *Novum Organum*, his philosophical masterpiece. Bacon was created Baron Verulam in 1618 and Viscount St. Albans in 1621.

That year, however, the chronically debt-ridden Bacon was banished from court after confessing to having taken bribes. He spent the rest of his life in a highly active retirement, during which he wrote another volume of *Essays;* an expanded version of his 1605 *The Advancement of Learning*; a *History of Henry VII* (1622); and one of literary history's earliest novels, *The New Atlantis* (1623—published in 1627).

According to possibly credible legend, his death in 1626 was the result of one of his own experiments. While researching the effect of cold on preserving meat, it is said that he caught a chill, developed pneumonia, and died.

The New Atlantis

Bacon's novel has a pretty thin plot by modern standards. A shipload of European sailors get lost in the Pacific somewhere west of Peru and stumble upon an island Bacon calls Bensalem. The people on it are governed by a pervasive spirit of "generosity and enlightenment, dignity and splendor, piety and public spirit." They devote their lives to discovering and creating works for the benefit of humankind, and their greatest public monument is "Salomon's House," a publicly supported university dedicated to the pursuit of science, both pure and applied.

Masonic author Manly Hall believed that the title of Bacon's novel was taken from the "New Atlantis" of the ancients, a utopia whose secrets were preserved in the Hermetic and Cabalistic traditions and transmitted via the Rosicrucians to the Freemasons. Moreover, he asserted that Bacon did not invent the idea of a utopian "New Atlantis" being established in America (or, at least, in the American hemisphere). He took this idea directly from ancient lore for the purpose of dramatizing the Masonic "Great Plan," which was (Hall wrote) to build an ideal commonwealth—a New Atlantis—in the New World.

PASSWORDS

"Ipsa scientia potestas est." (Knowledge is power.)

—Sir Francis Bacon, "De Hæresibus" ("Of Heresies"), in *Meditationes Sacræ (Sacred Meditations),* 1597

A Freemason? A Rosicrucian?

Hall was perhaps the first Masonic writer to argue that Bacon was one of the founding fathers of Freemasonry. This is almost certainly an overstatement, but it is a matter of historical fact that he often gathered with a circle of friends at London's Gray's Inn to discuss politics and philosophy. These discussions were conducted so regularly that historians make frequent reference to a "Baconian circle." Some have asserted that this circle was involved with the Rosicrucians, and they even suggest that Bacon intended readers of his *New Atlantis* to conclude that the island was governed by Rosicrucians. There is some evidence suggesting that Bacon believed his ideas on advancing learning were very much in harmony with Rosicrucian principles, although there is no corroborating evidence that the "Baconian circle" was a Rosicrucian society.

The Masonic connection is somewhat more substantial. In 1618, Bacon leased York House, a vast mansion located on London's famous Strand. Here he frequently hosted lavish banquets attended by the most influential and learned men of his day—making up what conspiracy theorists would likely identify as the "power elite." On January 22, 1621, these men, whom Bacon had so often treated, treated him to a York House dinner to celebrate his sixtieth birthday. Some historians have identified this as "a Masonic banquet," to which Rosicrucians were invited (indeed, they may have been the only guests). The great English poet and dramatist Ben Jonson (1572–1637), friend to both Bacon and Shakespeare, composed a Masonic ode.

American Ventures

Some students of secret societies argue that Bacon, a Mason and probably a Rosicrucian, embodied his knowledge of the ancient utopia of Atlantis and the New Atlantis in his "American" utopian novel. Even more, he sought to transform the vision of his fictional work into reality.

In his imagined Bensalem, women enjoyed equal rights with men, slavery was non-existent, church and state were separate, and both politics and religion were regarded as matters of individual conscience and absolutely unrestricted by law. Chronically and critically in debt all his life, Bacon also banned debtor's prison from his utopia.

All the utopian elements Bacon imagined would be variously embodied in the English colonies of America and, even more, in the independent United States. This may not have been coincidental. As a politician and influential man of affairs, Bacon was instrumental in the creation of the English colonies in Virginia, the Carolinas, and Newfoundland. In 1609, he wrote a report promoting "The Virginia Colony," which was widely circulated throughout the government. The next year, he became a founding member of the Newfoundland Colonization Company, which dispatched John Guy (died 1629), a Bristol merchant, to Newfoundland to establish and govern a colony there.

As if these connections were not sufficient to prove that Bacon wanted to create a Masonic-Rosicrucian utopia in America, a number of students of secret societies have asserted that Sir Walter Raleigh (sponsor of Virginia colonization) and Captain John Smith (the military leader of the Jamestown colony) were Rosicrucians and Masons or Rosicrucian Masons. Others have suggested that virtually *all* the first crop of English colonists were Freemasons, making the impetus behind the English colonization of America unquestionably Masonic. The Freemason's purpose was to create a "New World" order or what the Great Seal of the United States, which some say is drawn directly on Masonic symbolism, proclaims as a *Novus Ordo Seclorum:* A New Order of the Ages.

The Masons Come to America

Apart from Bacon's interest in America, which may or may not have involved Freemasonry, the earliest trace of the Craft in America may be the image of a square and compass cut into a flat slab of stone that bears the date 1606 and is found on the shore of Goat Island, Nova Scotia. Many believe, however, that this is not the work of Freemasons, but is the headstone of a working French stonemason.

Reverend Edward Peterson claimed that Rhode Island had a Masonic lodge as early as 1658; however, according to the written records, the first accepted Freemason in the New World was John Skene, of the lodge at Aberdeen, Scotland. He was deputy governor of East Jersey from 1685 to 1690. The first indisputable reference to a native-born North American Freemason is Jonathan Belcher, who was born in Boston in 1681. He was initiated while travelling in Europe in 1704. Not long after this, the first lodge meeting in the Western Hemisphere was recorded at King's Chapel, Boston, in 1720. From this time on there are increasingly frequent references to things Masonic in colonial newspapers.

The Revolutionary Masons

There is no denying that colonial Freemasons were involved in the independence movement that culminated in the American Revolution. Many conspiracy theorists write that the revolution was almost entirely a Masonic operation. Manly P. Hall (*The Secret Teachings of All Ages*) noted that of the 56 signers of the Declaration of Independence, only 1 was known *not* to be a Freemason.

It is always more difficult to prove a negative (what somebody was *not*) than a positive (what somebody *was*); according to recent Masonic historians, only 9 signers have been confirmed as Masons and another 11 are "rumored" to have been. In any case, William Bramley has called the American Revolution "almost a 'Who's Who' of American colonial Freemasonry." Bramley, however, is a highly controversial conspiracy theorist, whose 1990 *Gods of Eden* argued that war as a human institution is actually the product of a conspiracy of extraterrestrial origin.

Yet even a widely regarded mainstream academic historian, Gordon Wood, has declared—in his Pulitzer Prize–winning 1993 *Radicalism of the American Revolution*—that "it would be difficult to exaggerate the importance of Masonry for the American Revolution. It not only created national icons that are still with us; it brought people together in new ways and helped fulfill the Republican dream of reorganizing social relationships. For thousands of Americans, it was a major means by which they participated directly in the Enlightenment."

A Masonic War

Some conspiracy theorists see the origin of the American Revolution not in Masonic meetings or even the Boston Tea Party of 1773, which was organized in a public house used as a Masonic lodge, but in a cataclysm that occurred some two decades earlier: the French and Indian War (1754–1763).

George Washington was 21 years old when he ponied up a hefty initiation fee to enter the Masonic lodge in Fredericksburg, Virginia. He rose meteorically through the degrees, passing from Apprentice to Fellow-Craft on March 3, 1753, and to Master Mason—the highest of the traditional Masonic orders in colonial America—on August 4, 1753, just 10 months after having been initiated. Whatever this says about Washington's commitment to the Craft, it suggests that his fellow Masons, presumably well-connected and locally prominent men, regarded him socially as "one of us."

Virginia's lieutenant governor, Robert Dinwiddie, certainly thought highly of young Washington. Late in 1753, he sent him, as a major of militia, to deliver an eviction notice to the French traders who had trespassed on "Ohio Country" territory (in modern western Pennsylvania) claimed by the British. The expedition ultimately resulted in a skirmish on May 28, 1754, between Washington's force and a French scouting party led by nobleman Joseph Coulon de Jumonville. A number of the Frenchmen were killed, including Jumonville. This, in turn, triggered a reprisal against Washington and his men on July 3 at a rude stockade Washington had hastily erected at Great Meadows, Pennsylvania, and aptly dubbed Fort Necessity.

Thus began the French and Indian War, which historians generally view as the North American theater of the Seven Years' War (1756–1763)—a conflict so extensive that many history books describe it as the first "world war."

Together, the French and Indian War and the Seven Years' War were a great financial drain on the British Empire and therefore highly destabilizing. Some conspiracy theorists believe that Washington the Freemason knew that his attack on the Jumonville party (the survivors later claimed to have been French "ambassadors") would provoke retaliation that, in turn, would trigger a war that would affect not only North America but engulf all of the French and British empires. In this view, the French and Indian War in North America and the Seven Years' War in Europe and elsewhere—the first "world war"—were the products of a Masonic plot. Furthermore, Washington and his fellow Masons understood that such a war would weaken the British Empire, greatly improving the odds of a successful outcome of a later war of rebellion by the American colonies. An American revolution was the ultimate objective of the colonial Freemasons.

To any mainstream historian's obvious objection that the great majority of the colonists who fought for independence were not Masons, were unaware of any Masonic motives, and would have had no reason to support them had they known of them, conspiracy theorists answer that all of this is true. Only the Masonic inner circle was in the know. Everyone else assumed that they were fighting to free themselves of British tyranny and burdensome taxation. The Freemasons wanted them to think this—in fact, they didn't care what the masses were fighting for. The only important thing was that they fought.

Revolutionary Goals

The quick answer to why the Masons wanted an American Revolution is expressed in what many claim is the Masonic-inspired Great Seal of the United States. It was to create a *Novus Ordo Seclorum*, a "New Order of the Ages" or (as the Latin is sometimes translated) a "New Worldly Order."

But there is more. The Freemason membership included a large number of financiers and bankers. According to many students of secret societies, eighteenth-century Freemasonry was also heavily influenced by the tradition of the Knights Templar and may even have been a modern survival of the Templars. As seen in Chapter 12, the Knights Templar were the first major international bankers.

The greatest power of a banker is the capacity to extend credit and collect interest. The British Parliament had not only levied taxes on its American colonies, it also passed laws forbidding the colonies from printing their own money. This made the colonies wholly dependent on the mother country for cash, and it made the individual colonists wholly dependent on British bankers for credit. The American Freemasons wanted to change this, so that the international banking connections of the Craft would be in a position to finance America, to profit from the transactions, and to gain control of the American purse strings. In this, conspiracy writers see everything from a revival and extension of Templar power, to the aggrandizement of the "Jewish international banking network," to the laying of the foundations for what would become in 1913 the Federal Reserve System (see Chapter 9).

The Great Seal and the Masons

Many, including Masons, anti-Masons, and others, have claimed that the Great Seal of the United States is of obvious Masonic origin.

Details often cited include (among others):

- On the obverse of the seal is an eagle whose dexter (right) wing has 32 feathers, the number of ordinary degrees in Scottish Rite Freemasonry.

- The sinister (left) wing has 33 feathers, the additional feather corresponding to the 33rd Degree of the Scottish Rite.

- There are nine tail feathers, corresponding to the number of degrees in the Chapter, Council, and Commandery of York Rite of Freemasonry.

- The glory above the eagle's head is divided into 24 equal parts, thereby recalling the Mason's gauge, which is also divided into 24 equal parts.

- On the reverse of the seal is the all-seeing eye within a triangle surrounded by a golden glory, imagery that recalls Masonic emblems.

- That the pyramid on the Great Seal is unfinished (truncated) suggests the death of Hiram Abiff, the legendary chief architect of King Solomon's Temple, who was (according to the Masons) murdered by three men who tried to force him to divulge the Master Masons' secret password.

- The blaze of glory on either side of the seal recalls the "Great Light in Masonry," the informing faith of the Masons.

The Masonic Service Association of North America denies any Masonic meaning to the symbols of the great seal and points out the following:

- A "pyramid, whether incomplete or finished … has never been a Masonic symbol."

- While it is true that "the all-seeing eye came to be used officially by Masons as a symbol for God … this happened towards the end of the eighteenth century, after Congress had adopted the seal."

- "The combining of the eye of providence overlooking an unfinished pyramid is a uniquely American, not Masonic, icon, and must be interpreted as its designers intended. It has no Masonic context."

- "The Great Seal of the United States is not a Masonic emblem, nor does it contain hidden Masonic symbols."

Most historians believe the designers of the Great Seal and the Masons borrowed their symbols from parallel sources and that the Great Seal was not drawn from Masonic tradition.

Creating the Great Seal took a long time and was subject to much debate. It was first commissioned by the Continental Congress immediately after the signing of the

Declaration of Independence on July 4, 1776. The first design committee consisted of Benjamin Franklin, who was a Mason, and John Adams and Thomas Jefferson, who were not Masons. The design they submitted was rejected, and, over the years, two more committees drew up designs. Finally, in 1782, almost six years after the Continental Congress had called for a Great Seal, the third committee's design was submitted to Charles Thomson, secretary to the Continental Congress and a non-Mason. Thomson, with the help of another non-Mason, lawyer and scholar William Barton, modified the design and submitted it to Congress, which tinkered with it further before adopting it on June 20, 1782.

Francis Hopkinson (1737–1791), author, composer, signer of the Declaration of Independence, and possible contributor to the design of the first American flag, assisted the second design committee. Hopkinson was a Mason, and he is credited with having contributed to the reverse of the Great Seal the unfinished pyramid with a radiant eye, which is a recognizable Masonic image. Prior to its incorporation on the Great Seal, the design was used on the Continental $50 bill, which Hopkinson also designed.

As for the mottos on the Great Seal, their sources are readily identified—and non-Masonic. *Annuit coeptis*, which appears above the radiant eye, means "He has smiled upon our undertakings" and is quoted from Virgil's *Aeneid*. *Novus Ordo Seclorum* ("A New Order of the Ages") is from the same Roman poet and comes from his fourth *Eclogue*, verse 5.

Behind Another Revolution

Freemasonry came to France when English merchants who did business there founded lodges, beginning with one at the English Channel port of Dunkirk. In 1733, the Grand Orient de France (GOdF) was founded and soon became the largest and most important Masonic organization in France.

PASSWORDS

"If … the [French] Revolution was prepared in the lodges of Freemasons … let it always be added that it was *Illuminized Freemasonry* that made the Revolution, and that the Masons who acclaim it are Illuminized Masons, inheritors of the same tradition introduced into the lodges of France in 1787 by the disciples of [Illuminati founder Adam] Weishaupt, 'patriarch of the Jacobins.'"

—Nesta Helen Webster, *The French Revolution: A Study in Democracy*, 1919

Attached to the GOdF was the Lodge Les Neuf Soeurs, which was opened in 1776 and based on the Société des Neuf Soeurs, active in the Paris Academy of Sciences since 1769 as a cultural organization. The lodge was highly influential in organizing French support for the American Revolution. Benjamin Franklin was a member of Les Neuf Soeurs when he served as an American agent in Paris during this period. After the American Revolution, the lodge was instrumental in fomenting the intellectual movements that whipped up the French Revolution. Prominent French revolutionary figures including Voltaire, Marquis de Condorcet, Mirabeau, Georges Danton, and the Duc d' Orléans were all members of the lodge.

Conspiracy historians stress that the French Revolution was the work of "Illuminized Freemasonry"—that is, of the Illuminati working through the Freemasons. The purpose of the revolution was the goal always at the heart of the Illuminati: to bring a new order to the world by toppling both religious and secular leaders and replacing national governments with a single, universal, global republic of reason.

In the slogan of the French Revolution, "Liberty, Equality, Fraternity," the last word was the most important and most revelatory. The Freemasons—or the Illuminati via the Freemasons—sought to transform the entire world into one vast fraternity, transcending and superseding states, churches, bishops, princes, and kings. It would be a world entirely ordered by the inner circle of Freemasonry, the select few—bankers, financiers, and other wielders of covert power and influence—who shared what Manly P. Hall called the *Arcanum Arcanorum*, the "Secret of Secrets," at the heart of the Craft.

It was a secret that, passing through the Illuminati, the Rosicrucians, and the Knights Templar—all intertwined with one another in any case—reached back to the most powerful secrets behind Christianity (the truth of the Holy Grail, the true lineage of Jesus), behind Judaism, and behind all religion. The secret reached back through the lost Atlantis and the plan for a New Atlantis, back to the very beginning of civilization, to Sumer, and—at least some believe—to an extraterrestrial race of beings whose messengers came to Earth some 450,000 years ago.

The Least You Need to Know

- Some conspiracy theorists argue that the origins of the United States can be traced to the New Atlantis, an ancient plan for a New World Utopia, which reemerged in *The New Atlantis,* a seventeenth-century novel by Francis Bacon. Bacon was connected with the Rosicrucians and Freemasonry and championed the English colonization of North America.

- Freemasonry was active in America before and during the American Revolution; many conspiracy theorists and some mainstream historians argue that the independence movement was in large measure the work of Freemasons.

- Freemasons were unquestionably active in fomenting and conducting the French Revolution; some conspiracy theorists believe that the Illuminati acted through Freemasonry to topple king and church in France.

- The public purposes of the American and French revolutions mask the true goal of the Masonic (and Rosicrucian and Illuminist) inner circles that fomented these rebellions: to bring the many under the control of the few—the power elite at the core of the secret societies.

Conspiracy, Italian Style

In This Chapter

- The Carbonari—secret society and revolutionary cell
- The Carbonari becomes the Young Italy movement
- Giuseppe Mazzini's global ambitions
- The "3WW" conspiracy theory

It is safe to say that few Americans—perhaps few people outside of Italy—give much thought these days to the Risorgimento, the unification of Italy from the diverse states that made up the Italian peninsula from 1866 to 1871. But as students of the New World Order (NWO) see it, this Italian nationalist movement is a stunning example of a new order of government created by a secret society, the Carbonari, who (most conspiracy theorists believe) either allied with or were an outgrowth of "Illuminized" (Illuminati-controlled) Freemasonry.

Mainstream historians differ with the conspiracy theorists on various major points concerning the Carbonari and the Risorgimento, but even they acknowledge the importance of this secret society in the Italian independence movement. The Italian revolutions of the nineteenth century culminating in unification are, therefore, significant as a "new world order" movement unquestionably dependent on covert conspiracy.

But for some, there is even more to the story. Much of the NWO literature incorporates an idea first outlined in *Occult Theocrasy* [sic] by New York socialite and conspiracy writer Edith Starr Miller (1887–1933) and published posthumously in 1933. The idea was further developed in 1955 by the popular Canadian NWO conspiracy theorist William Guy Carr, who claimed that Albert Pike (1809–1891), a highly placed Freemason and Masonic scholar, conspired with former Carbonaro Giuseppe Mazzini (1805–1872)—a founding father of the modern Italian state. They conspired to move beyond Italian national unification to one-world government based on the principles of Illuminized Freemasonry. Toward this end (Carr wrote), Pike and Mazzini developed a Masonic plan for fomenting three world wars.

The Charcoal Burners

The names of many secret societies, not surprisingly, resonate with mystery and romance—Knights Templar, Rosicrucians, and so on—but the names of two of the most politically significant (and therefore most truly powerful) evoke neither the age of chivalry nor mystical religion, but rather ordinary trades. There are the Freemasons, of course, and, even more humbly, the *Carbonari*.

An Italian word meaning "charcoal burners," the name reflects a most elemental trade practiced extensively in the mountains of the Abruzzi and Calabria regions. Charcoal, an essential fuel, was traditionally produced by collecting wood, drying it, then slow-burning it in a kiln over several days. In the Italian mountains, these kilns were primitive, earth-covered mounds or sometimes nothing more than holes in the ground. The work was hard, dirty, and basic. Yet it produced a brilliant, magical effect: at night, the dark hills came alive with the starry glow of hundreds of fires, as if the heavens had been brought to Earth.

DEFINITION

Carbonaro is an Italian word meaning "charcoal burner," a person whose trade is making charcoal for fuel by gathering, drying, and slowly burning wood. The plural, **Carbonari,** was used as the name of an important nineteenth-century revolutionary secret society.

In early nineteenth-century Italy, no group inspired more fear in the ruling classes or more hope in people opposed to what they regarded as ruling-class tyranny. What most frightened those who thrived on the status quo was how thoroughly democratic the Carbonari were. The organization included and apparently united peasants, nobles, soldiers, army officers, small landowners, government officials, and priests. Like most other secret societies, including Freemasonry (of which many believe it was an offshoot), the Carbonari had a mysterious hierarchy and an elaborate ritual replete with arcane Christian symbols and symbols from the trade of charcoal-burning.

Organization and Ritual

The Carbonari lodge was called a *baracca* (hut) and its interior space was the *vendita*, in which coal was sold. The surrounding district of a particular vendita was the *foresta* (forest). Carbonari addressed one another as *buon cugino* (good cousin), which distinguished members from outsiders, who were called *pagani* (heathens). Like Freemasons, Carbonari made themselves known to one another by a secret "grip" or handshake.

In the manner of the Freemasons, the Carbonari were divided into hierarchical degrees, but whereas Freemasons *work* three degrees, the Carbonari work only two: apprentice and master. The minimum period of an apprenticeship was six months, but Freemasons could enter the Order immediately as masters.

DEFINITION

The verb **work** has a special meaning in hierarchical secret societies, such as the Freemasons or Carbonari. Such organizations are said to "work" a certain number of degrees. For example, basic Freemasonry "works" three degrees: apprentice, fellow-craft, and master.

Officers included the Master, Secretary, Orator, and the Master's First and Second Assistants. All members gathered in the vendita, furnished with simple benches running parallel to the long dimension of the room, which was prescribed to be wainscoted with wood and paved with brick. At the head of the parallel benches was the Master. Seated to his right were the lesser Masters (members who had been admitted to the Master degree), all of whom were distinguished by special hats. To the Master's left sat the bare-headed Apprentices.

Whereas Masons called God the Great Architect of the Universe, the Carbonari referred to Him as the Grand Master of the Universe, designating Christ as the Honorary Grand Master (though sometimes, in more conventional Christian style, as the Lamb). Such echoes of Freemasonry were amplified by the presence of various symbols also suggestively Masonic. The Master's desk, a rough block of wood, was adorned by the following, arranged in a line: cloth; water; salt; a cross; leaves of certain trees; sticks; fire; earth; a crown of white thorns; a ladder; a ball of thread; and three ribbons, one each of blue, red, and black. Behind the desk was a triangle set off by rays and bearing the initials of the password of the Master's degree. To the left of the desk was another triangle bearing the coat of arms of the particular vendita.

To the right were three triangles painted with the initials of the sacred words of the Apprentice.

History

Nobody knows exactly when the Carbonari was established, but the Order first came to light in Naples early in the reign of Joachim-Napoléon Murat (1767–1815), husband of Caroline Bonaparte, whose brother Emperor Napoleon I of France named him (among other things) king of Naples and Sicily in 1808. It was in the city of Naples that the Alta Vendita ("high lodge") of the Carbonari was based.

As is the case with many other secret societies, the Carbonari laid claim to an ancient ancestry. According to its self-created legend, in Scotland during the Middle Ages, during the reign of a certain Queen Isabella (not the Spanish monarch who sent Columbus to the New World), certain dissidents banded together, disguised themselves as charcoal-burners, and delivered their message of revolt across the countryside along with their charcoal. This went on until sometime in the early sixteenth century, when a few of the charcoal-burners by chance encountered the king of France, Francis I (1494–1547), who had been hunting in a forest. The legend describes it as the borderland between France and Scotland, with an absence of geographical savvy that eclipses the legend's ignorance about Scottish history. Francis heard their grievances and took them under his royal protection. Thereafter they flourished, spreading through Germany, England, and ultimately Italy.

PASSWORDS

"Property boundaries shall be erased, all possessions shall be reduced to communal wealth, and the one and only patria, most gentle of mothers, shall furnish food, education, and work to the whole body of her beloved and free children. This is the redemption invoked by the wise. This is the true re-creation of Jerusalem. This is the manifest and inevitable decision of the Supreme Being."

—Oath sworn by Carbonari Masters, as organized by Freemason and Italian revolutionary Filippo (Philippe) Buonarroti (1761–1837) in 1818

Professed Values

Each Carbonaro vowed to maintain "Good Cousinship" based on "religion and virtue," and pledged not to argue against—or, for that matter, to discuss—religion.

More important, they vowed to maintain secrecy concerning the mysteries of the Order and the business transacted within the vendita.

Actual Aims

Despite the professed respect for religion, the Carbonari were opposed to the established church; however, the Order took St. Theobald, patron saint of charcoal-burners, as its own patron. From the beginning, the main purpose of the Carbonari was political, although that political purpose was framed in the symbolism of Christianity. Each Carbonaro swore a solemn oath to redeem "the Lamb" (synonym for Christ) from "the Wolf"—that is, from the tyranny of the powers that be.

In the manner of a revolutionary cell rather than a secret society, the Carbonari had a flag of red and blue and black, which became famous throughout the Italian peninsula as the banner of revolution through 1831, when the now-familiar red, white, and green standard was adopted as the emblem of unification. The original banner embodied the overriding political purpose of the Carbonari: to unify Italy under either a constitutional monarchy or a republic. Toward this end, they would employ any and all means necessary, including assassination and armed rebellion.

Nineteenth-century Italian politics was notoriously chaotic, and just about everyone seems to have tried either to suppress the Carbonari or to use the Order for their own ends. In 1814, the Carbonari vowed to secure a constitution for the Kingdom of Naples by force of arms. The lawful ruler, Ferdinand, opposed the Order, but Murat, whom Napoleon imposed on the kingdom, initially embraced the Carbonari as a means of strengthening his grip on the throne. After Napoleon's final fall, Murat fled to his native Corsica, then incited a rebellion in Calabria and was defeated by Ferdinand, who ordered his execution.

Yet Ferdinand did not sit easily on the throne. After the fall of Napoleon I and the restoration of the Bourbons, the Carbonari grew in strength and power throughout the Kingdom of Naples and from there spread into the neighboring territories, seeking not only the overthrow of governments but also an end to the supremacy of the pope, whose cardinals had already issued bans against both Freemasonry and the Carbonari.

The Carbonari promoted the Neapolitan revolution of 1820, which resulted in the king's agreement to institute constitutional government. On the strength of this triumph, the Carbonari movement spread to Piedmont, which provoked the Austrian emperor to intervene by sending some 50,000 troops into Italy. They suppressed the Carbonari and scotched the Neapolitan constitution.

The Austrian invasion drove the Carbonari underground but also gave them a new and expanded nationalist following. In 1831, Carbonari rebelled in the Papal States, achieving considerable success in Romagna and Le Marche and overthrowing the rulers of Parma and Modena. When Austria again intervened, however, the Carbonari withdrew, and many of its members were absorbed into the "Young Italy" movement led by Giuseppi Mazzini.

INTEL

The most famous Carbonari include Charles-Louis-Napoléon Bonaparte (1808–1873), nephew of Napoleon I, who fought against the Austrian occupiers of Italy and went on to become Napoleon III, last emperor of France; the Marquis de Lafayette (1757–1834), French hero of the American Revolution; and Lord Byron (1788–1824), the English romantic poet, ladies' man, and champion of Greek independence. The Carbonaro whose membership proved to be of greatest consequence was Giuseppe Mazzini (1805–1872). With Giuseppe Garibaldi (1807–1882), Mazzini was a prime architect of Italian independence and unification.

Ferdinand

Ferdinand was born Ferdinando Antonio Pasquale Giovanni Nepomuceno Serafino Gennaro Benedetto in Naples in 1751, the third son of Charles, King of Naples and Sicily (and later Charles III of Spain, King of Sicily). In Italy before unification, rule was confusing at best. On August 10, 1759, King Charles succeeded his brother to become King Charles III of Spain. This put him in an awkward position because he was bound by an existing treaty not to hold the titles to all three kingdoms—Spain, Naples, and Sicily. He resolved this problem by abdicating on October 6, 1759, in favor of Ferdinand, his two elder brothers having been disqualified by "imbecility" (developmental disability) in the case of the Infante Felipe, and destined inheritance of the Spanish throne in the case of the middle son, Charles.

At his coronation on October 6, 1759, Ferdinand was styled Ferdinand III of Sicily *and* Ferdinand IV of Naples. He did not have a smooth ride. The Kingdom of Naples was abolished on January 23, 1799, and replaced by the Parthenopaean Republic, which proved shorter-lived than its grandiose name would suggest. The republic fell on June 13, 1799, and Ferdinand was restored to the throne until the day after Christmas

1805, when France's Napoleon I proclaimed Ferdinand deposed and replaced him with his own brother Joseph Bonaparte on March 30 of the following year. When the Austrians won the Battle of Tolentino on March 3, 1815, Ferdinand was restored to the Neapolitan throne yet again. The following year, with the merger of the thrones of Sicily and Naples as the Two Sicilies, Ferdinand became Ferdinand I, king of the Two Sicilies, and reigned until his death on January 4, 1825.

The Soul of Italy

Today remembered as the "Soul of Italy," Giuseppe Mazzini (1805–1872) was born in Genoa, the son of a college professor who supported the radical French Jacobins. Young Mazzini studied law and developed a practice among the poor while also aspiring to write plays and novels. In 1826, he wrote a nationalist essay titled "On Dante's Patriotic Love" and went to work for a Genoese nationalist newspaper. When authorities shut the paper down, Mazzini joined the Carbonari in 1830, only to be arrested in October of that year in a general crackdown on the secret society. While he was in prison, Mazzini conceived of Young Italy to take the place of the Carbonari.

From Italian Unification to One-World Government

During the 1820s, the Carbonari had spawned revolutionary offshoots in France (the Charbonniers), Spain (Spanish Carbonari), and Germany (the Totenbund, or Band of Death) dedicated to the overthrow of tyranny—all were short-lived. From 1830 to 1831, Mazzini hoped that Young Italy, which absorbed the Carbonari, would create a popular uprising that would unite all Italy and then give rise to a revolutionary movement across all of Europe. Ultimately this would unite Europeans in a vast, transnational brotherhood. Some NWO conspiracy theorists point to this as an early attempt to bring about, via a secret society, one-world government.

A series of insurrections during the 1830s failed. Mazzini was ultimately exiled to England, from which, in 1837, he continued to labor not only for Italian liberation and unification, but for the same throughout Europe. He founded Young Germany, Young Poland, Young Switzerland, and, finally, Young Europe. He also corresponded with revolutionary leaders in South America, and his Young European movement certainly inspired junior officers in the Turkish army to create what would become by the end of the nineteenth century the "Young Turks." This movement would finally overthrow the corrupt Ottoman dynasty and create the modern republic of Turkey.

Mazzini was instrumental in the revolutions of 1848, which shook Europe to its core. Although these failed, the relationship he established with Giuseppe Garibaldi helped lay the foundation for *Il Risorgimento*, the creation of the modern Italian state, which was largely completed by 1871.

> **DEFINITION**
>
> **Il Risorgimento** is Italian for "The Resurgence" and is applied to the nineteenth-century movement to bring together as a single nation the diverse states of the Italian peninsula. Historians do not agree precisely on beginning and end dates for the Risorgimento, but many see its beginning in the Carbonari insurrections that started in 1820.

3WW

The political designs of the Carbonari, a secret society with ties to the Freemasons (perhaps even an offshoot of the Craft), are matters of historical record. It is also well known that Giuseppe Mazzini was a Carbonaro and used the Carbonari as the foundation on which he built Young Italy, with which he intended ultimately to create what he referred to as "the United States of Europe." That Mazzini subsequently reached out to South American revolutionary leaders suggests that his ambitions for unification also extended beyond Europe.

Some NWO conspiracy theorists proceed from these historical facts to speculate that Mazzini, like other Carbonari, was willing to achieve his purposes by any means necessary. This included a plan not merely for Italian uprisings, but for three world wars that would progressively ready the planet for global government. Conspiracy writers refer to this scheme by a kind of shorthand: *3WW*.

The Pike Connection

In 1955, William Guy Carr (1895–1959), former Royal Canadian Navy intelligence officer and the author of controversial yet popular early books on the NWO conspiracy, presented what he claimed was either the transcription or a summary (Carr did not make clear which) of a letter written to Mazzini on August 15, 1871, by a prominent American Freemason, Albert Pike. The letter laid out a plan for three world wars that were the steps (according to Pike) required to bring about a one-world government.

Albert Pike (1809–1891) was born in Boston and studied at Harvard, but, an advocate of slavery, he joined the Confederate army at the outbreak of the Civil War and served as a brigadier general. Earlier, as a U.S. Army officer in the U.S.-Mexican War (1846–1848), Pike had been involved in a duel with his commanding officer; in the Civil War, his Confederate commanding officer charged Pike (whose command included Indians) with allowing his troops to scalp soldiers in the field and with having personally misappropriated funds. This time, instead of challenging the officer to a duel, Pike fled the prospect of court martial, sending his resignation from a hiding place somewhere in the Arkansas hills. Although he was subsequently apprehended, his resignation was accepted and he was discharged.

Pike had been active in the Freemasons well before the Civil War, and in 1859 became Sovereign Grand Commander of the Scottish Rite's Southern Jurisdiction. After the war, he may also have been active for a time in the Ku Klux Klan (Masonic historians deny this) and, in 1871, he wrote *Morals and Dogma of the Ancient and Accepted Scottish Rite of Freemasonry*, effectively the foundation document of the Scottish Rite.

Some conspiracy theorists (see www.terrorism-illuminati.com) believe that Pike established Supreme Councils of the Scottish Rite as an Illuminati front in London, under the leadership of Queen Victoria's foreign secretary Lord Palmerston; in Berlin, led by no less a figure than Otto von Bismarck; and in Rome, under Mazzini. It is further alleged that Pike also established 23 subordinate councils in other strategic places across the globe.

The Pike-Mazzini Letter

This brings us to the letter Carr claimed Pike wrote to Mazzini on August 15, 1871, prescribing three world wars as the necessary preconditions of an Illuminist-Masonic one-world government.

- A "First World War" would be required to enable the Illuminati to overthrow the Russian czars and replace their power with a government founded on "atheistic-Communism." Pike specified that "divergences caused by 'agentur' [agents] of the Illuminati between the British and Germanic Empires" would be used to foment the war. In the aftermath of the war, communism would be expanded and used to undermine and destroy other governments and to weaken religions.

- A "Second World War" would be fomented through the conflict between fascists and political Zionists. The result of the war, according to Pike, would be the destruction of "Nazism" so that the state of Israel could be established in Palestine. Also, the war would continue the international expansion of communism to the point that it equaled global Christendom, "which would be then restrained and held in check until the time we would need it for the final social cataclysm."

It is necessary to pause here to point out some obvious anachronisms. According to the *Oxford English Dictionary*, *fascism* was not a word in use before 1919, *Zionist* did not appear in print before 1896, and *Nazism* was a product of the 1920s. The letter from Pike to Mazzini was purportedly written in 1871. Carr did not make clear whether he is presenting a faithful transcription of the letter (in which case, the use of these terms argues powerfully against the document's authenticity) or paraphrasing, summarizing, and interpolating—in which case, the "letter" becomes Carr's text rather than the verbatim thoughts of Albert Pike. With these observations in mind, we proceed to World War III:

- A "Third World War" was to be fomented on the basis of conflicts the "agentur" of the Illuminati would stir up between political Zionists and the leaders of Islam. The objective of the war, from the point of view of furthering one-world government, would be the mutual destruction of Islam *and* political Zionism, including the state of Israel. At the same time, the other nations of the world, divided against one another over the struggle, would be provoked to fight to the point of complete exhaustion on all sides.

- In the wake of World War III (Pike allegedly explained to Mazzini), "We shall unleash the Nihilists and the atheists, and we shall provoke a formidable social cataclysm which in all its horror will show clearly to the nations the effect of absolute atheism, origin of savagery and of the most bloody turmoil." This will prompt the majority to become "disillusioned with Christianity," sending them into "the true light through the universal manifestation of the pure doctrine of Lucifer," which will simultaneously destroy both Christianity and atheism.

The Conspiracy Paradox

In his day, William Guy Carr was a very popular author. His *Pawns in the Game* sold half a million copies when it was first published in 1955, putting it squarely into mainstream bestseller territory. Even today, the 3WW thesis is still widely discussed in the NWO conspiracy literature. Yet, based on the absence of the actual 1871 Pike-Mazzini letter, Carr's own inconsistency (see Carr's footnote in the next section), and the anachronistic language of the purported letter itself, the document has strained the credulity even of many conspiracy writers.

Flimsy Evidence ...

In *Pawns in the Game* (1955), Carr explained that he had learned of the Pike-Mazzini letter from a well-known anti-Masonic writer, Cardinal Caro y Rodriguez, who served as cardinal of Santiago, Chile, from 1939 to 1958 and was the author of *The Mystery of Freemasonry Unveiled*. Carr also noted (without citing sources) that the letter was briefly on display at the British Museum in London. In his later book, *Satan, Prince of This World* (published posthumously in 1966), Carr included a footnote: "The Keeper of Manuscripts recently informed the author that this letter is NOT catalogued in the British Museum Library. It seems strange that a man of Cardinal Rodriguez's knowledge should have said that it WAS in 1925."

Recent writers on Pike and Mazzini's role in the NWO admit that the British Museum disclaims ever having owned or exhibited the letter, that no one has ever found the letter, and that there is no proof that the letter ever existed. Several Masonic websites (see, for example, www.freemasonry.bcy.ca/anti-masonry/pike_mazzini.html) offer evidence that the letter was a fraud. This notwithstanding, many conspiracy theorists continue to cite the Pike-Mazzini letter as Carr originally presented it, presumably accepting it as authentic.

Indeed, Carr was not the first to claim correspondence between Pike and Mazzini. In her *Occult Theocrasy* [sic], posthumously published in 1933, Edith Starr Miller (1887–1933) included a letter she claimed that Mazzini wrote to Pike on January 22, 1870:

> We must allow all the federations to continue just as they are, with their systems, their central authorities, and their diverse modes of correspondence between high grades of the same rite, organized as they are at the present, but we must create a super rite, which will remain unknown, to which we will call those Masons of high degree whom we shall select. With regard to our brothers in Masonry, these men must be pledges to the strictest secrecy. Through this supreme rite, we will govern

all Freemasonry which will become the one international center, the more powerful because its direction will be unknown.

Some critics of Carr and 3WW trace both his work and that of Miller to the so-called "Taxil hoax," which was revealed in 1897. Léo Taxil was the pen name of the French author Marie Joseph Gabriel Antoine Jogand-Pagès (1854–1907), who wrote a number of sensationalist anti-Catholic books only to feign conversion to Catholicism, apparently in response to an 1884 encyclical of Pope Leo XIII accusing the Freemasons of assisting Satan.

In the aftermath of the encyclical, Taxil published a massive four-volume history of Freemasonry, loaded with "eyewitness" accounts of Masonic Satanic rituals—all, however, fictitious. This was followed by *The Devil in the Nineteenth Century*, which included the wild "eyewitness" accounts of one Diana Vaughan, purportedly an adherent of Satanic Freemasonry, as well as first-person accounts of her personal encounters with Satan. Taxil also claimed that the Masons themselves distinguished between Satan and Lucifer, claiming that the "true and pure philosophical religion is the belief in Lucifer … the God of Light and God of Good." Both Miller and Carr after her made much of the Luciferian elements of Freemasonry in its conspiracy to dominate the world.

On April 19, 1897, Taxil convened a press conference in Paris, promising to produce Diana Vaughan. Instead, to the assembled reporters, he confessed to having fabricated much of what he had "revealed" about the Freemasons and humbly thanked the Catholic Church for giving his books so much publicity.

... and Solid History

The vast majority of NWO conspiracy material is either difficult or impossible to prove or disprove. The believers believe, the nonbelievers do not, and seldom does either side venture very far beyond their own assumptions and conjectures.

In the case of Mazzini and Pike, however, it seems fairly easy to dismiss the alleged correspondence between the two men as fantasy, if not outright fraud. Yet, even having done this easy thing, it is very hard to dismiss the well-documented history that leads up to the fiction. The letter of 1871 may be insubstantial, but the strains of the Carbonari conspiracy that contributed to it are the stuff of solid fact. Here was a secret society that clearly aimed to unite a nation. In the end, even after Carbonari had ceased to exist, the Carbonari succeeded. And for at least one of their number,

Giuseppe Mazzini, the union of Italy was only a beginning. From one Italy, he hoped humanity would take a step toward one world. For this aspiration, the evidence is straightforward and ample.

The Least You Need to Know

- The Carbonari were a combination secret society and revolutionary cell, whose members were dedicated to liberating the disparate states of Italy from foreign control and unifying them into a single independent nation.

- The Carbonari were likely influenced by—and may have even developed directly from—the Freemasons; conspiracy theorists believe that the Illuminati used the Freemasons to control the Carbonari.

- Giuseppe Mazzini, an early architect of Italian unification, was a member of the Carbonari and, after the secret society had been suppressed, he used it as the foundation for his Young Italy movement, which, in turn, became the basis for organizations aimed at liberating and unifying other countries and even creating a "United States of Europe."

- The 3WW conspiracy theory, which asserts that Mazzini conspired with the American Freemason Albert Pike to plan three world wars that would prepare the way for a one-world government under the Illuminati, is based on an almost certainly fraudulent letter from Pike to Mazzini. Nevertheless, the Carbonari were a politically powerful secret society, and Mazzini, a Carbonaro, did have globalist ambitions.

Internationale

In This Chapter

- The role of communism in the NWO
- Alternative views of the rise of communism
- Role of Wall Street in the Bolshevik Revolution
- Relation of the Carbonari, Freemasons, Illuminati, and Rosicrucians to modern communism

Few books that set out to expose the NWO reach a wide audience. For the most part, that's the way their authors like it. Exclusion from the publishing "mainstream" is not only to be expected, but is a certification of truth and authenticity. After all, mainstream publishers are part of mainstream media, which is part of the machinery of the New World Order (NWO) conspiracy. William Guy Carr's *Pawns in the Game* and *Red Fog over America*, both published in 1955, are rare exceptions. Both sold far into the six figures before Carr died in 1959—*Pawns* reportedly topped a half million sales—and continues to sell in reprints.

The gist of these books is that a conspiracy involving Jewish bankers (the Rothschilds chief among them) and the Illuminati, driven by Lucifer, used twentieth-century technology (chiefly radio) to create a covert network centered on the Bilderberg Group (see Chapter 3) to bring about a one-world government. The origins of the conspiracy reach back into the ancient past, according to Carr, but post–World War II Soviet communism is its most dramatic contemporary manifestation. And that revelation, unveiled during the height of the Cold War, was doubtless what made Carr a bestseller. During the 1950s, communism spread across Europe like a dark red stain and, as many saw it, infiltrated the West, especially the United States, at every level: in business, in the media, and in government. It was a conspiracy as vast as it was mysterious. Where had the conspiracy come from? Who was behind it?

Writers like Carr offered answers; what's more, their answers neatly linked a scary new world to the distant past. The conspiracies, they said, had been around for a very long time. During the Cold War, which began at the end of World War II and lasted until the collapse of the Soviet Union at the start of the 1990s, just about everyone who wrote about the NWO wrote about the rise of communism.

Communism: The Ultimate One-World Conspiracy

Bestseller though Carr was, many found, and many still find, much that he had to say offensive. Like his leading influence Nesta Helen Webster (see Chapter 16), his theory rests on a hard bed of anti-Semitism. In other respects, his vision may seem paranoid, deluded, just plain silly, or at the very least far-fetched. Yet who can deny that communism is (or was) a movement toward one-world government—perhaps even the ultimate one-world conspiracy?

In the *Communist Manifesto* of 1848, Karl Marx and Friedrich Engels called for the creation of a classless society through the centralization by the state of finance, industry, transportation, and property. As their thought developed beyond the *Manifesto*, Marx and Engels proposed as the ultimate goal a dissolution of the all-powerful state and the joint possession of all wealth ("capital") by the working class—that is, by those who actually produce the capital. In this view, workers owe their loyalty not to any state or empire, but to their own class, which by definition transcends borders, nationality, ethnicity, and religion and is truly global.

PASSWORDS

"Workers of the World, Unite! You Have Nothing to Lose But Your Chains."

—Communist Party slogan from Marx and Engels, *The Communist Manifesto*, 1848

In its ultimate manifestation, communism *is* one-world government. And this is precisely the common object conspiracy theorists find in all of history's major secret societies. The ancient orders (the Knights Templar, the Illuminati, the Rosicrucians) and the Freemasons, like the Council on Foreign Relations (CFR), the Bilderberg

Group, the Trilateral Commission (TC), and the United Nations, all seek to transcend nationhood and national allegiance along with religious belief to create a flat world over which the secret power elite will exercise total control.

Every secret society has an outer circle and an inner circle, what Masonic historian Manly P. Hall called the *Arcanum Arcanorum:* the "Secret of Secrets." The generations who lived with or under Soviet communism called the inner circle the *Kremlin*, the ancient Moscow citadel, older than the czars. The likes of Vladimir Lenin and Joseph Stalin aspired to control not just the fate of hundreds of millions of Russians, but that of the peoples of the world. For not until everyone was persuaded to give their allegiance to their class rather than their country, their king, or their God would the Communist revolution be complete. One-world rule is the essence of communism.

> **DEFINITION**
>
> **Kremlin** (Russian for "fortress" or "citadel") may denote any central fortification in historic Russian cities, but it is most frequently used to refer to the Moscow Kremlin, the center of czarist, Communist, and current Russian government.

The Rise of Communism: A Tale of Two Histories

One-world rule is the essence of communism. For NWO theorists, one-world rule is also the essence of history's great conspiratorial secret societies. Is this a striking coincidence or a matter of evolution, of cause and effect? Is twentieth-century communism the spawn of a covert history driven by the members of secret societies?

Communist History: The Mainstream Version

Karl Marx did not claim to have invented communism. Rather, he saw it as the natural state of humankind at its most primitive level of social organization, when people subsisted exclusively on what they could hunt and gather. Only when communities became capable of stepping beyond subsistence by producing a surplus did communal possession of commodities give way to private property, a system in which some had more than others.

Throughout history, various religious sects and other groups espoused communal ownership of property and criticized the privileges of nobility. A number of Christian monastic orders were Communist insofar as they renounced private property. Sir Thomas More's (1478–1535) celebrated *Utopia*, written in 1516, envisioned an ideal society based on communal ownership. Since then, utopian organizers have founded a number of communelike communities, the most famous of which are Robert Owens's New Harmony, in Indiana (1825), and the Transcendentalists' Brook Farm (1841–1847), in Massachusetts.

But it took the rise to dominance of the *factory system* created by the Industrial Revolution to spur the development of communism on a large scale. The 1848 *Communist Manifesto* of Marx and Engels, written in a year during which unrest and revolution swept Europe, was in large part a response to the misery created by factory life. A handful of capitalists controlled the means of production and thereby controlled those who actually performed production, effectively transforming the masses into wage slaves.

DEFINITION

The **factory system** arose first during the Industrial Revolution and soon spread to other developed nations. Wage workers were gathered into a central factory to serve the machines that produced a product. Working hours were dawn to dusk, six days a week. The labor, trained but unskilled, reduced each worker to an item of disposable, replaceable commodity.

Marx and Engels proposed a revolution to restructure society so as to put the means of production in the hands of the workers. Their theory of communism was urban and industrialized. It was based on the assumption that the *proletariat*—the urban laboring masses—were not only intensely discontented with their way of life, but because they worked together in factories and cities, could be readily organized for revolution.

The earliest Russian Marxist thinker, Georgi Plekhanov (1857–1918), believed that Russia, because it was far less industrialized and urbanized than Western Europe, would not be ready for a full-out proletarian revolution for some time. He therefore proposed a kind of staged political evolution rather than an outright revolution, in which the autocratic rule of the czars would transition into a constitutional democratic government, which, in the fullness of time, would become Communist. Others—most notably Vladimir Ilych Lenin (1870–1924)—believed that Russia, despite lagging behind the West, could vault over the democratic period and leap directly into communism.

> **DEFINITION**
>
> The **proletariat** (Latin, *proletarius,* citizen of the lowest class) is the Marxist label for the lower social class of the laboring masses.

After the first of the Russian revolutions of 1917 toppled Czar Nicholas II (1868–1918), the revolutionaries split into two broad factions: the Mensheviks, who favored Plekhanov's democratic transition, and the Bolsheviks, who wanted Lenin's full Communist revolution even in the absence of a fully developed urban capitalist society. This led to a second revolution, the Bolshevik Revolution of 1917, which brought Lenin and his followers into power.

Immediately after the second revolution of 1917, the Bolsheviks changed their name to the Communist Party, which set itself up as the one and only party of Russia. Civil war broke out (1918–1922), during which the party nationalized all property in Russia and all factories and railroads were put under central control. Incompetent administration quickly brought massive shortages, which exacerbated the Civil War. In an effort to end the counterrevolution, Lenin in 1921 introduced the "New Economic Policy," which restored a limited degree of capitalism. Only in 1928, with the ascension of Joseph Stalin (1878–1953) to absolute leadership of the Communist Party, was the New Economic Policy ended and capitalism eliminated completely.

Even as the ruinous Russian Civil War ground on, Lenin created the Third International (the Communist International, or Comintern) in 1919, which was an attempt to spread communism throughout Europe. With the end of the Civil War in 1922, the former Russian Empire became the Union of Soviet Socialist Republics (USSR), and Moscow's Kremlin became the center not only of Soviet government, but of the Comintern and therefore world communism.

Soviet influence spread during the years following World War I. The forces of fascism and Nazism threatened to extinguish communism during World War II, but thanks to an alliance with the democratic powers of the West (which, though anti-Communist, regarded Hitler as the more immediately destructive common enemy), the Soviet Union emerged victorious. After World War II, the alliance between the Soviets and the Western democracies quickly dissolved, and Soviet-backed communism took hold throughout Eastern Europe. Mao Zedong triumphed in China, but his alliance with the Soviets would fade as he began to lead his nation along an ideological course sharply different from that of the Kremlin. Elsewhere in Asia, North Korea, North Vietnam, Laos, and Cambodia all embraced communism, as did Cuba in the Caribbean.

By the early 1980s, the high point of Communist global government, nearly 30 percent of the planet lived in Communist countries. Contrary to what some in the West—especially the United States—believed, this did not represent a monolithic world state controlled by the Kremlin. Nevertheless, the Communist "empire" dwarfed both the Roman and the British empires at their height and may therefore be regarded as history's nearest approach to one-world government.

PASSWORDS

So comrades, come rally
And the last fight let us face
The Internationale unites the human race.
So comrades, come rally
And the last fight let us face
The Internationale unites the human race.

—*"The Internationale,"* anthem of international communism and socialism, lyrics translated from French, Eugène Pottier, 1871

Communist History: The Alternative Version

Marx and Engels, poor men themselves, wrote on behalf of the exploited and down-trodden proletariat. The revolution they predicted and prescribed was to be a revolt of the masses against the capitalists. Obviously, the capitalists, of all people, should have been the most vehemently opposed to communism.

Astoundingly, this was not the case. NWO writers, including G. Edward Griffin, William T. Still, and David Icke, among others, argue that (in Still's words) "wealthy Wall Street bankers ... were willing to finance a revolution in Russia."

Some writers link Wall Street's support of the Bolshevik Revolution to the theory, widely held as early as 1917, the year of the revolution, that Bolshevism was the work of a "Jewish conspiracy"—more precisely, a conspiracy of Jewish bankers. Even the U.S. Department of State drew up a document titled "Bolshevism and Judaism" (State Department Decimal File, 861.00/5339) dated November 13, 1918. It reported that the revolution in Russia had been engineered "in February 1916" with finance from

Jewish American financiers and financial firms. The list is reproduced verbatim from the State Department document:

(1) Jacob Schiff—Jew

(2) Kuhn, Loeb & Company—Jewish Firm

Management: Jacob Schiff—Jew

    Felix Warburg—Jew

    Otto H. Kahn—Jew

    Mortimer L. Schiff—Jew

    Jerome J. Hanauer—Jew

(3) Guggenheim—Jew

(4) Max Breitung—Jew

(5) Isaac Seligman—Jew

The report even stated that Jacob Schiff publicly announced his financial support of the revolution and for the Jewish revolutionary Leon Trotsky in particular. "There is now definite evidence that Bolshevism is an international movement controlled by Jews," the report firmly stated, though it provided no documentary evidence.

Doubtless, many supporters of the Bolshevik Revolution were Jewish; but the point is not that Jews supported the revolution, but that Wall Street did. Indeed, contrary to the assertion in the State Department document, Jacob Schiff was among those American financiers who spoke out against the Bolshevik Revolution. John Pierpont "Jack" Morgan Jr. (1867–1943) and John D. Rockefeller (1839–1937), on the other hand, actually promoted the cause. American-based finance for the Bolshevik Revolution was not a Jewish conspiracy, but a Wall Street one.

Clarence W. Barron (1855–1928), the financial journalist who founded *Barron's* magazine, recorded a conversation he had aboard the Atlantic steamer SS *Aquitania* on February 1, 1919, with American oil magnate E. H. Doheny. The men Doheny named in the conversation, William Boyce Thompson, Thomas Lamont, and Charles R. Crane, were all major Wall Street players of the period:

> *Spent the evening with the Dohenys in their suite. Mr. Doheny said: If you believe in democracy you cannot believe in Socialism. Socialism is the poison that destroys democracy. Democracy means opportunity for all. Socialism holds out the hope that a man can quit work and be better off. Bolshevism is the true fruit of socialism and if*

you will read the interesting testimony before the Senate Committee about the middle of January that showed up all these pacifists and peace-makers as German sympathizers, Socialists, and Bolsheviks, you will see that a majority of the college professors in the United States are teaching socialism and Bolshevism and that fifty-two college professors were on so-called peace committees in 1914. President Eliot of Harvard is teaching Bolshevism. The worst Bolshevists in the United States are not only college professors, of whom President Wilson is one, but capitalists and the wives of capitalists and neither seem to know what they are talking about. William Boyce Thompson is teaching Bolshevism and he may yet convert Lamont of J.P. Morgan & Company. Vanderlip is a Bolshevist, so is Charles R. Crane. Many women are joining the movement and neither they, nor their husbands, know what it is, or what it leads to. Henry Ford is another and so are most of those one hundred historians Wilson took abroad with him in the foolish idea that history can teach youth proper demarcations of races, peoples, and nations geographically.

None of the men Doheny mentions were Jewish.

Why would Wall Street capitalists support a movement dedicated to their own destruction? According to the alternative history of the revolution, it is because the American capitalists believed they could control a Communist state—with a centralized command economy—more completely than they could a capitalist one.

Outsiders Get Inside

There can be no doubt that it was a very bad thing to be a wealthy capitalist living in Russia during the throes of the Bolshevik Revolution and the Civil War that followed it. But Wall Street is not in Moscow. Morgan, Rockefeller, and the other Wall Street supporters of the Bolshevik Revolution were Americans, beyond the reach of Lenin's secret police and the Soviet Red Army. From the physical safety of their outside position, they were able to get inside the revolution without getting hurt.

Big-time capitalists crave monopolies. That was true of Morgan and his railroads and Rockefeller and his oil trust. A truly democratic economy fosters competition, especially when it is bolstered by anti-trust legislation. A command economy, in contrast, in which the financial strings are pulled by members of a Kremlin inner circle, can be approached, purchased, bribed, and controlled. If an American-based capitalist can make an ally of the inner-circle powerbrokers of a Communist state, he may well be able to reduce the command economy to a kind of financial colony or client state under his control. Holding the purse strings, he may become the puppet master. If it is possible to have a monopoly on railroads or on oil, why not a monopoly on an entire national economy?

Deeper Background

According to the alternative view of the history of the Bolshevik Revolution, American capitalists, in contrast to the mainstream historians who wrote about them, were able to wiggle out of the intellectual straitjacket that automatically opposes "capitalism" to "communism." Where conventional historians saw only irreconcilable differences, the financiers—the ones who actually helped to create the history—saw the makings of a marriage, if not of love, at least of convenience.

The Proto-Bolsheviks

Some NWO conspiracy writers are not content to explain the Russian revolutions of 1917 as (at least in part) the work of American capitalists. They propose that the rich and powerful were involved in the rise of communism long before the days of Lenin or even Marx.

Conspiracy theorists tend to see many historical secret societies as contributing to a historical movement that eventually created modern communism. The most important of these is the Carbonari (see Chapter 17), a secret society they believe was a political instrument of Illuminized Freemasonry (see Chapters 13 and 15). The popular historian of secret societies, Arkon Daraul went so far as to write in his *History of Secret Societies* that the "Bolsheviks and their theoreticians of the Communist persuasion are ... offspring of the Charcoal-burners."

Who Is Arkon Daraul?

Anyone interested in secret societies knows the name Arkon Daraul, whose 1961 *History of Secret Societies* remains the most popular book on the subject. Fittingly, "Arkon Daraul" is a pseudonym—and no one is quite sure of its owner's true identity. Nevertheless, it is widely believed that the name was invented by Idries Shah (1924–1996), internationally known as a Sufi teacher and an author of popular books on spirituality, anthropology, travel, and what is best characterized as pop psychology. He was widely respected by such figures as British writers Robert Graves and Doris Lessing. More controversially, he was the secretary and companion of Gerald Gardner, founder of modern Wicca, a religion based on witchcraft.

Shah was born in India, the scion of Afghan nobility, but was raised primarily in England. After establishing himself as an author on the subjects of magic and witch-craft, he founded Octagon Press in 1960, which issued translations of classic works of Sufi literature in addition to some of his own original works, including his important 1964 work of history, *The Sufis.*

Shah promoted Sufism as an alternative to Islam and a kind of universal wisdom. His Institute for Cultural Research, which he founded in London in 1965, incorporates Sufism, but is open to the study of human behavior and of culture generally.

A Bridge to Bolshevism

The International Workingmen's Association (IWA), often referred to as the First International, brought together a number of socialist political groups and trade unions in 1864 in London. Karl Marx, who had moved to London in 1849 to escape the reper-cussions of the failed revolutions of 1848, embraced the IWA, and became its leader. Many conspiracy writers see the organization as a direct outgrowth of the Carbonari and the Freemasons and as an even more direct precursor of modern communism. As such, the IWA figures as the bridge that connects Illuminism, Freemasonry, and the Carbonari on the one hand with modern communism on the other.

In this view, Marx's leadership of the IWA puts him at the end of one line of secret societies that were bent on replacing the existing regimes with a new world order and at the head of another—the line that leads to the revolution the leaders of Bolshevik Russia hoped would engulf the world. Certainly, it came closer to doing so than any other conspiracy (so far).

The Least You Need to Know

- For many believers in an NWO conspiracy, the rise of communism was the work of the greatest one-world government conspiracy, and for this reason books on the NWO were especially popular during the Cold War and the "Red Scare" that accompanied it.

- Whereas conventional historians see the origin of communism in a revolt of the proletariat—the laboring class—against the capitalist ruling class, NWO historians emphasize the role of Wall Street capitalists in backing the Bolshevik Revolution.

- Some NWO literature pictures Karl Marx as the intellectual bridge between the Carbonari (seen as an instrument of the Freemasons, Illuminati, and Rosicrucians) and modern communism by virtue of his writings as well as his leadership of the nineteenth-century International Workingmen's Association, or First International.

Roosevelt's Revolutions

In This Chapter

- Why Roosevelt was elected
- The New Deal as an NWO conspiracy
- Roosevelt as a "Great Dictator"
- The president's motives in World War II
- The Pearl Harbor conspiracy theory

Look at the newsreel images from April 14, 1945: the funeral procession of President Franklin Delano Roosevelt. The camera pans on the grief-stricken faces of the silent crowds lining the streets of Washington, D.C., as the cortege passes. The public weeping, the terrible weight of collective despair—all testimony of a national affection rarely accorded its chief executive.

Elected to an unprecedented four terms, FDR led the United States through the Great Depression and most of World War II. The people were profoundly grateful. Many, perhaps most, believed him to have been a great leader. But just six years later the states ratified the Twenty-Second Amendment to the U.S. Constitution to ensure that no other man or woman would ever again serve more than two terms as President of the United States.

The presidents who have had the most profound effect on the nation—leaders such as Lincoln, Wilson, and FDR—have elicited the most profound gratitude, admiration, and devotion as well as the greatest suspicion, fear, and even hatred. As many New World Order (NWO) writers see it, FDR was the prime architect of the one-world government movement in the twentieth century, first through the sweeping economic and social policies of the Depression era and then through his role in World War II.

New Deal or New World Order?

After a brief recession immediately following World War I, the 1920s roared through America, bringing to many an unprecedented level of prosperity. Finding themselves with some brand-new disposable income, large numbers of Americans disposed of it in stock speculation, often dangerously overextending themselves by purchasing securities "on margin" for as little as 10 cents on the dollar. Before long, a great deal of the stock, held by dimes against dollars, was just so much paper.

Flush with finance, factories ginned up production, which soon outstripped the buying power of consumers. More merchandise was being dumped into the marketplace than could be sold. As prices fell and unsold goods piled up, factories laid off workers. Without a wage, you can't buy a thing, and so the consumer market contracted even more. In a shrinking marketplace, there is no demand for workers. The cycle could not have been more vicious.

Crash!

By the fall of 1929, stock prices oscillated wildly. On October 29, "Black Tuesday," the bottom fell out. From a high of 358.77 points on October 11, the Dow Jones Industrial Average fell to 212.33, a decline of nearly 41 percent. (It would go much lower. In 1932, the Dow fell to a mere 40.56 points, 89 percent below the October 11, 1929 figure.)

Amid the panic, brokers "called" their margin loans, demanding full payment on now-worthless stocks. Many investors were wiped out. As for the working man, by 1933 one in four would be jobless. Even those who prudently put their cash into savings accounts faced the reality that 1,300 banks failed in 1930. Within three years, another 3,700 would go belly up.

"Prosperity Is Just Around the Corner"

Following the crash, the thirty-first president of the United States, Herbert Hoover, did little more than attempt to reassure Americans that "prosperity was just around the corner." As the Depression deepened, he proposed a number of emergency relief programs, however, insisting that private charities and state and local governments provide funding that they did not have. Federal aid was out of the question. Hoover feared that big-government intervention would undermine individual liberty and integrity, sapping the initiative of the individual citizen.

The 1932 Election

Little wonder that Hoover drew much of the blame for the Great Depression. When he stood for reelection in 1932, his Democratic opponent proclaimed his intention to do everything Hoover refused to do. At the Democratic National Convention in Chicago, he pledged to deliver to the American people a "new deal." It would be a federally funded, federally administered program of relief and recovery on a vast scale.

Most Americans in 1932 had been raised on the values Herbert Hoover represented: self-reliance in a business environment little regulated or ameliorated by the government. These seemed to be the values most compatible with democracy and the Constitution. But values can change dramatically when people are hungry and frightened. FDR defeated Hoover by a landslide.

A Hundred Days and Beyond

In what the press called the "Hundred Days," the first three months of the Roosevelt administration, the president sent to Congress a dazzling series of legislative initiatives. The Federal Deposit Insurance Corporation (FDIC) was established to protect depositors from losing their savings in the event of bank failure; the authority of the Federal Reserve (see Chapter 9) was expanded; the Home Owners Loan Corporation was created to help beleaguered homeowners avoid foreclosure; and a Federal Securities Act created the Securities and Exchange Commission (SEC) to regulate stock transactions in a bid to prevent the kind of speculation that led to the 1929 crash.

> **PASSWORDS**
>
> "The New Deal was a coup d'état designed by plutocrats, for installing an oligarchy, to achieve an autocracy, administered by quisling bureaucrats. The Wilsonian internationalist hallucination was consummated by Roosevelt."
>
> —"SARTRE," *Global Gulag* website (http://batr.org/gulag/081903.html), August 19, 2003

These acts were followed by the creation of the Civilian Conservation Corps (CCC), which put many thousands of unemployed young men to work under U.S. Army supervision on projects in national forests, parks, and public lands; and the National Recovery Act (NRA), which established the Public Works Administration (PWA) and introduced strict employment and labor regulations. The Tennessee Valley Authority

(TVA) was set up to build roads, dams, and hydroelectric plants in some of the nation's poorest states.

After the Hundred Days came many more programs, including the Works Progress Administration (WPA) in 1935, a massive federally subsidized employment program. That same year, Social Security was introduced, federally funding pensions through payroll and wage taxes. After FDR won a second term in 1936, the so-called "Second New Deal" introduced extensive labor reforms.

PASSWORDS

"The conclusion is inescapable that, traditional as the words may have been in which the New Deal expressed itself, in actuality it was a revolutionary response to a revolutionary situation. … The searing ordeal of the Great Depression purged the American people of their belief in the limited powers of the federal government and convinced them of the necessity of the guarantor state."

—Carl N. Degler, *Out of Our Past,* 1959

Open to Criticism

Although a majority of the American people supported it, the New Deal was controversial when it was introduced. Even though key aspects of it—such as the FDIC, SEC, and Social Security—remain very important elements of modern American life, it is still controversial today even among many mainstream historians and economists, who endlessly debate the effectiveness of the New Deal in coping with the Depression.

Among NWO conspiracy theorists, there is no controversy. The New Deal was un-American. It was unadulterated socialism, even outright communism. It brought a small army of radical leftists into positions of limitless bureaucratic power. The result was not a higher level of economic security and democratic freedom, but the increased dictatorship of the central government and the conversion of the nation into a *collectivist state*. By means of the New Deal, the federal government invaded every aspect of American life and commerce, transforming a nation of hardy individualists into the subjects of a vast, centrally planned, centrally controlled project of social engineering. The purpose of consolidating American government was to enable the next step: consolidation of world government.

> **DEFINITION**
>
> A **collectivist state** emphasizes human interdependence, valuing group goals over individual goals.

In the Age of Great Dictators

The 1930s—which saw the rise of Adolf Hitler in Germany, the consolidation of the dictatorship of Benito Mussolini in Italy, and the expansion of military-dominated government in Japan—was sometimes called the "Age of Great Dictators." Traditional historians contrast FDR to such figures, portraying him as the great champion of democracy.

Roosevelt, like most American presidents who enjoy substantial electoral victories, believed he had a popular mandate to continue his New Deal transformation of the American government, economy, and society. The president's critics argued—and continue to argue—that he took this "mandate" as license to expand his power beyond constitutional limits. NWO writers argue that, far from offering a democratic contrast to the "Great Dictators," FDR himself aspired to be the greatest of them all.

The Court-Packing Scheme

FDR was reelected in 1936 by a sweeping margin, carrying 46 of 48 states and providing long coattails that made the Democratic majorities in both houses of Congress even larger. Throughout his first term, the U.S. Supreme Court, a majority of whose justices had been appointed during the three conservative Republican administrations that had preceded Roosevelt's, offered the most formidable resistance to the legislation of the New Deal.

In 1935, the Supreme Court found unconstitutional key parts of the National Industrial Recovery Act, which gave the president great power to regulate industry and create certain cartels and monopolies for the purpose of stimulating economic recovery. In 1936, the court also struck down the Agricultural Adjustment Act Amendment of 1935, which gave the president wide latitude in regulating farm production and using federal money to subsidize aspects of it.

Concerned that these two decisions presaged others that would soon strike down the Social Security Act and the National Labor Relations Act, mainstays of the New

Deal, FDR moved to reorganize the Supreme Court to ensure a friendlier body by "packing" it with liberal appointees.

> **INTEL**
>
> Defenders of the president point out that his "court-packing scheme" was far less radical than what some congressional Democrats wanted: a constitutional amendment to take away from the court its principal power: judicial review— the authority to deliver binding opinions on the constitutionality of an act or its application. FDR wanted to do no more (though it was a lot!) than expand the court from 9 to 15 justices and allow him to appoint a new justice whenever a justice reached the age of 70 and declined to retire.

Over the Line

Even ardent supporters of the president believed his court-packing scheme was an intolerable attack on the Constitution, and he was compelled to step back from it. Instead of giving him credit for withdrawing the initiative, however, the president's critics pointed to it as a token of his ambition to make the executive branch supreme over both the legislative and the judicial branches, thereby destroying the balance of powers vital to the American democracy.

NWO theorists go even further. The court-packing scheme, they say, drew back the curtain to reveal the true nature of the wizard who controlled Oz. FDR was bent on gaining total and exclusive control of the U.S. government, so that nothing could stop him from collectivizing and centralizing every aspect of national life. Court packing was a brazen step toward national dictatorship, and that dictatorship would be, in turn, a step toward merging the United States into a global government.

Slouching Toward War

On September 1, 1939, Germany invaded Poland, starting World War II. As in July 1914, when World War I broke out in Europe, the overwhelming majority of Americans wanted nothing more than to stay out of it. Throughout the 1930s, as Europe edged toward war for the second time in little more than 20 years, Congress enacted a series of neutrality acts, ostensibly designed to preserve American neutrality, but each of which tended to bring the United States closer to entering the conflict. This eventually led to the Lend-Lease Act of 1941, by which the United States became what FDR called "the arsenal of democracy." It supplied Britain, the

Soviet Union, and smaller allies with arms, ships, tanks, aircraft, and other materials of war.

CFR

No sooner had the war begun in Europe than the Council on Foreign Relations (CFR) approached the U.S. State Department with an offer to largely assume responsibility for long-range planning. The CFR undertook a "War and Peace Studies Project," which concluded that by early 1940, the United States should immediately declare war on Germany. NWO conspiracy theorists assert that the CFR had been founded to promote one-world government and was now, at the invitation of the Roosevelt State Department, attempting to steer America into a war that would bring its goal to realization (see Chapter 2).

The CFR had two motives, according to conspiracy writers. The first was to create a permanent alliance between the United States and Great Britain—a step toward global government. The second was to promote a war that, like other wars, would be tremendously profitable for the financiers, bankers, and industrialists who controlled the CFR.

Armed Neutrality

Much as Wilson had done before him, Roosevelt moved steadily toward a policy of "armed neutrality." The Neutrality Act of 1939 permitted the cash sale of arms and strategic materials to any belligerent the president did not specifically exclude. Still anxious to prevent U.S. entry into the war, Congress authorized the president to designate "combat areas" through which U.S. citizens and vessels were not permitted to travel. It was hoped that this would avoid the kind of *Lusitania*-type incident that helped propel the nation into World War I.

On November 17, 1941, however, the act was amended to permit the arming of merchant vessels and also to permit those vessels to carry cargoes into belligerent ports. By this time, the U.S. and German navies were engaging in sporadic armed exchanges in the Atlantic, which historians characterize as an undeclared naval war.

The Churchill-Roosevelt Courtship

Within days of Britain's declaration of war on Germany, Roosevelt wrote to Winston Churchill, who at the time was first lord of the Admiralty, thereby initiating a correspondence in which Churchill skillfully courted an Anglo-American alliance. Roosevelt let himself be courted, even though America at the time had no end of isolationists, including one of its most admired heroes, Charles A. Lindbergh (an admirer of Hitler and Mussolini), who warned against "meddling with affairs abroad."

Polls taken as late as 1939 showed that only 7.7 percent of Americans favored entering the war. Nevertheless, on June 10, 1940, the day Mussolini's Italy declared war on Britain and France, President Roosevelt gave the commencement address to the University of Virginia Law School Class of 1940, pledging "in our American unity" to "pursue two obvious and simultaneous courses: we will extend to the opponents of force the material resources of this nation; and, at the same time, we will harness and speed up the use of those resources in order that we ourselves in the Americas may have equipment and training equal to the task of any emergency and every defense. Signs and signals call for speed—full speed ahead." Churchill, who heard the speech on radio, greeted it enthusiastically.

On September 2, 1940, FDR agreed that the U.S. Navy would transfer 50 obsolescent World War I–era destroyers to the British Royal Navy in exchange for 99-year leases on British naval and air stations in Antigua, the Bahamas, Bermuda, British Guiana, Jamaica, Newfoundland, St. Lucia, and Trinidad. With this, U.S. neutrality effectively came to an end. The destroyers-for-bases deal paved the way for "An Act to Promote the Defense of the United States," better known as the Lend-Lease Act, which FDR signed on March 11, 1941. Armed with Lend-Lease, the president was authorized to give aid to any nation whose defense he deemed critical to that of the United States. It empowered the government to accept payment "in kind or property, or any other direct or indirect benefit which the President deems satisfactory."

 PASSWORDS

"Work is America's answer to the need of idle millions … Work, not charity … peaceful work, not regimentation to build the machines of war."

—Inscription at the WPA Pavilion, New York World's Fair, 1939

Gearing Up

Throughout 1940, President Roosevelt successfully asked Congress for ever-increasing war appropriations to vastly expand the army, the U.S. Army Air Corps, and the navy. Congress obliged, in part because the spending rapidly pulled the nation out of the Great Depression.

Not only did Congress raise the national debt ceiling by what was at the time a stupefying $4 billion to $49 billion to accommodate defense spending; FDR also signed, on July 20, 1940, the Two-Ocean Navy Act, anticipating that vast armadas would be required to fight both the Germans in the Atlantic and the Japanese in the Pacific. On September 16, he signed the Selective Training and Service Act of 1940, creating the first peacetime conscription in U.S. history. By October 16, 16.4 million American men had registered for the draft.

The Atlantic Charter

Lend-Lease took the United States as close to a formal alliance with Britain as it could get without an actual diplomatic agreement. That came during August 9 through 12, 1941, when the president and Prime Minister Churchill met aboard naval vessels of the United States and Great Britain off the coast of Newfoundland. There they drafted the Atlantic Charter, which boldly set forth eight principles of American and British policy in war as well as peace.

PASSWORDS

"When you see a rattlesnake poised to strike you, you do not wait until he has struck before you crush him."

—Franklin D. Roosevelt, September 11, 1941, in a speech justifying the unde-clared naval war against Germany

Day of Infamy

Both mainstream historians and those who see history through the lens of the NWO conspiracy point to FDR's long preparation for war as giving the lie to the myth that the Japanese attack on Pearl Harbor thrust the United States into the war unexpect-edly on December 7, 1941.

There can be no denying that, for a long time, President Roosevelt had been looking for a way to overcome popular opposition and enter the war. Mainstream historians say that this was because he believed that, after Germany conquered Britain and controlled its mighty Atlantic fleet, the United States would be vulnerable to attack and conquest. NWO writers, however, believe that his motive was the motive of the CFR and other "secret societies" that wanted to foment a profitable war and, at the same time, move ever closer to one-world government. To do this, Communist Russia had to be saved from defeat by fascist Germany, because the ideology and political apparatus of communism were global, whereas fascism was nationalistic.

Just as FDR courted war with Germany in the Atlantic, the NWO theorists believe, he deliberately provoked the Japanese in the Pacific. The president, they say, both anticipated and hoped for an attack that would force the United States to enter the war.

Sticking It to Japan

Roosevelt approved war loans to China, which had been engaged in the Sino-Japanese War since 1937. He also covertly approved the creation of the American Volunteer Group (AVG), better known as the Flying Tigers, an elite cadre of "civilian" mercenary pilots (they had actually resigned from the military for the purpose of joining the Tigers) who fought an air war against China's Japanese invaders.

Seeking to pressure Japan into withdrawing from China, the U.S. Department of State on July 1, 1938, sent letters to U.S. aircraft manufacturers and exporters expressing opposition to the sale of aircraft to countries that were using the planes to attack civilian populations. Secretary of State Cordell Hull called this a "moral embargo," which he extended in 1939 to raw materials essential to airplane manufacturers as well as to plans, plants, and technical information for the production of aviation gasoline. When aircraft companies responded favorably to the moral embargo, it was extended even further to discourage U.S. financial firms from extending credit to Japan. Finally, in July 1939, the Roosevelt administration notified Japan that it intended to terminate a master trade treaty in force since 1911, an unmistakable warning that a full embargo would not be far behind.

When Japan refused to yield to economic pressure and instead joined Germany and Italy in September 1940 in the so-called Tripartite ("Axis") Treaty, Congress—at the president's urging—passed an Export Control Act on July 2, 1940, authorizing him to curtail or ban the export of all war materials. Under this act, the export to Japan of aviation gasoline and most types of machine tools was ended, and in September, iron and scrap steel exports were banned.

Mainstream historians generally accept FDR's rationale for the embargo as an alternative to going to war to end Japanese aggression. Conspiracy theorists, however, believe that the true purpose was to goad Japan into an attack that would allow Roosevelt to declare war.

The Pearl Harbor Conspiracy Theory

Whether FDR wanted it to or not, the embargo not only failed to deter Japanese aggression, it made Japan's militarist government all the more determined to seize vital sources of raw materials in Asia and the Pacific. By attacking the United States with overwhelming force, Japan hoped to compel the Roosevelt government into acquiescing in its aggressive policies. Even as Japanese diplomats continued to meet with Secretary Hull in Washington, D.C., the attack on Pearl Harbor became inevitable.

Many conspiracy theorists believe that, given the highly developed state of U.S. military intelligence, which included thorough knowledge of the key Japanese diplomatic codes, it is impossible to believe that the president was unaware of the impending attack on Pearl Harbor. Moreover, conspiracy theorists hold that:

- FDR and his secretary of state knew that diplomatic talks were doomed and that the Pearl Harbor attack was a foregone conclusion. Yet they kept this information secret.

- FDR ordered the U.S. Pacific Fleet to move from San Francisco, where it was relatively safe, to Pearl Harbor, Hawaii Territory, where it was vulnerable. (Mainstream military historians believe that the move was intended to provide a line of naval defense that did not expose the U.S. mainland to direct attack.)

- FDR and his advisers were aware that a large Japanese task force had dropped out of sight as it approached Hawaii, yet they took no action, other than to order U.S. Army Chief of Staff General George C. Marshall to send the top commanders at Pearl Harbor an oddly ambiguous message warning of possible hostility, yet adding that "the United States desires that Japan commit the first overt act." Some writers see this as a bald admission that the administration desired an attack.

- In the days leading up to December 7, 1941, warnings of the impending attack came from a variety of sources, but were largely ignored.

- Finally, mainstream historians frequently remark on the navy's good fortune that its fleet of aircraft carriers was out at sea during the Pearl Harbor attack and therefore escaped the fate that befell the American battleships moored there. Conspiracy theorists believe that luck played no part in this. They argue that FDR and his naval advisers (correctly) believed that aircraft carriers would win the Pacific War and therefore were unwilling to sacrifice them, whereas the battleships were expendable. The absence of the carriers was planned.

Roosevelt the Warmonger

There is no proof that FDR conspired in the attack on Pearl Harbor. There is no proof that he did *not* conspire in it. Common sense argues strongly against his complicity, unless you believe in the NWO conspiracy and Roosevelt's involvement in it.

If you do believe that FDR was committed to the CFR's goals as conspiracy theorists define them, then you can conclude that his purposes in entering the war consisted of the following:

- To prevent fascist Germany and quasi-fascist Japan from crushing Communist Russia, because the survival of communism would promote the development of a centrally controlled global government.

- To create a postwar global government. According to NWO writers, the United Nations (see Chapter 6), which FDR was instrumental in creating and promoting, was (and remains) a tool of one-world rule.

- To generate astronomical war profits for the power elite who control the CFR (and would soon control the United Nations). The profits would enable the CFR power elite to take control of global affairs as a one-world shadow government.

If these things are true, as many conspiracy theorists believe they are, then one of the most beloved of American presidents was in reality a dictator, whose ambition and evil were more than a match for the likes of Mussolini, Hitler, the Japanese militarists, and Joseph Stalin.

The Least You Need to Know

- Herbert Hoover's refusal to use the federal government to intervene to ameliorate or end the Great Depression paved the way for Franklin D. Roosevelt's presidential victory in 1932.

- FDR's New Deal brought the federal government deeply into the lives of every American and consolidated political, economic, and social power on an unprecedented scale. NWO conspiracy theorists believe this was a deliberate step toward bringing the United States into a one-world government.

- NWO conspiracy theorists hold that Roosevelt was (like Mussolini, Hitler, and Stalin) a "Great Dictator" who purposely brought America into World War II to generate profits for the power elite (represented by the CFR). He was a member of the CFR and created a permanent Anglo-American alliance that would facilitate global government after the war.

- Conspiracy writers theorize that President Roosevelt deliberately provoked Japan to attack the United States and that he was complicit in rendering Pearl Harbor vulnerable to a "sneak attack." His objective was to overcome all popular and political objections to the United States' entry into World War II.

From Third Reich to Fourth

20

In This Chapter

- Varied definitions of Fourth Reich
- Fascism as a merger of the state and corporate capitalists
- The Fourth Reich's rebirth in America
- Postwar Nazi escape networks
- U.S. corporate complicity in the Holocaust

"Fourth Reich" is a buzzword among conspiracy theorists, and, like many buzzwords, it means different things to different people—albeit all related to the Third Reich, Adolf Hitler's Nazi regime, which spanned 1933 to the surrender of Germany in World War II on May 7–8, 1945.

For some New World Order (NWO) writers, Fourth Reich is a synonym for the NWO itself, pointedly conveying what they regard as the fascist quality of globalism. For others, including the substantial fraction of NWO theorists who believe that the one-world government movement is a Jewish or Zionist plot, the Fourth Reich is nothing less than a modern manifestation of "Jewish fascism," a bizarre, short-lived political movement from the 1930s that called for the establishment of a state of Israel based on the principles of Mussolini and Hitler (minus the anti-Semitism).

Finally, there is the work of Edwin Black, investigator of American corporate complicity in the Holocaust, and Jim Marrs, most popular of all current NWO writers, which has led to the theory that certain Nazis who survived the collapse of the Third Reich in World War II, in conspiracy with sympathizers in the United States and elsewhere, have been working covertly to create an actual Fourth Reich that embodies Third Reich principles, values, and goals. Emanating from the United States, this NWO is ultimately intended to be global in scope.

PASSWORDS

"Heute Deutschland, morgen die Welt!" ("Today Germany, tomorrow the world!")

—Nazi Party slogan attributed to Adolf Hitler, 1930s

Behind the Buzz

The idea of a Fourth Reich as a Jewish conspiracy based on the Jewish fascist movement not only partakes of the anti-Semitic strain of some NWO literature, but is too far-fetched to make an intellectually compelling case for the actual existence of a Fourth Reich.

More instructive, at least, is the use of the term *Fourth Reich* as a synonym for the NWO as a whole. Nazism, associated with Adolf Hitler and Germany, and fascism, associated with Benito Mussolini and Italy, were widely perceived as so closely related ideologically that *fascism* was and still is often used synonymously with *Nazism*. There are significant differences, especially in the Nazis' heavy reliance on Germanic-Nordic racial mythology, but the similarities are more significant.

Jewish Fascism

Unlikely though it may seem in retrospect, a faction of Zionists (Jewish activists working to create a state of Israel in Palestine) during the 1930s embraced the example of Italian dictator Benito Mussolini and sought to establish Israel on the pattern of fascist Italy. This faction, known as Brit HaBirionim, was a subset of the Zionist Revisionist Movement (ZRM), which had been created by the Russian-born Jewish journalist Abba Ahimeir (1897–1962).

Brit HaBirionim espoused an ideology known as Revisionist Maximalism, which Ahimeir brought into being in 1930. Disillusioned with the Soviet regime ushered in by the Bolshevik Revolution, the Revisionist Maximalists favored fascism's anti-communism, and Ahimeir not only supported Mussolini, but also Hitler—even as he denounced Hitler's anti-Semitic policies.

Not surprisingly, Ahimeir's strange position alienated and outraged most of the Jewish community, prompting Ahimeir to quickly backpedal, but the movement he had founded nevertheless collapsed in 1933. It resurfaced briefly under new leadership in 1938, but was of no historical significance. It would doubtless be forgotten today were it not for the small number of NWO theorists who have attempted to base on it an implausible theory of a Jewish-backed Fourth Reich.

Fascism as a Definition of the NWO

Hitler built his Nazi Party on the ideological foundation of fascism. Although Hitler added a mythology of racial superiority and racial destiny that do not figure prominently in fascism, the underlying political, social, and economic ideology of Nazism is fascist.

Begin with the word *fascism*. It comes from the *fasces*, an emblem of ancient Roman government. The *fasces* is a bundle of sticks bound around the handle of a battleaxe, the blade head of which protrudes through the bundle.

The significance of the *fasces* symbol is this: any individual stick is brittle, weak, and easily broken. Tightly bound together, however, a bundle of sticks is strong and unbreakable. Bound around a battleaxe, the unbreakable bunch is a mighty force to be reckoned with. This was the essence of fascism: the individual is weak and easily broken; bound together in a mighty state, however, individuals create an unbreakable whole. The state does not exist to serve the individual; the individual exists to serve the state. Liberal democracy is centered on the individual. Fascism is centered on government—the state.

INTEL

Like many symbols of Roman government, the *fasces* also appears as an icon of American democratic government. A pair of *fasces* flank the American flag behind the Speaker's chair in the U.S. House of Representatives, and the official seal of the U.S. Senate features a pair of crossed *fasces*. The reverse side of the "Mercury" dime, which circulated from 1916 to 1945, featured a *fasces* superimposed over an olive branch.

For most NWO theorists, this description of fascism could easily serve as a description of globalism, which has as its aim the complete subordination of the individual to government on a global scale—the total absorption of the individual into the state.

The similarity doesn't end there. Both communism and fascism are totalitarian forms of government in which the individual is subordinated to—indeed, swallowed up by—the state. However, whereas communism nationalizes all business, industry, and finance, fascism is a merger of state and corporate power. Benito Mussolini even suggested that fascism might be called *corporatism*. Because the partnership between the state and capitalism promised to be tremendously profitable, many Italian and German moguls, magnates, and tycoons eagerly supported the likes of Mussolini and Hitler.

DEFINITION

Corporatism was offered by Benito Mussolini as a synonym for fascism because the word conveyed the concept of a state in powerful partnership with corporate capitalists.

NWO theorists regard the globalist movement—rule of the many by the few—as much the same thing: a partnership of state and capital to create a power elite. They point out, however, that whereas the leaders of fascist Italy and Germany's Third Reich had the upper hand over the corporations—were, so to speak, the senior partners in the merger—it is the corporations that dominate the Fourth Reich shadow government of the United States.

Today's Fourth Reich is ruled by the CEOs of great corporations. The elected government and all its functions are pure theater, a show to distract the masses. Republican president, Democratic president, it makes no difference: the course of the government remains essentially unchanged.

Fascism as the Source of the NWO

Some conspiracy theorists use the writings of Edwin Black and Jim Marrs to take the Fourth Reich concept beyond mere definition and analogy. For them, fascism—specifically Nazism—is the actual historical source of a rising Fourth Reich, which they see as the key element of the NWO.

The Fall of the Third Reich

Adolf Hitler proclaimed that the Third Reich—the Third German Empire, after the First Reich (the Holy Roman Empire, which lasted from 800 to 1806) and the Second Reich (Germany as a unified state under Kaisers Wilhelm I and II, 1871–1918)—would last for a thousand years. By February 1945, however, when the Third Reich was barely 12 years old, the Red Army was 35 miles east of Berlin. Although the situation for Germany was hopeless, Hitler ordered his soldiers to defend the capital "to the last man and the last shot," and even mustered the Volksstürm, a home guard made up of old men and children, to aid in its defense.

Together with the remnants of the regular German army, these last-ditch forces were arrayed in four concentric rings around Berlin, the outermost ring 20 miles out from the center city; the second 10 miles; the third deployed along the S-Bahn, the city's suburban rail system; and the innermost ring, called the Z-ring (Z for *Zitadelle*, or

Citadel), arranged within the center of the city itself. The *Zitadelle* ring was intended to protect the government buildings and the *Füherbunker*, the underground shelter that housed Hitler and his immediate staff below the ruins of the Reich Chancellery, the administrative center of the government.

The army and Volkssturm resisted the Russians with suicidal determination, but on April 20, 1945, Adolf Hitler's birthday, Soviet tanks rolled over the main Berlin ammunition depot and then the military communications center. Holed up in his bunker, Hitler gave members of his inner circle permission to leave Berlin, if possible. He himself, he said, would remain in the city to the end.

By April 25, Berlin was completely encircled. A delusional Hitler continued to issue orders to his mostly nonexistent armies. On April 29, Lieutenant General Karl Weidling, commanding the capital's defenses, reported to Hitler that he would be out of ammunition by the next day. On that day, April 30, 1945, the Red Army stormed the Reichstag, the seat of German government.

By this time, according to thousands of mainstream history books, Adolf Hitler was already dead. In his bunker beneath the Reich Chancellery, he'd shot himself in the head while simultaneously biting down on a capsule of cyanide. His former mistress—and now bride of a single day—Eva Braun, had poisoned herself. Aides carried their bodies into the Chancellery courtyard, deposited them into a bomb or artillery crater, doused them with gasoline, and ignited the makeshift pyre.

 PASSWORDS

"National Socialism will use its own revolution for establishing a new world order."

—Adolf Hitler, during World War II

The mainstream accounts are based on eyewitness reports from within the bunker. Late in the morning of April 30, 1945, with Soviet forces less than a third of a mile from the bunker, Hitler conferred for the last time with General Helmuth Weidling, commander of the Berlin Defense Area, who reported the situation as hopeless. Hitler then lunched with two secretaries and his personal cook, after which he and Eva Braun, whom he had married the day before, said their farewells to various fellow occupants of the bunker, including Josef Goebbels and his family, Martin Bormann, bunker staff, and several military officers. The couple then retired to Hitler's personal study.

At about 3:30 in the afternoon, witnesses reported hearing a loud gunshot. Hitler's valet, Heinz Linge, accompanied by Bormann, waited several minutes before opening the door to the study. Linge reported the aroma of burnt almonds, characteristic of the presence of prussic acid, a form of hydrogen cyanide. Otto Günsche, Hitler's SS adjutant, inspected the bodies that were seated on a sofa. Hitler, he said, had shot himself. Because Eva Braun was unwounded, he assumed she had poisoned herself with cyanide.

A number of witnesses later reported seeing the two bodies carried up through the bunker's emergency exit to the Chancellery garden. Here they were splashed with gasoline and set afire. They were not completely consumed, however, and Soviet shelling made it impossible to complete the cremation. Subsequently, the charred corpses were deposited into a shell crater, where Soviet troops later found them.

The Alternative History

Rumors that Hitler had faked his suicide and slipped out of Berlin began to circulate almost simultaneously with news of his death. Even though charred bodies were discovered in the Chancellery courtyard, and although witnesses claim to have seen the bodies of Hitler and Braun, there is no irrefutable forensic evidence of their identity. This fed speculation that Hitler made his way out of the city and out of the country, taking refuge in some country over which the victorious Allies had no control. Around him may have coalesced a resurgent Nazi movement, the seeds of the Fourth Reich.

INTEL

Soviet-era records released after the fall of the Soviet Union revealed that the bodies of Hitler and Eva Braun (as well as those of propaganda minister Josef Goebbels, his wife and six Goebbels children, General Hans Krebs, and Hitler's dogs) were secretly buried, presumably by East German or Soviet intelligence officials, near Rathenow, Brandenburg, at the time in East Germany. The records further reveal that in 1970, these remains were exhumed and cremated, the ashes disposed of in the Elbe River. The Russian Federal Security Service, successor to the Soviet-era KGB, reported holding in its archives a fragment of Hitler's skull, which was put on public display in 2000. The skull fragment has what is apparently a bullet hole. In 2009, however, DNA analysis revealed that the fragment came from the body of an unidentified woman younger than 40 years old. Thus, to this day, no remains of Adolf Hitler have been recovered.

Hitler's Legacy

In the end, Hitler's personal survival matters to Fourth Reich theorists far less than the survival of his legacy. The legacy is twofold. It consists of the many prominent Nazi leaders who escaped capture after the war. Some simply slipped through Allied fingers, while others struck deals with the Allies to serve as anti-Communist and anti-Soviet spies and informants, or to provide access to the advanced weapons technology the Germans produced during the war. It also consists of ideas and people willing to embrace them: the ideas of racial superiority and racial destiny, of global domination, and of government in partnership with business—the ideas that gave rise to the Third Reich in the first place.

Around this legacy—Nazi people and Nazi ideas—the Fourth Reich is said to have coalesced. The point is this: Germany was unquestionably defeated in World War II. National Socialism (Nazism) survived.

Safe Haven

The principal Nuremberg Tribunal, the war crimes trials of 1945 to 1946, tried 22 of the highest-profile Nazi leaders captured in Germany. Of these, 19 were found guilty and given sentences ranging from imprisonment to death. Those tried in these highly publicized proceedings represented a very small fraction of the Nazi leadership. The Allied public was not informed about the many more ex-Nazis who were never tried—not because they died or somehow escaped capture (though a significant number did escape), but because they were given safe haven.

ODESSA

Thanks largely to *The Odessa File*, the 1972 bestselling novel by Frederick Forsyth made into a successful movie two years later, ODESSA—an acronym for Organisation der ehemaligen SS-Angehörigen ("Organization of Former Members of the SS")—is the most famous secret network dedicated to sheltering top Nazis from capture and prosecution after the war.

It is widely thought that ODESSA, organized by SS officers, successfully established escape routes ("ratlines") by which former SS members made their way to friendly havens in South America and the Middle East. According to Paul Manning (author of the 1981 *Martin Bormann: Nazi in Exile*), as many as 10,000 former German military leaders, including Hitler's private secretary Martin Bormann, used ODESSA to escape to South American refuges.

The Spider

Die Spinne ("The Spider") was another network, led in part by Otto Skorzeny, the brilliant Nazi commando chief who successfully liberated Benito Mussolini from anti-fascist captivity late in the war. (Mussolini was subsequently recaptured by Italian partisans and executed, along with his mistress, Clara Petacci. Their corpses were grotesquely hung by the heels in a Milan public square.)

Between 1945 and 1950, Die Spinne enabled fugitive Nazis to find refuge in Francisco Franco's fascist Spain and Juan Perón's fascist Argentina. Chile and Paraguay were also safe havens. Well into the late 1960s, Argentina continued to harbor extensive communities of German Nazi immigrants and their descendants.

Operation Paperclip

In 1945, the Joint Intelligence Objectives Agency of the U.S. Office of Strategic Services (OSS), precursor agency of the CIA, launched Operation Paperclip, a program for the recruitment and extraction of German scientists from Nazi Germany to the United States immediately after the end of the war in Europe. The operation was authorized at the highest level by President Harry S. Truman, who took care to stipulate that all former Nazis were to be barred from the program. Because the most valuable targets of Operation Paperclip had been prominent Nazis, including scientists of the caliber of Wernher von Braun (developer of the German V-2 rocket weapon and subsequently father of the U.S. manned space program), OSS operatives covertly scrubbed, purged, and bleached their Nazi records before admitting them to the program and bringing them to the United States.

The scientists of Operation Paperclip were instrumental in creating and advancing the U.S. aerospace program after World War II. In a very real sense, the towering achievement of *Apollo 11* landing the first human beings on the moon was rooted in Nazi efforts to produce the most advanced weapons of mass destruction here on Earth.

Nazi Nexus

Edwin Black is a wide-ranging investigative reporter, not an NWO proponent, researcher, or theorist. Nevertheless, his *Nazi Nexus* (2009) follows up on some of his earlier books—*The Transfer Agreement* (1984), *IBM and the Holocaust* (2001), *War Against the Weak* (2003), and a host of newspaper and magazine articles—to argue that five corporate American giants, Ford Motor Co., the Carnegie Institution, the Rockefeller Foundation, General Motors, and IBM were complicit in the Holocaust, the Nazi genocide of six million Jews during World War II.

Made in the USA

Black argues that Henry Ford's anti-Semitic theories of an age-old Jewish global conspiracy actively inspired Adolf Hitler as early as the 1920s, and served to guide his own Nazi programs of genocidal persecution. Black goes on to assert that the Nazi theory of racial superiority was at least partly grounded in research on *eugenics* conducted and promoted in the United States by the Carnegie Institution and Rockefeller Foundation.

DEFINITION

Eugenics is the study and practice of selectively breeding human beings, including culling out those judged undesirable, for the purpose of improving the human species.

This work included recommendations that all those judged "unfit" should be culled from the gene pool through restrictions on marriage, sterilization, confinement to concentration camps, and even euthanasia. Black presents research documenting Rockefeller Foundation prewar funding of Nazi medical researchers, including eugenicist Otmar Freiherr von Verschuer, who went on to conduct experiments at the Auschwitz extermination camp in 1944 with the assistance of Dr. Josef Mengele, the Holocaust's infamous "Angel of Death."

Black documents the role of U.S.-based General Motors in covertly expanding its German subsidiary Opel during the years leading up to World War II. By the outbreak of the war, Opel was Germany's biggest maker of cars and trucks and was largely devoted to building military vehicles.

While Ford stimulated anti-Semitic ideology, the Carnegie Institution and Rockefeller Foundation promoted eugenics and General Motors funded the manufacture of military vehicles; IBM (according to Black's research) supplied Nazi Germany with the advanced information technology that enabled the identification of Jews across occupied Europe, thereby facilitating first persecution then genocide. Black asserts that, operating from the United States and, later, from offices in Paris and Geneva,

IBM played a key role in planning not only the identification of Jews, but their social expulsion, the state confiscation of their assets and real property, their confinement to ghettos, their deportation, and ultimately their extermination.

The Neo-Nazi Misnomer

Most Americans are familiar with the term "Neo-Nazi" to describe any number of white supremacist, anti-Semitic "skinhead" groups, who often dress in Nazi-style uniforms and prominently exhibit swastikas and other symbols associated with National Socialism.

The work of Edwin Black suggests that the "Neo" in "Neo-Nazi" is a misnomer because there is really nothing *new* about Nazis in the United States. We know from both Mussolini and Hitler that fascism and Nazism required corporate participation. Black suggests that some of the most significant corporations that participated in creating and promoting the Third Reich were not German, but American.

Whereas Black documents corporate America's connection to Nazism before and even during World War II, Jim Marrs and others who write about the Fourth Reich focus (though with far less documentation and far more speculation) on postwar relations between American corporate interests and ex-Nazis and other elements of the former Third Reich. They argue that the gangs of brown-shirted, armband-wearing men and women who occasionally parade before television news cameras are not the Nazis who wield real power in America.

The true Nazis, those who seriously aim to dominate the world, are directly linked to ex-Nazis who actually made their way via ODESSA, Die Spinne, and Operation Paperclip to safe havens outside of conquered Germany after the war. These individuals wear business suits, not uniforms. They do not carry signs or swing clubs at street-corner rallies. They sit behind expansive desks in the corporate corner-offices in which they have been quietly working since the end of World War II. Their goal is to establish in America various aspects of fascism and Nazism, especially those related to what Mussolini called "corporatism." They aim to exercise corporate control of American life and to ensure that a select cadre of CEOs and chairmen of the board will exercise the real governing power in the nation. These individuals are the power elite, which owes allegiance to no nation. Paraphrasing Adolf Hitler himself, they may proclaim (albeit in a whisper rather than a shout): *Today, America. Tomorrow, the world.*

The Least You Need to Know

- The term "Fourth Reich" has more than one meaning in the NWO conspiracy literature, the most important of which is the idea that ex-Nazis and their followers are working covertly, with the complicity of industrialists and financiers, to resurrect Hitler's defeated Third Reich in America as the Fourth Reich.

- Most NWO theorists would agree that, as a merger of the state and corporate capitalists, fascism operates in the same manner as the one-world government conspiracies they attempt to document.

- Journalist Edwin Black has documented what he believes is the complicity of at least five major American corporations in the Holocaust, the Third Reich's central crime against humanity.

- NWO researcher Jim Marrs and others have concluded that powerful corporate figures and Nazi protégés are currently at work in the United States to create a Fourth Reich. They propose to complete the mission of global domination begun by Adolf Hitler.

Wars Cold and Hot

In This Chapter

- The consolidation of executive power with undeclared wars
- The Korean War as a step toward one-world government
- The Vietnam War as a "cash cow" for the power elite

As discussed in Chapter 6, New World Order (NWO) conspiracy theory interprets the Yalta Conference of February 4 through 11, 1945, among President Franklin D. Roosevelt, Prime Minister Winston Churchill, and Premier Joseph Stalin as the vehicle by which the future United Nations was created for the purpose of overriding the U.S. Constitution to give the president power to declare war without seeking congressional approval. This would put one man, the president of the United States, in position to lead the nation to abandon sovereignty by acting in obedience to the United Nations (UN).

After national subordination to the UN became an established fact, it would be a fairly short trip from traditional nationhood to one-world government. The Korean War and the Vietnam War, the two major "hot wars" of the Cold War era, were key steps in this journey.

The Korean "Conflict"

When it was fought, from June 25, 1950, to July 17, 1953, everyone called it the Korean War—except for President Harry S. Truman, who was always careful to refer to it as a "police action" or the Korean Conflict. He had good reason for being finicky about semantics. Declaring *war* is a power the U.S. Constitution reserves for Congress; however, as the constitutionally designated commander in chief of the armed forces, the president has the authority to use military force in situations other than declared war. The Constitution does not require Congress to declare a "police action" or a "conflict."

Truman was not the first president to take it upon himself to order troops to fight without a congressional declaration of war, but the Korean Conflict was the first substantial war the United States fought (480,000 soldiers, airmen, sailors, and marines fought; 35,516 were killed) in which Congress played no declarative role. Since the Korean War, the United States has fought extended, large-scale military campaigns in Vietnam, Iraq (twice), and Afghanistan without declaring war. In fact, since Korea, a constitutional declaration of war has become almost unthinkable.

NWO conspiracy theorists are hardly alone in voicing alarm, even outrage, at this abridgment of constitutional government. At the time of the Korean Conflict, President Truman gave a plausible reason for avoiding declaring war. He believed that to do so would draw both the Soviet Union and China into the fight, at the very least greatly expanding the conflict and, at worst, touching off World War III. Conspiracy theorists (and others) counter that Truman, followed by Lyndon Johnson, Richard Nixon, and the two Bushes, avoided seeking declarations of war not to avert a larger conflict, but to execute an end run around the Constitution and thereby assume total control over the single most significant executive power, the better to use that power in the service of one-world rule.

INTEL

Since World War II, the United States has not declared war. Beginning with the Korean War, the major undeclared wars have cost the nation some 101,000 killed (35,516 in Korea; 58,159 in Vietnam; 379 in the Persian Gulf War; more than 4,400 in Iraq; nearly 1,000 in Afghanistan). The total of wounded is about four times these numbers.

Korea: The Mainstream Story

According to generally accepted history, the Korean War narrative goes like this:

At the 1943 Cairo Conference among China, Great Britain, and the United States, the Allies agreed to make independence for Korea (which had been occupied by Japan since 1910) one of the objectives of their joint prosecution of World War II; however, they anticipated a postwar period of Allied military occupation and decided that this should be supervised by a joint international commission consisting of the United States, Great Britain, China, and the Soviet Union. At the Yalta Conference in February 1945, President Roosevelt attempted to get Soviet premier Stalin to agree to an international trusteeship to prepare Korea for independence after the defeat of Japan. Stalin neither objected to nor approved of the proposal.

At the Potsdam Conference during July 27 through August 2, 1945, President Truman tried again, but not until August 8, when the Soviets belatedly declared war on Japan, did Stalin announce his intention to establish a trusteeship for Korea. The sudden surrender of Japan following the atomic bombing of Hiroshima and Nagasaki made long-term Allied occupation of Korea unnecessary. The United States government, however, proposed that the Soviets receive Japan's surrender in Korea north of the 38th parallel and that the United States accept surrender south of this line.

The *partition* arrangement was intended to be strictly temporary—the Soviets had troops in the north, the Americans in the south. The division was a matter of logistical convenience. The Soviets, however, seized on the expedient to divide Korea politically and bring the northern portion into the Communist sphere of influence. Almost immediately, they began building fortifications along the 38th parallel, and although the United States and the Soviet Union agreed to set up a joint commission to help the Koreans create a provisional government, the Soviets refused to move forward with this work. In September 1947, therefore, the United States requested that the United Nations intervene to bring about Korean unification. Over Soviet objections, the UN decided that a unified government should be established for Korea following a general election. Moreover, after the government was established, the UN would dispatch a security force to Korea to protect it.

DEFINITION

In diplomacy and politics, to **partition** a country is to alter political borders so at least one national community's homeland is divided. Partition is typically a diplomatic rather than a military action, and it is usually intended to be temporary until permanent borders can be agreed on.

With Soviet encouragement, the North Korean Communists barred the UN commission from holding elections north of the 38th parallel. South of the parallel, the elections proceeded on May 10, 1948, creating the Republic of Korea (ROK) under President Syngman Rhee. When the UN affirmed the ROK as the only lawful Korean government, the Soviets proclaimed a rival government in North Korea, which became the People's Democratic Republic of Korea (DRK). Having set up the

DRK, however, the Soviets announced their intention to withdraw Red Army troops from the country by January 1, 1949.

Eager to demobilize after four years of World War II, the Truman administration welcomed the Soviet promise—though it pledged to Rhee that it would train and equip a security force for the South and provide economic aid. President Truman wanted to arm South Korea for defense without giving the appearance that the United States was sponsoring South Korean aggression, which might lead to full-scale war involving the North Koreans as well as the Soviets. Accordingly, the United States agreed to train and equip a very modest South Korean military without tanks, artillery, a navy, or an air force.

The weakly defended South made a tempting target for the Soviet-backed North, and, at 4 A.M. on the morning of June 25, 1950, the North Korean People's Army crossed the 38th parallel, brushed aside the inferior South Korean forces, and bore down on the South Korean capital of Seoul, which it quickly captured. In response, President Truman ordered General Douglas MacArthur, hero of World War II's Pacific theater and now commander of the U.S. Far East Command, to resupply the ROK army with equipment and ammunition, most of which had been abandoned in the South's headlong retreat from the invaders.

President Truman wanted to enable South Korea to fend off the Communists, yet to do so without escalating Korea into a world war. At first, the president ordered the U.S. Seventh Fleet to sail toward Korea, but then decided to redeploy most of it to Taiwan, to prevent the Chinese Communists on the mainland from attacking the U.S.-allied Chinese Nationalists' Taiwanese stronghold. Truman ordered MacArthur to use air and naval strikes against North Korean positions below the 38th parallel, then, on June 30, 1950, gave him permission to deploy all available U.S. forces to aid the ROK. Yet there was little available to him. Both ground and air forces, depleted by postwar demobilization, were under strength and underequipped.

The U.S. sponsored a UN Security Council resolution authorizing military action against North Korea. At the time, the Soviets were boycotting all UN organizations and committees that included Nationalist China (Taiwan) which they considered illegitimate, so the Soviet delegation was not present to veto the resolution. Thus President Truman had UN backing for a war. What was not clear was whether the objective would be to forcibly unify the country under Rhee or to simply preserve the sovereignty of the South on a divided Korean peninsula. Left undecided was whether UN forces, now commanded by MacArthur, would be permitted to operate north of the 38th parallel or would be constrained to remain on the defensive below that line. Furthermore, although MacArthur had supreme command of UN forces, he was constrained by international political considerations, which meant that important military decisions were often delayed or attenuated by UN debate.

Initially, North Korean forces overwhelmed both the ROK army and UN ground forces. In contrast to the situation on the ground, the U.S. Air Force was quickly able to establish air superiority and began bombing North Korean supply lines. A U.S. Navy blockade proved effective in reducing the flow of supplies to the North Korean invaders. But the North Koreans had penetrated deep into the South. Although this alarmed many U.S. leaders, General MacArthur saw it as an opportunity. Their deep penetration made them vulnerable to attack from the rear. MacArthur believed that if he could sever their supply lines and cut off their routes of retreat, he could squeeze the invaders between UN forces defending Pusan, south of the enemy, and forces he intended to land at Inchon, north of them.

The Inchon Landing was a high-stakes gamble, but on September 15, 1950, MacArthur pulled it off. It was the most brilliant military operation in his long and distinguished career. Soon, the invaders had been driven out of South Korea. The Inchon victory renewed the issue of whether or not to cross the 38th parallel and invade North Korea. In the end, President Truman decided to take the risk and on September 27, 1950, ordered MacArthur to pursue the North Korean forces, warning him, however, to stay away from the Yalu River (the border with Manchuria) and the Tumen River (the Soviet border). When China threatened to intervene, Truman called a conference with MacArthur on Wake Island. The general assured him that the Chinese threats were empty, and Truman authorized the advance to continue. On the night of November 25, Chinese forces hit the Eighth U.S. Army hard, and by November 28, all UN positions were caving in and quickly withdrew back to the 38th parallel.

MacArthur now lobbied for permission to attack China, but Truman and his advisors, including Secretary of Defense George C. Marshall, refused. Many U.S. planners believed that Korea was a Soviet ploy aimed at starting World War III. The Soviet objective, they believed, was to drain U.S. military strength, compelling a great reduction of U.S. forces in Europe, which would leave the member nations of the newly created NATO vulnerable to Soviet attack.

INTEL

NATO, the North Atlantic Treaty Organization, was formed on April 4, 1949, as a system of collective defense against Soviet aggression in Europe. At its founding, NATO was arguably a paper tiger—more a political organization than a credible military deterrent. NWO conspiracy theorists argue that the Truman administration incited the Korean War to force the NATO member states—at the time Belgium, the Netherlands, Luxembourg, France, the United Kingdom, Canada, Portugal, Italy, Norway, Denmark, Iceland, and the United States—to build up the military component of the alliance in earnest. Although mainstream historians, in contrast to NWO theorists, do not believe that Truman and his advisers deliberately provoked the war in Korea, they do acknowledge that the Korean War galvanized NATO, elevating it from a political association to a genuine military alliance.

Seoul fell to the Communists on January 4, 1951, but Matthew Ridgway, commanding the Eighth U.S. Army, believed that UN forces could exploit Chinese logistical shortcomings by pounding away at the stalled invaders. MacArthur disagreed and, once again, clamored for an attack on China. The Joint Chiefs of Staff responded by explicitly instructing him to *defend* his positions in Korea, albeit to defend them so as to inflict as many casualties on the enemy as possible.

Slowly, painfully, the strategy produced results, and President Truman notified MacArthur that he would announce his willingness to commence negotiations with the Chinese and North Koreans on the basis of the current positions of forces on either side of the 38th parallel. Outraged, MacArthur boldly preempted Truman's announcement by making an unauthorized public announcement of his own, declaring that, if the UN would expand the conflict to North Korea's coastal areas and interior strongholds, the Chinese would realize that they were at serious risk of suffering military defeat. Truman felt he had no choice but to withhold his peace initiative and await military developments. He did not want to wreck U.S. and UN military morale by engaging in an open dispute with his top combat leader.

But MacArthur did not let up. He followed up his announcement with a letter to Republican Speaker of the House Joseph W. Martin, knowing that Martin would make it public by reading it into the congressional record. In the letter, MacArthur defied the president by declaring the necessity of opening up a second front against China. He denounced what he regarded as a war without victory in Korea, and he closed his letter by declaring that there is "no substitute for victory."

The letter was an act of gross insubordination, which Truman deemed an attempt to subvert his constitutional role as commander in chief of the armed forces. Backed by the Joint Chiefs of Staff, Truman relieved MacArthur as commander of U.S. and UN troops on April 11, 1951. He was replaced by Ridgway, who continued to fight an anti-insurgent war through July 27, 1953, when an armistice was at long last signed.

PASSWORDS

"I fired [MacArthur] because he wouldn't respect the authority of the President .... I didn't fire him because he was a dumb son-of-a-bitch, although he was."

—Harry S. Truman, quoted in Merle Miller, *Plain Speaking* (1973)

Korea: The NWO Version

Conspiracy theorists, not surprisingly, interpret the Korean War differently from mainstream historians. Their principal claim is that the Truman administration, packed with Council on Foreign Relations (CFR) members (see Chapter 2), effectively provoked or invited a North Korean invasion by refusing to take a strong stand along the 38th parallel. They also believe that the Soviet boycott of the Security Council meeting at which the U.S.-sponsored intervention vote was taken was not really a protest of UN recognition of Taiwan, but a deliberate Soviet tactic to ensure that the United States would sacrifice its sovereignty to fight a United Nations war. After all, no one desired one-world government more than the Soviets.

Conspiracy theorists tend to see Douglas MacArthur as an unalloyed military genius who tried to warn Truman that the Chinese would invade South Korea, and they see Truman's dismissal of MacArthur as the result of a CFR conspiracy. They regard the many tactical and strategic restrictions placed on MacArthur and other commanders not as efforts to avert World War III, but as a strategy to intensify the Communist threat to validate the necessity of the newly created NATO. Like the United Nations, it was a big step toward the submergence of U.S. sovereignty into a collective that would ultimately lead to one-world rule.

Why Are We in Vietnam?

American involvement in the Vietnam War, the major Cold War "hot" conflict that followed the Korean War, is a story both complex and controversial. Officially, the war was an outgrowth of the Truman-era policy of *containment*, an effort to contain the aggressive spread of communism wherever and whenever it manifested itself.

> **DEFINITION**
>
> **Containment** was a foreign policy formulated during the administration of President Harry Truman whereby the United States used political, economic, and limited military means to counter Soviet attempts to expand its sphere of influence wherever and whenever these attempts occurred.

Conspiracy theorists, however, see the Vietnam War as a CFR-driven plot by which the United States, Britain, and France combined to achieve a kind of globalist hegemony in Southeast Asia. The result, the CFR hoped, would be a war that would feed the coffers of the bankers and moguls that constituted their membership. When President John F. Kennedy started to hint at his intention to begin withdrawing from Vietnam, he was assassinated, making way for the presidency of Lyndon B. Johnson, who (coming from a state rife with defense contractors) was much more amenable to a profitable military escalation.

Vietnam, as conspiracy theorists interpret it, was the ideal war from the CFR point of view. It was bound to be long—if not interminable—yet would not likely touch off a universally destructive thermonuclear World War III; therefore, it would create a long-term demand for costly military hardware, serving the CFR as a kind of "cash cow." This would enable the organization's members to buy more and more power as they worked toward subverting elected government and replacing it with one-world rule.

During the Korean War, the risk of China or the Soviets escalating the conflict to a global scale seemed very real. For this reason (according to NWO conspiracy theorists), the CFR-controlled Truman administration was eager to negotiate a quick end to the war, and so the Korean War lasted just three years. In the case of the Vietnam War, however, both the Chinese and the Soviets gave clear signals that they did not intend to fan the conflict into a larger war; therefore, the fighting could go on and on without risk of provoking a nuclear holocaust. By means of his negotiations ("triangular diplomacy," he called it) with the Soviets and the Chinese, Nixon's national security adviser and, later, secretary of state, Henry Kissinger (a member of the CFR and the Bilderberg Group) made sure that Vietnam would be a "safely" contained conflict.

PASSWORDS

"I don't think that unless a greater effort is made by the [South Vietnamese] government to win popular support that the war can be won out there. In the final analysis, it is their war. They are the ones who have to win it or lose it .... [It] is the people and the government [of South Vietnam] itself who have to win or lose this struggle. All we can do is help .... But I don't agree with those who say we should withdraw. That would be a great mistake."

—President John F. Kennedy, television interview with Walter Cronkite, September 2, 1963

A fundamental principle among conspiracy theorists (as seen in Chapters 1 and 2) is that the CFR and other globalist secret societies populated by the power elite believe that war is an economic necessity, a necessary condition to enable the march toward rule of the many by the few. Just not *too much* of a war.

The Least You Need to Know

- NWO conspiracy theorists argue that the undeclared wars that followed World War II (including Korea, Vietnam, the Persian Gulf War, and the Iraq War) were attempts to elevate the executive branch of American government over the legislative and judicial branches. It would effectively concentrate power in the hands of presidents whose administrations have been dominated by members of a conspiracy dedicated to creating one-world government.

- As conspiracy theorists see it, the Korean War was not a war against Communist aggression, but a means of galvanizing support for the weak NATO alliance. The ultimate objective of moving toward the submergence of national sovereignties is a large military collective—a Free World versus the Iron Curtain.

- A leading tenet of the NWO conspiracy theory is that the power elite who work toward one-world government recognize war as an economic necessity because war profits are required to finance their plots to acquire more power and more control over elected national governments.

New World Order: Bush 41 and After

In This Chapter

- Permanent role of war in the NWO
- The globalist agenda of George H. W. Bush
- The 9/11 terrorist attacks as part of the NWO conspiracy
- Questions of motive for the Iraq wars
- Pax Americana

Karl Marx understood that the object of any Communist government is world government—that is, government of a state defined not by national, tribal, or ethnic allegiance, but by identification with one's class without regard to geography. This is the ultimate form of totalitarian government—at least in theory. But as totalitarian dictators from Hitler to Stalin discovered, there is a problem with the theory. Governments require enemies.

People will accept rule, even oppressive rule, when they feel united against some threat. For Hitler, it was the Jews; for Stalin, it was the capitalist West. Political writer George Orwell explained the situation dramatically in his postwar novel of a totalitarian anti-utopia, *1984*. Oceania, the vast totalitarian state against which Orwell's hero, Winston Smith, abortively rebels, holds onto its governing power by maintaining the nation's population in a perpetual state of low-level war. The identity of the enemy doesn't much matter, just as long as it is perceived as evil and implacable.

As conspiracy theorists understand the drive toward American totalitarianism, rule of the many by the few likewise requires a perception of perpetual war against some evil and implacable enemy. Without it, people begin to think for themselves, and when that happens, they start to question the authority of their leaders.

"It Is Iraq Against the World ..."

Under the dictator Saddam Hussein (1937–2006), Iraq had long claimed the small, oil-rich nation of Kuwait as a province. Suddenly, on August 2, 1990, the Iraqi army, the fourth largest ground force in the world, invaded Kuwait pursuant to Hussein's proclamation of annexation. In less than a week, Kuwait was completely occupied. The United States, its allies, and much of the world now feared that Iraq would go on to mount an attack southward into Saudi Arabia, giving Hussein a stranglehold on much of the world's oil supply. Even if the dictator chose to press the attack no further, his seizure of Kuwait put him in a position to threaten Saudi Arabia on an ongoing basis and thus control the flow of oil.

President George H. W. Bush responded to the invasion by freezing Iraqi assets in American banks and by cutting off trade with the country. The Bush administration acted swiftly to obtain UN resolutions condemning the invasion and supporting military action against it.

PASSWORDS

"A line has been drawn in the sand."

—George H. W. Bush, August 8, 1990

The Globalist

President Bush and Secretary of State James Baker forged an unprecedented *coalition* among 48 nations. Of these, 34 provided military forces, with the United States making the largest contribution. In this remarkable assemblage, New World Order (NWO) conspiracy theorists have identified the seeds of one-world government. Those inclined to dismiss conspiracy theories dismiss this interpretation as well. Yet even the most skeptical have to admit that, in George Herbert Walker Bush, the conspiracy believers had found a president who neatly filled the globalist bill.

DEFINITION

A **coalition** is an alliance of a temporary, ad hoc nature. The Bush administration was careful to call the nations united against Saddam Hussein's Iraq a "coalition" in contrast to an "alliance," which implies a more permanent union. Nevertheless, NWO conspiracy theorists interpret coalition as a code word for something approaching global government.

Bush was born to privilege in Massachusetts in 1924 and grew up in Greenwich, Connecticut. His father, Prescott Bush, was a Wall Street banker, U.S. senator, and one of seven directors of the Union Banking Corporation (UBC), which was controlled by the Thyssen family of Germany. For NWO conspiracy theorists, this is sufficient to certify George H. W. Bush as a member of a globalist banking family.

Some NWO writers claim that Prescott Bush was an active Nazi supporter. Although such claims are almost certainly unsupported by the facts, it is true that Prescott Bush, in his capacity as a UBC director, had direct dealings with Fritz Thyssen, a Nazi industrialist. Thyssen, it must be pointed out, broke with the Nazi Party early in World War II (among other things, he objected to the persecution of the Jews) and attempted to flee Germany, but was arrested and spent the rest of the war first in a sanatorium and then in the Sachsenhausen and Dachau concentration camps.

INTEL

During the war, journalist Emery Reves published in the United States a biography of Fritz Thyssen, *I Paid Hitler*, which portrayed him as one of the cadre of Nazi industrialists who funded the rise of Hitler and the Third Reich. After the war, Thyssen attempted to clear his name, but was nevertheless tried as a Nazi supporter and, despite his break with the party, accepted responsibility for abusing Jewish employees during the 1930s. He voluntarily paid compensation to certain former employees, but was acquitted of most charges against him.

After distinguished service as a U.S. Navy aviator in World War II, Bush entered Yale University, where, like his father before him, he became a member of Skull and Bones (see Chapter 7). After graduation, Bush used his father's business connections to enter the oil business in Texas, made his own fortune, and then entered politics, becoming a U.S. representative from the 7th District of Texas.

After losing a bid for Texas governor, Bush, a wealthy, connected politician from a long-established and influential Republican family, was named ambassador to the United Nations in 1971 by Richard Nixon and then envoy to China by Nixon's successor, Gerald R. Ford. Both of these posts were "globalist" in nature, but in 1976 came the appointment conspiracy theorists find most suspicious of all. Bush was named director of the CIA.

Bush ran for president in 1980 and was then nominated as Ronald Reagan's running mate in the general election. Thus, the former CIA director became one of a number of Council on Foreign Relations (CFR) and Trilateral Commission (TC; see Chapter 4) members of the Reagan administration.

Tough Act to Follow

George H. W. Bush was widely perceived as a competent, if lackluster, vice president. When he received the Republican nomination for president in 1988, he began his run trailing Democratic nominee Michael Dukakis, but soon pulled ahead. Nevertheless, he excited little enthusiasm, and his public-approval ratings sagged early in his presidency.

It must be conceded that Ronald Reagan was the proverbial tough act to follow. Despite political scandal in his second term—the botched "Iran-contra" arms-for-hostages deal—Reagan was widely credited with bringing the Soviet Union to the verge of collapse and the Cold War to its climactic turning point. For some 50 years, the Soviet Union had been the perpetual, evil, and implacable threat against which the United States and its leaders had (perhaps in *1984* fashion) defined themselves. Now that threat was fading as fast as George H. W. Bush's ratings.

The First New World Order Speech

Then came Saddam Hussein's invasion of Kuwait. Bush began the U.S. build-up in the Middle East ("Operation Desert Shield") on August 7, 1990, in response to a Saudi request for military aid to defend against possible Iraqi invasion. By September, American forces were augmented by those of the coalition members and were now at sufficient strength to deter an invasion of Saudi Arabia.

On September 11, 1990, President Bush addressed a joint session of Congress. He explained America's goals: "Iraq must withdraw from Kuwait completely, immediately, and without condition. Kuwait's legitimate government must be restored. The security and stability of the Persian Gulf must be assured." He also explained that these goals were "not ours alone," but had "been endorsed by the United Nations Security Council five times in as many weeks. Most countries share our concern for principle. And many have a stake in the stability of the Persian Gulf. This is not, as Saddam Hussein would have it, the United States against Iraq. It is Iraq against the world."

As conspiracy theorists interpret this last sentence, Iraq had now officially replaced the Soviet Union as the implacable, evil enemy against which not just the United States but the entire world was united—united as *one* world. Indeed, Bush went on to explain how he had *joined with* "Soviet President Gorbachev … to build a new relationship [and to affirm] to the world our shared resolve to counter Iraq's threat to peace." He quoted from an agreement he and Gorbachev reached in Helsinki: "'We are united in the belief that Iraq's aggression must not be tolerated.' … Clearly, no longer can a dictator count on East-West confrontation to stymie concerted United Nations action against aggression. A new partnership of nations has begun."

It is an intellectual foundation of NWO conspiracy theory that the long revolutionary movement toward one-world government has proceeded by a Hegelian process. German philosopher Georg Wilhelm Friedrich Hegel (1770–1831) believed that history moved forward through a *dialectic*, in which a particular power, interest, position, or idea encountered its opposition, resulting in an interaction that produced a new power, interest, position, or idea. Expressed formulaically, the progression was *thesis + antithesis = synthesis*. For conspiracy theorists, the Iraq War provided the moment of synthesis for U.S.-led democratic capitalism (thesis) and Soviet-dominated totalitarian communism (antithesis). This synthesis, made possible by the Iraq situation ("It is Iraq against the world") was a catalytic moment in the creation of one-world government.

DEFINITION

Dialectic, in Hegelian philosophy, is the process by which history moves forward through the "synthesis" of opposing views, ideas, powers, interests, or political positions—opposites that are referred to as "thesis" and "antithesis."

President Bush, the globalist, made no secret of what the impending collapse of the Soviet Union and the end of the Cold War meant:

> *We stand today at a unique and extraordinary moment. The crisis in the Persian Gulf, as grave as it is, also offers a rare opportunity to move toward an historic period of cooperation. Out of these troubled times, our fifth objective—a new world order—can emerge …*

There it was. The NWO was no longer the hidden objective of a secret conspiracy, but the declared objective of an American president.

The Second New World Order Speech

Preparation for the Persian Gulf War consumed months. An intensive campaign of air strikes began on January 17, 1991, and was followed by ground operations beginning on February 24. The ground war was over in about 100 hours. A cease-fire was declared at 8 A.M. on February 28, shortly after Iraq capitulated.

Kuwait was liberated, and coalition casualties were minimal: 95 killed, 368 wounded, 20 missing in action. Iraqi casualties were perhaps as many as 50,000 killed and another 50,000 wounded; 60,000 Iraqi troops were taken prisoner. Huge quantities of Iraqi military hardware were destroyed, as were communication equipment and military bases, barracks, and other facilities.

George H. W. Bush achieved a record-breaking approval rating of 89 percent among the U.S. electorate, and with this bolstering him, he addressed another joint session of Congress on March 6, 1991. "Until now," he declared, "the world we've known has been a world divided—a world of barbed wire and concrete block, conflict, and cold war." But …

> *Now, we can see a new world coming into view. A world in which there is the very real prospect of a new world order. In the words of Winston Churchill, a "world order" in which "the principles of justice and fair play … protect the weak against the strong …." A world where the United Nations, freed from cold war stalemate, is poised to fulfill the historic vision of its founders. A world in which freedom and respect for human rights find a home among all nations.*

New World Order Breakthrough (*Not!*)

There is much grist for the conspiracy theory mill in the Persian Gulf War and George H. W. Bush's involvement in it. Yet, despite the war and all the other apparatus of the NWO—the secret societies, the globalist organizations, the Korean and Vietnam wars, and the rest—we have yet to see an end to nations and nationhood.

Does this mean that the NWO conspiracy, after all these centuries, has been ineffective? Some conspiracy theorists answer this question by arguing that the manifestations of nations and nationhood we see today are surface phenomena only. The real power is wielded by a one-world shadow government of bankers, moguls, and the like, which we cannot see. Other conspiracy believers argue that true one-world government remains a work in progress and has yet to arrive.

In the short run, the "new world order" that President Bush spoke of seems to have been a disappointing fizzle. For George H. W. Bush himself, the Persian Gulf War yielded no long-term benefits. His 89 percent approval rating rapidly dissolved in a growing economic crisis to which he seemed oddly indifferent. He lost his 1992 bid for a second term to relative newcomer Democrat Bill Clinton—and by a substantial margin. Even Iraq remained unfinished business. Despite the fact that Saddam Hussein had suffered the most complete and lopsided defeat in modern military history, he remained Iraq's dictator—and was therefore a target for the next President Bush.

Whatever NWO conspiracy theorists make of it, George H. W. Bush was clear in his definition of a "new world order." He defined it as the following:

> *A new era—freer from the threat of terror, stronger in the pursuit of justice, and more secure in the quest for peace. An era in which the nations of the world, East and West, North and South, can prosper and live in harmony …. A world where the rule of law supplants the rule of the jungle. A world in which nations recognize the shared responsibility for freedom and justice. A world where the strong respect the rights of the weak.*

The False Flag of 9/11

Has this "new world order" arrived? Hardly. And what did arrive arrived with a terrible newness, a shock beyond the imagination of just about everyone, conspiracy theorists included.

On September 11, 2001, 19 Middle Eastern young men, all associated with the al-Qaeda terrorist organization, hijacked four U.S. commercial jet airliners at American airports and commandeered them as human-guided cruise missiles. Two were crashed into the Twin Towers of the World Trade Center in New York City, one plowed into the Pentagon outside of Washington, D.C., and the fourth crashed in a field near Shanksville, Pennsylvania, apparently after passengers and flight crew attempted to wrest control from the hijackers. It is believed that this aircraft targeted the Capitol or the White House.

INTEL

It remains surprisingly difficult to find a definitive count of casualties from the attacks of September 11, 2001. The most generally agreed upon figure is 2,996, which includes the 19 hijackers. Subtracting them, we are left with 2,977 victims, of whom 236 were non-U.S. nationals, leaving an American death toll of 2,741.

Conspiracy Views

Such is the mainstream account of the attacks of 9/11. Conspiracy theorists, naturally, have formulated alternative versions. As in the conspiracy view of Pearl Harbor (see Chapter 19), some believe that key government officers had foreknowledge of the 9/11 attacks and purposely chose not to act on this intelligence. Some go beyond the Pearl Harbor model to argue that certain officials, again with foreknowledge of the attacks, took active steps to reduce or weaken U.S. defenses to make certain that the hijacked planes would get through and the attacks would succeed. A smaller number of theorists speculate that some elements within the government actually planned the attacks and, to carry them out, either operated in conjunction with al-Qaeda or used their own agents and framed al-Qaeda.

In either case, as conspiracy theorists see it, 9/11 was a *false-flag operation*—the work of certain elements within the U.S. government and/or military.

DEFINITION

False-flag operation, a phrase found throughout conspiracy literature, describes an event, act, or scheme perpetrated by friendly forces but made to look like the work of enemies. The purpose of false-flag operations is to move one's own country to respond as if it had actually suffered an enemy attack.

Why?

Why would anyone inside the U.S. government want to create the appearance of an act of Islamic terrorism? The motive most widely suggested is to provide justification for the invasion of Afghanistan and Iraq, with the object of gaining control of the extensive oil reserves in these regions.

Secondarily, some believe the 9/11 attacks were orchestrated to force an increase in military spending while also increasing the power of the central government, especially the president, by restricting domestic civil liberties in the name of security.

NWO conspiracy theorists acknowledge these motives, but typically add that the attacks were primarily the work of a group of neo-conservatives ("neocons") within the Bush administration and were intended to justify military action against Iraq. This would give the United States strategic control over the Middle East, the supplier of much of the world's energy needs. It would also put those who control American commerce and wealth at the center of an NWO in which the United States and its power elite would enjoy global hegemony.

As the Roman Empire presided over a Pax Romana and the British Empire over a Pax Britannica, so the United States would be at the heart of a Pax Americana.

PASSWORDS

"All the world now faces a test, and the United Nations a difficult and defining moment. Are Security Council resolutions to be honored and enforced, or cast aside without consequence? Will the United Nations serve the purpose of its founders or will it be irrelevant?"

—George W. Bush, speech before the UN General Assembly, September 12, 2002, pressing for UN action against Iraq

The Leading Theories

As with the JFK assassination, the conspiracy literature that has grown up around 9/11 is daunting in its volume. Adequate coverage is far beyond the scope of this book. Aside from theories that elements within the government either passively allowed the attacks to occur or actively instigated or collaborated with them, three more theories are frequently offered:

- The World Trade Center "attack" had been planned by elements of the government years earlier. Although it appeared to be the result of the impact of two airliners, the "attacks" were in reality a pair of controlled demolitions. Some believe that explosives were secretly planted at strategic structural points in the building anytime from days to years before September 11, 2001. Others have theorized that the explosives were built into the structure when it was constructed from 1966 to 1973 and that detonation of the built-in explosives only awaited an opportune moment.

- The Pentagon was attacked by a conventional cruise missile launched by some element within the U.S. government and/or military. The airliner impact was a deliberate misdirection to cover up the actual weapon used. Some conspiracy theorists have noted that security camera video of the impact fails to show an airliner, and they claim that no aircraft debris was recovered from the site.

- Elements within the government and/or the military orchestrated a wide-ranging standdown of alert forces—NORAD and other air defense facilities—and arranged for the airliner attacks, either in collaboration with al-Qaeda agents or with agents under al-Qaeda cover.

- 9/11 was the product of an international Jewish conspiracy. Some 9/11 conspiracy theorists contend that 4,000 Jewish employees absented themselves from work at the World Trade Center on September 11. This (according to some theorists) is evidence that Israel was responsible for the attacks and had issued a warning to certain Jews prior to them. Some theorists assert that Israeli agents had foreknowledge of the attacks.

- The attacks were a joint operation of the CIA and the Mossad, the Israeli secret service.

- The attacks were a joint operation of American neocons and Israeli agents.

- The attacks were perpetrated by reptilian, shape-shifting extraterrestrial humanoids (according to British NWO theorist David Icke, who believes that the global elite are actually of such an extraterrestrial race).

- The attacks were perpetrated by a drug industry cartel as part of a population reduction conspiracy.

PASSWORDS

"We SHELL not EXXONerate Saddam Hussein for his actions. We will MOBILize to meet this threat in the Persian GULF until an AMOCOble solution is reached. Our plan is to BPrepared. Failing that, we ARCOming to kick his ass."

—Speech ascribed to President Bush on a poster issued by DemocracyMeansYou.com, February 2003

Oil Wars

The 9/11 conspiracy theories may be seen either as occupying a universe all their own or as constituting a specialized subset of a larger NWO conspiracy literature. In any case, however, one does not have to be a believer in a 9/11 conspiracy or an NWO conspiracy to accept the fact that, for whatever reason, the administration of George

W. Bush intensively used 9/11 as a rationale for invading both Afghanistan and Iraq. Moreover, even those most skeptical about conspiracies continue to scratch their heads over presidential assertions of a connection between 9/11 and the decision to go to war in Iraq. Whereas the extremist Taliban regime had harbored and supported al-Qaeda in Afghanistan, thereby making that nation an arguably justifiable target for war, there was never compelling evidence that Saddam Hussein and Iraq had played any role in the 9/11 attacks.

The fact is that many people, not just conspiracy writers, believe that the Persian Gulf War of 1990 to 1991 and the Iraq War that began in 2003 and (as of 2010) has yet to end had nothing to do with freedom, democracy, defeating the dangerous tyrant Saddam Hussein, or combating terrorism, but, instead, were and are all about oil.

NWO theorists contend that, like the wars in Korea and Vietnam, the two Iraq wars were conceived as engines for draining revenue from an elected government (the United States) and siphoning it into the coffers of the CFR and similar cabals of the powerful few who already form a shadow American government and who want to ensure that the shadow spreads worldwide.

Even those most skeptical about conspiracy theories have to admit that the Persian Gulf War fought near the end of the twentieth century and the Iraq War that began the twenty-first century, present an abundance of dots crying out to be connected. Consider that both the forty-first president, George Herbert Walker Bush, and the forty-third, George Walker Bush, were Bonesmen (see Chapter 7) and oilmen. The senior Bush became famous—some would say infamous—for using the phrase "new world order" to describe the global political environment after the collapse of the Soviet Union, and both Bushes prosecuted their Iraqi wars with the backing of the United Nations and with military forces they each referred to as "coalitions."

In the case of the elder Bush and the Persian Gulf War of 1990 to 1991, the coalition was a genuine military entity consisting of actual armed forces from 34 countries; the junior Bush's much less popular Iraq War (2003–) included what the president called a "coalition of the willing," putatively consisting of 49 countries, but only 4 of which, besides the United States, actually contributed troops to the invasion. (Later, 33 countries provided very small numbers of troops to support occupation operations.) Conspiracy theorists regard the coalition concept in both wars as attempts to create a one-world military force.

The "Join or Die" Fraud

The concepts of the nation-state and nationhood have been around at least since the Renaissance, and persuading people to trade in their long-held national identity for global citizenship is a tough sell. During the long Cold War, the motivator (as NWO theorists see it) was the threat of Communist aggression. Politicians and pundits spoke of a "Free World" versus the "Iron Curtain countries" or the "Soviet bloc." The gist of the slogan popular during the American Revolution was often applied during the Cold War: *Join or die*.

With the collapse of the Soviet Union, holy war—*jihad*, religiously motivated terrorism—became the new motivator. Moderate, democratic, "Christian" nations were under attack and were therefore compelled to band together to oppose "Islamic extremist" states and nonstate entities (such as al-Qaeda) that supported and perpetrated terrorism. Again, it was a case of *Join or die*.

Most NWO theorists recognize that religiously motivated terrorism is a genuine threat; however, they believe that it has also been fraudulently exploited as a rationale for moving toward one-world rule.

The Open Question

For the reader who has not yet made up his or her mind about the reality of a global conspiracy, the ultimate significance of the new world order that George H. W. Bush spoke of, remains an open question. Is it nothing more than a phrase intended to reflect a geopolitical environment, long divided between two ideologically opposed superpowers, dominated after 1991 by just one? Or is it a means for the wealthy few to become even wealthier by profiting from war (supplying weapons as well as "mercenaries" and "contractors") and then reaping the spoils of that war (that is, oil profits)?

Most NWO believers accept the second interpretation as the valid one, but take its implications beyond war profits as ends in themselves. Rather, they see the money as the vehicle used to finance a secret, insidious, unstoppable movement toward one-world rule—a movement whose origins may be traceable to the dawn of civilization or even a time *before* civilization.

The Least You Need to Know

- Globalization requires the centralization of government authority and control, which is facilitated by a perceived threat against which individuals are willing to unite; therefore, continual war is a prerequisite for the advancement of the NWO.

- Many NWO conspiracy theorists believe President George H. W. Bush was a committed globalist who engineered the Persian Gulf War (1990–1991) as a means of uniting much of the world in a U.S. effort to establish itself as the leading power in the energy-rich Middle East.

- Some NWO conspiracy theorists argue that the terrorist attacks of 9/11 were exploited or even planned and executed by elements within the U.S. government. This justified the invasion of oil-rich Afghanistan and Iraq and used them as stepping stones for establishing American domination of the Middle East.

- Control of Middle Eastern energy resources would establish a global "Pax Americana"—effectively consolidating one-world government in the hands of an American government ruled from the shadows by an oil-financed power elite.

Who's Who in the New World Order

Acheson, Dean (1893–1971)   U.S. secretary of state (1949–1953) under President Harry S. Truman; an architect of U.S. Cold War strategy; member of the Council on Foreign Relations.

Adams, Samuel (1722–1803)   Key architect of the American Revolution; his revolutionary secret society network, the Sons of Liberty (a.k.a. Committees of Correspondence) drew heavily on Freemasons for members, though Adams himself was not a Mason.

Aldrich, Nelson W. (1841–1915)   Republican senator from Rhode Island (1881–1911); chaired the Senate Finance Committee and was often called "General Manager of the Nation"; instigated and guided the creation of the Federal Reserve System (1913); daughter Abby married John D. Rockefeller Jr.

Annunaki   Collective name for Sumerian deities; some believe the Annunaki were extraterrestrials who bestowed their vast knowledge on the Sumerians—a secret at the heart of the ancient mysteries.

Bacon, Sir Francis (1561–1626)   English philosopher, scientist, statesman, and author whose utopian novel *The New Atlantis* (published in Latin, 1624; in English, 1627) is said to have influenced many secret societies, which in turn influenced aspects of the New World Order conspiracy.

Bailey, Alice (1880–1949)   Neo-Theosophist often identified as the founder of the New Age movement, which is sometimes associated with the New World Order conspiracy.

Baruch, Bernard (1870–1965)   U.S. financier, political consultant, and adviser to Presidents Woodrow Wilson and Franklin D. Roosevelt; a founding member of the Council on Foreign Relations.

Bernhard, Prince, of Lippe-Biersterfeld (1911–2004)   Prince consort to Queen Juliana of the Netherlands; a globalist, Bernhard was cofounder of the Bilderberg Group and a founder of Rotary International.

Blanchfort, Bertrand de (ca. 1109–1169)   Sixth grand master of the Knights Templar and reformer of the Order.

Blavatsky, Helena Petrovna (1831–1891)   Principal founder of Theosophy and the Theosophical Society, which inspired the New Age movement and other movements associated with the New World Order.

Brzezinski, Zbigniew (b. 1928)   Polish-born U.S. political scientist and national security adviser to President Jimmy Carter; a globalist, he played a leading role in the creation of the Trilateral Commission.

Bundy, McGeorge (1919–1996)   National security adviser to presidents John F. Kennedy and Lyndon Johnson (1961–1966), Bundy was a Council on Foreign Relations member and one of the architects of the Trilateral Commission.

Bush, George H. W. (b. 1924)   Forty-first president of the United States, Bush was a globalist whose administration included many members of the Council on Foreign Relations; at Yale, Bush was a prominent member of Skull and Bones.

Bush, George W. (b. 1946)   Forty-third president of the United States and son of George H. W. Bush; like his father, "W" was a Bonesman at Yale.

Carter, Jimmy (b. 1924)   Thirty-ninth president of the United States; recruited for his administration a large number of Council on Foreign Relations and Trilateral Commission members, most prominently his National Security Adviser, Zbigniew Brzezinski.

Casey, William (1913–1987)   CIA director (1981–1987); member of the Council on Foreign Relations.

Churchill, Winston (1874–1965)   World War II prime minster of the United Kingdom; a Freemason who was (at one time) deeply involved in a global eugenics movement.

Clinton, Bill (b. 1946)   Forty-second president of the United States; closely associated with the Council on Foreign Relations and the Trilateral Commission; championed the creation of NAFTA (North American Free Trade Agreement) among Canada, the United States, and Mexico, sometimes condemned as a destructive step toward globalization.

Constantine I (ca. 272–337)   Roman emperor instrumental in the establishment of the Christian Church as the dominant religion in the Roman Empire and under whom the Eastern and Western empires reunified; a prototypical one-world government ruler.

Drosnin, Michael (b. 1946)   Author of *The Bible Code* (1997), which popularized the theory that the Bible contains coded prophecies—a concept important to some New World Order conspiracy writers, who believe that suppressed religious truths remain accessible through coded expression in the Bible, Cabalistic texts, and other scriptural material.

Dulles, Allen Welsh (1893–1969)   World War II U.S. spymaster; CIA director (1953–1961); member, director, and secretary of the Council on Foreign Relations; brother of John Foster Dulles.

Dulles, John Foster (1888–1959)   U.S. secretary of state (1953–1959) under President Dwight Eisenhower; founding member of the Council on Foreign Relations; brother of Allen Welsh Dulles.

Eckart, Dietrich (1868–1923)   Early member of the Nazi Party; mentor to Adolf Hitler; member of the Thule Society, which formulated plans for world domination that inspired Hitler and the Nazis.

Eisenhower, Dwight D. (1890–1969)   Supreme Allied Commander in Europe during World War II and thirty-fourth president of the United States. Eisenhower's Farewell Address in 1961 warned the nation against the "military-industrial complex," which threatened to become a shadow government.

Epperson, A. Ralph   Leading New World Order conspiracy writer; believed the Freemasons are at the heart of the conspiracy.

Ford, Henry (1863–1947)   Ford Motor Company founder; globalist; his four anti-Semitic pamphlets collectively titled *The International Jew* (1920) influenced Adolf Hitler's plans for world domination.

Franklin, Benjamin (1706 [O.S., 1705]–1790)   Publisher, inventor, philosopher, political theorist, statesman, writer, and architect of the American Revolution; with George Washington, Franklin is America's most famous Freemason Founding Father.

Gardner, Laurence   Revisionist historian and Knights Templar authority often cited to support a variety of conspiracy theories, including those relating to the New World Order.

Gibson, Donald (b. 1945)   Author of *The Kennedy Assassination Cover-Up* (1999), which argued that JFK was assassinated on orders of a cabal of wealthy men whose efforts to dominate U.S. government and foreign affairs were at odds with the Kennedy presidency.

Gisors, Jean de (1133–1220)   Norman nobleman alleged to have been the first grand master of the Priory of Sion, a secret society alleged to have guarded (and to still guard) the secret that Christ married Mary Magdalene and had children by her, whose descendents are still living.

Goldwater, Barry, Jr. (1909–1998)   "Mr. Conservative"; five-term U.S. senator from Arizona; Republican presidential candidate in 1964; and early outspoken critic of the Council on Foreign Relations, globalism, and one-world government.

Greider, William   Economist critic of the Federal Reserve (*Secrets of the Temple: How the Federal Reserve Runs the Country*, 1987) and of the economic hazards of globalism (*One World, Ready or Not: The Manic Logic of Global Capitalism*, 1997).

Griffin, G. Edward (b. 1931)   Libertarian author; documentary filmmaker; and critic of globalism, the Federal Reserve, and the United Nations.

Haig, Alexander, Jr. (1924–2010)   NATO commander, White House chief of staff (under President Nixon), and secretary of state (under President Reagan); prominent member of the Council on Foreign Relations.

Hall, Manly P. (1901–1990)   Canadian American mystic and Freemason. Author of *The Lost Keys of Freemasonry* (1923) and *The Secret Teachings of All Ages: An Encyclopedic Outline of Masonic, Hermetic, Qabbalistic and Rosicrucian Symbolical Philosophy* (1928), both considered major contributions to the history and evolution of secret societies.

Hamilton, Alexander (1757–1804)   First U.S. secretary of the treasury; created the Bank of the United States as a means of centralizing and controlling the national economy, seen by many as a precursor of the Federal Reserve System.

Hancock, John (1737–1793)   Founding Father, revolutionary activist, powerful merchant, and Freemason.

Harriman, W. Averell (1891–1986)   Son of railroad tycoon E. H. Harriman; served as Franklin Roosevelt's special envoy to Europe, as ambassador to the Soviet Union, ambassador to Great Britain, secretary of commerce (under President Truman), and New York governor; member of the Council on Foreign Relations.

Hegel, Georg Wilhelm Friedrich (1770–1831)   German philosopher whose "dialectical method" offered an alternative to dogma and influenced a number of secret society organizers in the nineteenth century.

Hitler, Adolf (1889–1945)   Nazi German dictator, mass murderer, instigator of World War II, and would-be leader of a German-controlled one-world government (which he called the "new world order"); some New World Order conspiracy theorists believe that followers are even now building a Fourth Reich on the ashes of his Third Reich, with the object of global domination.

House, Edward Mandell (1858–1938)   Adviser and confidant to President Woodrow Wilson; founding force behind the Council on Foreign Relations.

Hugues de Payens (ca. 1070–1136)   First grand master of the Knights Templar.

Icke, David (b. 1952)   British author who writes on a wide variety of conspiracy subjects, including the "global elite" and the "Reptoid hypothesis," the idea that a "Babylonian Brotherhood," spawn of a reptilian species from the constellation Draco, governs the world.

Jackson, Andrew (1767–1845)   Seventh president of the United States; hailed by critics of central government, central banking, and the Federal Reserve System because he successfully dismantled the Second Bank of the United States, thereby democratizing the economy (for a time).

Kissinger, Henry (b. 1923)   Powerful national security adviser and secretary of state under President Nixon; a globalist associated with the Council on Foreign Relations, the Bilderberg Group, and the Trilateral Commission.

Lindbergh, Charles August (1859–1924)   Father of the famed aviator; U.S. congressman from Minnesota's 6th district (1907–1917). A vehement opponent of the creation of the Federal Reserve System, he argued that it would become an all-powerful shadow government.

Lippmann, Walter (1889–1974)   Extraordinarily influential political commentator and founding editor of *The New Republic*; adviser to President Woodrow Wilson; instrumental in the creation of the Council on Foreign Relations.

Marshall, George C. (1880–1959)   U.S. Army chief of staff, secretary of state, and secretary of defense, who championed the creation of the so-called Marshall Plan; some see the political and economic unity it imposed on Europe as a springboard to the European Union (EU), a step toward full-scale global government.

McNamara, Robert (1916–2009)   Secretary of defense under Presidents John F. Kennedy and Lyndon B. Johnson; president of the World Bank from 1968 to 1981; member of the Council on Foreign Relations, Bilderberg Group, and Trilateral Commission.

Milner, Alfred (1854–1925)   British colonial administrator instrumental in founding Chatham House (Royal Institute of International Affairs), and UK counterpart to the U.S.-based Council on Foreign Relations.

Molay, Jacques de (d. 1314)   Last (23rd) grand master of the Knights Templar.

Morgan, John Pierpont (1837–1913)   U.S. magnate who covertly championed the establishment of the Federal Reserve, presumably as a source of finance for his banking interests.

Morgan, Captain William (1774–1826?)   Anti-Mason activist who was abducted and presumably killed after announcing his intention to reveal Masonic secrets in a book he was about to publish; his death spurred the founding of the Anti-Masonic Party and resulted in the suppression of Freemasonry in the United States for a time.

Pike, Albert (1809–1891)   Prominent nineteenth-century U.S. Freemason who admitted that Masonry had secret aspects distinct from its public face.

Plato (428/427–348/347 B.C.E.)   Greek philosopher whose concept of the ideal society (the subject of *The Republic*) influenced Cecil Rhodes in his founding of the Round Table movement.

Pythagoras (ca. 570–ca. 495 B.C.E.)   Greek philosopher whose mysticism inspired Freemasonry and the Illuminati, thereby rooting these secret societies to ancient mysteries.

Rhodes, Cecil (1853–1902)   British mining magnate and empire builder in Africa; Rhodes's Round Table movement was the impetus behind the Council on Foreign Relations, Chatham House, and other globalist organizations and initiatives.

Rockefeller, David (b. 1915)   Grandson of oil baron John D. Rockefeller Sr.; banker and globalist; a Bilderberger who cofounded the Trilateral Commission and has long been a lightning rod for anti-globalist writers, conspiracy theorists, politicians, and activists.

Roosevelt, Franklin D. (1882–1945)   Thirty-second president of the United States, who served from 1933 until his death (in his *fourth* term) on April 12, 1945. His massive program of New Deal legislation, replete with a menu of government "alphabet agencies," is condemned by some as the beginning of American big government and the unconstitutional concentration of governing authority in the executive branch.

Rothschild, Mayer Amschel (1744–1812)   Founder of the Rothschild international banking dynasty. Universally described as a founding father of international finance, he is condemned by some as a founding father of a New World Order conspiracy designed to concentrate wealth and power in the hands of the very few.

Rothschild, Nathan Mayer (1777–1836)   Son of Mayer Amschel Rothschild; founded the powerful English branch of the Rothschild financial dynasty.

Rusk, Dean (1909–1994)   Secretary of state under Presidents John F. Kennedy and Lyndon B. Johnson; a Bilderberger and member of the Council on Foreign Relations.

Ruskin, John (1819–1900)   Although best known as an art critic and master of English prose, Ruskin was also a utopian social thinker whose ideas, inspired by Plato's *Republic*, influenced the imperial and globalist thought of Cecil Rhodes when he founded the Round Table movement.

Sitchin, Zecharia (b. 1922)   Israeli American author; his *12th Planet* (1976), based on Sumerian mythology, argues that the extraterrestrial Annunaki visited Earth 450,000 years ago, bringing with them advanced knowledge and creating the Mesopotamian civilization.

Truman, Harry S. (1884–1972)   Thirty-third president of the United States, Truman, a Freemason, sponsored the Marshall Plan and other global initiatives.

Vanderlip, Frank A. (1864–1937)   American banker and assistant secretary of the treasury under President William McKinley; member of the secret Jekyll Island group, which laid out the Federal Reserve Act of 1913.

Warburg, Paul M. (1868–1932)   Jewish, German American banker who championed the creation of the Federal Reserve in 1913; closely associated with the Rothschild international banking dynasty.

Washington, George (1732 [O.S. 1731]–1799)   Commanding general of the Continental Army in the American Revolution and first president of the United States. The "father of his country" was a prominent Freemason.

Weishaupt, Adam (1748–1830)   German philosopher who founded the Order of the Illuminati, considered by many the progenitor of modern secret societies bent on creating one-world government.

Wilson, Woodrow (1856–1924)   Twenty-eighth president of the United States; ushered in the Federal Reserve System and championed ratification of the Sixteenth Amendment, which brought the federal income tax; led the nation into World War I and the creation of the League of Nations, which some see as an overture to genuine global government.

The New World Order in Pop Culture

B

The New World Order conspiracy has provided inspiration (fodder?) for a large number of novels, television shows, and movies. The following list contains some highlights.

Novels (Including Comic Books and Graphic Novels)

Dan Brown, *Angels and Demons* (2000): Features the Illuminati.

Dan Brown, *The Lost Symbol* (2009): Plot line includes Masonic conspiracies.

DC Comics, *Vandal Savage:* A group calling itself "the Illuminati" razes the city of Atlantis.

Leo Tolstoy, *War and Peace* (1869): Protagonist Pierre Bezukhov tries to convert his Masonic lodge into an Illuminati chapter.

Robert Anton Wilson, *The Historical Illuminati Chronicles*, consisting of *The Earth Will Shake* (1982), *The Widow's Son* (1985), and *Nature's God* (1991): Principal character is a young Italian Freemason.

Robert Shea and Robert Anton Wilson, *The Illuminatus! Trilogy* (1975): Includes an occult group called Illuminates of Thanateros, clearly modeled on the Illuminati.

Umberto Eco, *Foucault's Pendulum* (1988): Features a number of secret societies, including the Illuminati and the Rosicrucians.

Movies

Angels and Demons (2009), Ron Howard, director: Film adaptation of the Dan Brown novel, which focuses on an attack by the Illuminati.

Conspiracy Theory (1997), Richard Donner, director: Plot revolves around the theme of a secret shadow government.

Eyes Wide Shut (1999), Stanley Kubrick, director: Makes frequent reference to both the Illuminati and Freemasonry.

Lara Croft: Tomb Raider (2001), Simon West, director: The bad guys call themselves the Illuminati, and they have a scheme to create and run a one-world government. The villains and Lara Croft's dad agree: the Illuminati have been around for thousands of years, and their purpose has always been to take over the world.

Monsters vs. Aliens (2009), Conrad Vernon and Rob Letterman, directors: The film not only makes reference to the Illuminati, but also features Masonic-like symbols.

National Treasure (2004), Jon Turteltaub, director: Nicolas Cage contends with references to the Illuminati, the Freemasons, and the Knights Templar.

Network (1976), Sidney Lumet, director: We discover that the fictional UBS television network is owned by a conglomerate that is part of a global corporate system that exists as an economically based shadow world government.

Rollover (1981), Alan J. Pakula, director: Plot involves the Federal Reserve as well as a mysterious Arab-owned multinational corporation that secretly manipulates the global economy with catastrophic results.

TV

Bones (2005–present): Dr. Jack Stanley Hodgins (T. J. Thyne) is obsessed with conspiracy theories and often makes connections between the forensic cases he works and the Illuminati.

Conspiracy Theory with Jesse Ventura (2010–present): In this nonfiction documentary series, former pro wrestler and Minnesota governor Jesse Ventura leads a team of expert investigators on missions to examine "the most frightening and mysterious conspiracy allegations of our time." Although show subjects are not limited to New World Order conspiracy theories, topics often revolve around this material. Ventura approaches the subject with a willingness to believe; however, the show is well researched and endeavors to present and represent multiple points of view.

The Simpsons (1989–present): In an episode titled "Homer the Great," Homer Simpson joins a secret society, which parodies Skull and Bones, the Illuminati, and the Freemasons rolled into one. The members reveal what conspiracy theorists have long asserted—that they secretly rule the world.

The X-Files (1993–2008): Exploits UFO cover-up conspiracies.

Recommended Books and Websites

The following are some of the most influential resources for those seeking to delve more deeply into the New World Order. Some may be difficult to find.

Books

Alford, Alan F. *Gods of the New Millennium: Scientific Proof of Flesh & Blood Gods.* Walsall, UK: Eridu Books, 1996.

———. *The Temple and the Lodge.* New York: Arcade, 1989.

Allen, Gary. *None Dare Call It Conspiracy.* Cutchogue, NY: Buccaneer Books, 1976.

———. *The Rockefeller File.* Seal Beach, CA: '76 Press, 1976.

Anonymous. *Report from Iron Mountain: On the Possibility and Desirability of Peace.* New York: Dial Press, 1967.

Baigent, Michael, Richard Leigh, and Henry Lincoln. *Holy Blood, Holy Grail.* New York: Dell, 1983.

Bamford, James. *The Puzzle Palace: A Report on NSA, America's Most Secret Agency.* New York: Penguin Books, 1983.

Beaty, Jonathan, and S. C. Gwynne. *The Outlaw Bank: A Wild Ride into the Secret Heart of BCCI.* New York: Random House, 1993.

Blair, John M. *The Control of Oil.* New York: Pantheon, 1976.

Boulay, R. A. *Flying Serpents and Dragons: The Story of Mankind's Reptilian Past.* Escondido, CA: The Book Tree, 1997.

Bowen, Russell S. *The Immaculate Deception.* Carson City, NV: America West Publishers, 1991.

Bramley, William. *The Gods of Eden.* New York: Avon Books, 1989.

Brzezinski, Zbigniew. *Between Two Ages: America's Role in the Technetronic Era.* New York: Viking, 1970.

Chatelain, Maurice. *Our Ancestors Came from Outer Space.* Garden City, NY: Doubleday, 1978.

Coleman, John. *Conspirators' Hierarchy: The Story of the Committee of 300.* Carson City, NV: America West Publishers, 1992.

Collier, James M., and Kenneth F. *Votescam: The Stealing of America.* New York: Victoria House Press, 1992.

Constantine, Alex. *Psychic Dictatorship in the U.S.A.* Portland, OR: Feral House, 1995.

Costen, Michael. *The Cathars and the Albigensian Crusade.* Manchester, UK: Manchester University Press, 1997.

Drosnin, Michael. *The Bible Code.* New York: Simon & Schuster, 1997.

Eddy, Patricia G. *Who Tampered with the Bible.* Nashville: Winston-Derek Publishers, 1993.

Epperson, A. Ralph. *The New World Order.* Tucson, AZ: Publius Press, 1990.

———. *The Unseen Hand: An Introduction to the Conspiratorial View of History.* Tucson, AZ: Publius Press, 1985.

Estulin, Daniel. *The True Story of the Bilderberg Group.* Waterville, OR: TrineDay, 2007.

Ferguson, Niall. *The House of Rothschild.* New York: Viking, 1998.

Fox, Hugh. *The Invisibles: A Dialectic.* New York and London: Horizon Press, 1976.

Gardner, Laurence. *Bloodline of the Holy Grail.* Rockport, MA: Element Books, 1996.

Garrison, Jim. *On the Trail of the Assassins.* New York: Warner Books, 1988.

Gatto, John Taylor. *Dumbing Us Down: The Hidden Curriculum of Compulsory Schooling.* Philadelphia: New Society Publishers, 1992.

Goldwater, Barry M. *With No Apologies.* New York: Morrow, 1979.

Greider, William. *One World, Ready or Not.* New York: Simon & Schuster, 1997.

————. *The Fearful Master.* Los Angeles: Western Islands, 1964.

————. *Secrets of the Temple: How the Federal Reserve Runs the Country.* New York: Simon & Schuster, 1987.

Griffin, Des. *Fourth Reich of the Rich.* Clackamas, OR: Emissary Publications, 1976.

Griffin, G. Edward. *The Creature from Jekyll Island: A Second Look at the Federal Reserve.* Westlake Village, CA: American Media, 1994.

Guirdham, Arthur. *The Cathars and Reincarnation.* Essex, UK: C. W. Daniel Company, 1970.

Gurudas. *Treason: The New World Order.* San Rafael, CA: Cassandra Press, 1996.

Hall, Manly P. *The Secret Teachings of All Ages.* Los Angeles: Philosophical Research Society, 1988. Reprint ed., 1928.

Hammer, Richard. *The Vatican Connection.* New York: Charter Books, 1982.

Hancock, Graham. *The Sign and the Seal.* New York: Touchstone, 1993.

Harris, Jack. *Freemasonry.* New Kensington, PA: Whitaker House, 1983.

Henry, William. *One Foot in Atlantis.* Anchorage, AK: Earthpulse Press, 1998.

Hoffman, Michael A., II. *Secret Societies and Psychological Warfare.* Dresden, NY: Wiswell Ruffin House, 1989.

Howe, Linda Moulton. *Glimpses of Other Realities—Volume II: High Strangeness.* New Orleans: Paper Chase Press, 1998.

Huntington, Samuel P. *The Clash of Civilizations and the Remaking of World Order.* New York: Simon & Schuster, 1996.

Icke, David. *... and the Truth Shall Set You Free.* Cambridge, UK: Bridge of Love Publications, 1995.

————. *The Biggest Secret.* Scottsdale, AZ: Bridge of Love Publications, 1999.

Jackson, Devon. *Conspiranoia!: The Mother of All Conspiracy Theories.* New York: Penguin Books, 1999.

Johnson, George. *Architects of Fear: Conspiracy Theories and Paranoia in American Politics*. Los Angeles: Jeremy Tarcher, 1983.

Katz, Howard S. *The Warmongers*. New York: Books in Focus, 1979.

Keith, Jim. *Black Helicopters Over America: Strikeforce for the New World Order*. Lilburn, GA: IllumiNet Press, 1994.

———. *Mind Control World Control: The Encyclopedia of Mind Control*. Kempton, IL: Adventures Unlimited, 1997.

———. *Secret and Suppressed: Banned Ideas & Hidden History*. Portland, OR: Feral House, 1993.

Lee, Martin A., and Norman Soloman. *Unreliable Sources: A Guide to Detecting Bias in News Media*. New York, NY: Carol Publishing Group, 1991.

Lewels, Joe. *The God Hypothesis*. Mill Spring, NC: Wild Flower Press, 1997.

Litchfield, Michael. *It's a Conspiracy*. Berkeley, CA: Earth Works Press, 1992.

Mackey, Albert Gallatin. *The History of Freemasonry*. New York: Gramercy, 1996.

———. *Dark Majesty*. Austin, TX: Living Truth Publishers, 1992.

Marrs, Jim. *The Rise of the Fourth Reich: The Secret Societies That Threaten to Take Over America*. New York: Harper, 2008.

———. *Rule by Secrecy: The Hidden History That Connects the Trilateral Commission, the Freemasons, and the Great Pyramids*. New York: Harper, 2000.

Marrs, Texe. *Circle of Intrigue: The Hidden Inner Core of the Global Illuminati Conspiracy*. Austin, TX: Living Truth Publishers, 1995.

Marsden, Victor E., tr. *Protocols of the Learned Elders of Zion*. London: Morning Post, 1934.

Maxwell, Jordan. *Matrix of Power: Secrets of World Control*. San Diego: The Book Tree, 2000.

McManus, John F. *The Insiders: Architects of the New World Order*. Appleton, WI: The John Birch Society, 1992.

Moore, William L., and Charles Berlitz. *The Philadelphia Experiment: Project Invisibility*. New York: Ballantine Books, 1979.

Morton, Frederick. *The Rothschilds: A Family Portrait*. New York: Atheneum, 1962.

Moscow, Alvin. *The Rockefeller Inheritance*. Garden City, NY: Doubleday, 1977.

Mullins, Eustace. *The Secrets of the Federal Reserve*. Staunton, VA: Bankers Research Institute, 1983.

————. *The World Order: A Study in the Hegemony of Parasitism*. Staunton, VA: Ezra Pound Institute of Civilization, 1985.

Pagels, Elaine. *The Gnostic Gospels*. New York: Vintage, 1981.

Parenti, Michael. *Inventing Reality: The Politics of the Mass Media*. New York: St. Martin's Press, 1986.

Perloff, James. *The Shadows of Power: The Council on Foreign Relations and the American Decline*. Appleton, WI: Western Islands Publishers, 1988.

Picknett, Lynn, and Clive Prince. *The Templar Revelation*. New York: Touchstone, 1997.

Piper, Michael Collins. *Final Judgment: The Missing Link in the JFK Assassination Conspiracy*. Washington, D.C.: The Center for Historical Review, 1994.

Pool, James. *Who Financed Hitler: The Secret Funding of Hitler's Rise to Power, 1919–1933*. New York: Pocket Books, 1997.

Powell, S. Steven. *Covert Cadre: Inside the Institute for Policy Studies*. Ottawa, IL: Green Hill Publishers, 1987.

Prados, John. *Keepers of the Keys: A History of the National Security Council from Truman to Bush*. New York: Morrow, 1991.

Pye, Lloyd. *Everything You Know Is Wrong*. Madeira Beach, FL: Adamu Press, 1997.

Ravenscroft, Trevor. *The Spear of Destiny*. York Beach, MA: Samuel Weiser, 1973.

Robertson, Pat. *The New World Order*. Dallas: World Publishers, 1991.

Sitchin, Zecharia. *Divine Encounters*. New York: Avon Books, 1995.

————. *Genesis Revisited*. New York: Avon Books, 1990.

————. *The 12th Planet*. New York: Avon, 1976.

————. *The Wars of Gods and Men*. New York: Avon, 1985.

Sklar, Holly. *Trilateralism: The Trilateral Commission and Elite Planning.* Brooklyn, NY: South End Press, 1999.

Speer, Albert. *Inside the Third Reich.* New York: Macmillan, 1970.

Still, William T. *New World Order: The Ancient Plan of Secret Societies.* Lafayette, LA: Huntington House Publishers, 1990.

Sutton, Antony C. *America's Secret Establishment: An Introduction to the Order of Skull & Bones.* Billings, MT: Liberty House Press, 1986.

———. *The Federal Reserve Conspiracy.* Boring, OR: CPA Book Publishers, 1995.

———. *Wall Street and the Rise of Hitler.* Seal Beach, CA: '76 Press, 1976.

Sutton, Antony C., and Patrick M. Wood. *Trilaterals Over Washington.* Scottsdale, AZ: The August Corp., 1979.

Tarpley, Webster Griffin, and Anton Chaitken. *George Bush: The Unauthorized Biography.* Washington, D.C.: Executive Itelligence Review, 1992.

Thorn, Victor. *The New World Order Exposed.* State College, PA: Sisyphus Press, 2003.

Turnage, C. L. *New Evidence the Holy Bible Is an Extraterrestrial Transmission.* Santa Barbara, CA: Timeless Voyager Press, 1998.

Valee, Jacques. *Revelations: Alien Contact and Human Deception.* New York: Ballantine Books, 1991.

Vankin, Jonathan. *Conspiracies, Cover-ups and Crimes: Political Manipulation and Mind Control in America.* New York: Paragon House, 1992.

Vankin, Jonathan, and John Whalen. *The Fifty Greatest Conspiracies of All Time: History's Biggest Mysteries, Coverups, and Cabals.* New York: Carol Publishing Group, 1995.

Waite, Arthur Edward. *A New Encyclopaedia of Freemasonry.* New York: Wings Books, 1996.

Webster, Nesta H. *Secret Societies and Subversive Movements.* 1924 reprint ed. Palmdale, CA: Omni Publications, 1998.

West, John Anthony. *Serpent in the Sky.* Wheston, IL: Quest Books, 1993.

Whaley, William J. *Christianity and American Freemasonry.* Milwaukee: Bruce, 1958.

Wilgus, Neal. *The Illuminoids.* New York: Pocket Books, 1978.

Wilson, Derek. *Rothschild: The Wealth and Power of a Dynasty.* New York: Scribner's, 1988.

Wilson, Robert Anton. *Everything Is Under Control: Conspiracies, Cults, and Cover-Ups.* New York: Harper Perennial, 1998.

Wise, David, and Thomas B. Ross. *The Invisible Government.* New York: Vintage, 1974.

Websites

There are thousands of websites substantially dedicated to the New World Order conspiracy. The following is a selection of places to begin.

Battling the New World Order: PublicEye.org
www.publiceye.org

Conspiracy Archive: New World Order
www.conspiracyarchive.com/NWO

David Icke.com
www.davidicke.com

Educate-Yourself
www.educate-yourself.org

Illuminati News
www.illuminati-news.com

The Insider: New World Order
www.theinsider.org/reports/new-world-order

Alex Jones' Infowars
www.infowars.com

Jim Marrs Website
www.jimmarrs.com

New World Order Information
www.newworldorderinfo.com

Power of Prophecy: The monthly newsletter ministry of Texe Marrs
www.texemarrs.com

Project for the New American Century
www.newamericancentury.org

Sherry Shriner: New World Order
www.sherryshriner.com

Upside Backwards
www.upsidebackwards.info/index.php

The Watcher Files: UFOs, Aliens, Reptilians, Secret Government
www.thewatcherfiles.com

Watcher Website Global Government
www.mt.net/~watcher/conspir.html

A New World Order Address Book

The following provides contact information for the modern organizations New World Order theorists identify as associated with the New World Order conspiracy.

AMORC (Ancient and Mystical Order Rosae Crucis)

Rosicrucian Order, AMORC
1342 Naglee Avenue
San Jose, CA 95191
Fax: 408-947-3677
membership@rosicrucian.org
programs@rosicrucian.org
info@rosicrucian.org
www.amorc.org

Bilderberg Group

Although the organization itself provides no contact information, maintains no website, and never issues press releases, it is publicly represented by:

American Friends of Bilderberg, Inc.
Contact: Murden & Company Inc.
1325 Avenue of the Americas, Suite 25
New York, NY 10019

Chatham House

The Royal Institute of International Affairs
Chatham House, 10 St. James's Square
London SW1Y 4LE UK
Telephone: +44 (0)20 7957 5700
Fax: +44 (0)20 7957 5710
contact@chathamhouse.org.uk
www.chathamhouse.org.uk

Communist Party USA

Communist Party USA National Office
235 West 23rd Street, 8th floor
New York, NY 10011
Telephone: 212-989-4994
Fax: 212-229-1713
cpusa@cpusa.org
www.cpusa.org

Council on Foreign Relations

New York Office:

The Harold Pratt House
58 East 68th Street
New York, NY 10065
Telephone: 212-434-9400
Fax: 212-434-9800

Washington Office:

1777 F Street, NW
Washington, DC 20006
Telephone: 202-509-8400
Fax: 202-509-8490
www.cfr.org

Ford Foundation

320 East 43rd Street
New York, NY 10017
Telephone: 212-573-5000
Fax: 212-351-3677
www.fordfound.org

Freemasons

United Kingdom:

United Grand Lodge of England
Freemasons' Hall
60 Great Queen Street
London WC2B 5AZ UK
Telephone: +44 20 7831 9811
www.ugle.org.uk/library-and-museum/

United States:

Supreme Council, 33°, Ancient Accepted Scottish Rite Northern Masonic Jurisdiction
PO Box 519
Lexington, MA 02420
Telephone: 781-862-4410
Fax: 781-863-1833
www.supremecouncil.org

The Supreme Council, 33°
1733 16th Street NW
Washington, DC 20009
Telephone: 202-232-3579
Fax: 202-464-0487
www.scottishrite.org
www.scottishriteamerica.org

Hermetic Order of the Golden Dawn, Inc.

The Hermetic Order of the Golden Dawn
PO Box 1757
Elfers, FL 34680
HOGDMAIL@aim.com
www.hermeticgoldendawn.org

Knights of Malta

Sovereign Military Order of Malta
Magistral Palace
Via Condotti, 68 - 00187
Rome, Italy
Telephone: +39.06.67581.1
Fax: +39.06.6797.202
info@orderofmalta.org
www.orderofmalta.org/english

Open Source Order of the Golden Dawn

www.osogd.org

Contact by e-mailing the Order's Cancellarius at cancellarius@osogd.org.

Rockefeller Foundation

New York Office:

The Rockefeller Foundation
420 Fifth Avenue
New York, NY 10018
Telephone: 212-869-8500
Fax: 212-764-3468

Bangkok Office:

The Rockefeller Foundation
21st Floor UBC II Building
591 Sukhumvit 33, Wattana
Bangkok 10110- Thailand
Telephone: 66-2-262-0091 to 95
Fax: 66-2-262-0098
Reference: RF/Thailand

Nairobi Office:

The Rockefeller Foundation
Eden Square Building, Block 1, 2nd Floor
Greenway Lane, off Westlands Road
PO Box 14531 Westlands, 00800
Nairobi, Kenya
Telephone: 254-20-3742-726 or 3742-727
Fax: 254-20-3675-260

Bellagio Center:

Bellagio Study and Conference Center
Villa Serbelloni
Bellagio (Lago di Como) 22021
Italy
Telephone: 39-031-9551
Fax: 39-031-955259
www.rockefellerfoundation.org

Rotary International
One Rotary Center
1560 Sherman Avenue
Evanston, IL 60201
Telephone: 847-866-3000
Fax: 847-328-8554 or 847-328-8281
www.rotary.org/en/Pages/ridefault.aspx

Skull and Bones

No contact information.

Societas Rosicruciana in America
PO Box 1316
Bayonne, NJ 07002
sria2000@aol.com
www.sria.org

Theosophical Society in America

Street Address:

Theosophical Society in America
1926 North Main Street
Wheaton, IL 60187

Mailing Address:

Theosophical Society in America
PO Box 270
Wheaton, IL 60187
Telephone: 630-668-1571 ext 300
Fax: 630-668-4976
info@theosophical.org
www.theosophical.org/national_center

Trilateral Commission

The North American Group:

Trilateral Commission
1156 15th Street, NW
Washington, DC 20005
Telephone: 202-467-5410
Fax: 202-467-5415
contactus@trilateral.org

The European Group:

Trilateral Commission
5, rue de Téhéran, 75008
Paris, France
Telephone: 33-1: 45 61 42 80
Fax: 33-1: 45 61 42 80
trilateral.europe@wanadoo.fr

The Pacific Asian Group:

Trilateral Commission
Japan Center for International Exchange
4-9-17 Minami-Azabu, Minato-ku
Tokyo 106, Japan
Telephone: 81-3: 3446-7781
Fax: 81-3: 3443-7580
admin@jcie.or.jp
www.trilateral.org

United Nations

www.un.org

Contact via the web form at www.un.org/en/contactus.

United States Federal Reserve System

www.federalreserve.gov

Contact via the web form at www.federalreserve.gov/feedback.cfm.

World Bank
The World Bank
1818 H Street, NW
Washington, DC 20433
Telephone: 202-473-1000
Fax: 202-477-6391
www.worldbank.org

Index

Numbers

3WW (three world wars), 218
  Pike, Albert, 218-219
  Pike-Mazzini letter
    details, 219-220
    legitimacy, 221-222
9/11 attacks
  casualties, 279
  conspiracy theories,
    281-282
  overview, 279
  U.S. government, 280-281
322 in Skull and Bones
  emblem, 84
1984, 273

A

Abgrall, Dr. Jean-Marie, 179
accepted masons, 189
aeons, 136
Age of Great Dictators,
  241-242
agendas
  AMORC, 174
  ancient secret societies
    and modern agencies,
    140
  Assassins, 152

Bilderberg Group, 38-40
CFR, 28, 243
Crusades, 144
  Eastern expansion of
    Christianity, 145
  Magdalene theory,
    146-147
  search for truths of
    Christianity, 145
FDR's desire for war, 248
Federal Reserve, 109, 115
Freemasons, 205
Knights Templar
  official mission, 147
  search for religious
    relics, 148
money, 7
Round Table movement,
  62
Societas Rosicruciana, 177
Trilateral Commission,
  51
U.S. government
  involvement in 9/11
  attacks, 280-281
Agnostus, Irenaeus, 173
Ahimeir, Abba, 252
alchemy, 175
Aldrich, Senator Nelson W.,
  108

America
  9/11 attacks
    casualties, 279
    conspiracy theories,
      281-282
    overview, 279
    U.S. government
      motives, 280-281
  1920s prosperity, 238
  banking history
    central banks, 110-113
    Federal Reserve Act of
      1913, 114
    one-man banking
      trust, 113
    Revolutionary War,
      111
  Bilderberg Group
    involvement, 35
  Bush, George H. W., 8
    1992 election, 278
    ambassador positions,
      275
    background, 275
    CIA director, 275
    coalition against Iraq,
      274
    first NWO speech,
      276-277
    following Reagan, 276
    new world order
      definition, 279

oil wars with Iraq, 283
Operation Desert
  Shield, 276
Persian Gulf War, 277
Reagan's vice
  president, 275
response to Iraq's
  invasion of Kuwait,
  274
second NWO speech,
  278
Skull and Bones
  member, 275
unfinished business in
  Iraq, 278
Bush, George W.
  oil wars with Iraq, 283
  Skull and Bones
  connection, 90
Commission to Negotiate
  Peace
  founding, 18
  Institute of
  International Affairs,
  21
  meeting with British
  scholars, 20
FDR. *See* FDR
Federal Reserve, 12,
  110-114
  founding, 108-110
  function, 115
  governing body, 116
  Great Depression, 115
  Jekyll Island secret
  meeting, 107-110
  New York City bank
  stockholders, 118
  power, 118
  structure, 117
Freemason lodges, 190
French and Indian War,
  203-205

Great Depression, 115,
  238-239
Jewish American
  financing for
  Bolshevism, 231
nuclear policies, 25
oil wars with Iraq, 283
origins. *See* New Atlantis
Pearl Harbor attack,
  245-247
Persian Gulf War, 277
presidents avoiding
  declarations of war,
  263-264
Revolution
  economy, 111
  Freemason
  involvement, 203-205
Truman. *See* Truman,
  President Harry S.
undeclared wars, 264
Wall Street financing
  for Russian revolutions,
  230-232
Washington, George, 204
Wilson, President
  Woodrow, 8
  Colonel House, 19-21
  Fourteen Points, 20
  presidency, 18
  Treaty of Versailles, 18
World War II. *See* World
  War II
American Volunteer Group
  (AVG), 246
AMORC (Ancient and
  Mystical Order Rosae
  Crucis), 171, 174
  connections, 179-180
  Initiatic Tradition, 175
  membership, 174
  objective, 174

ancestry
  Carbonari, 214
  secret societies, 12-13
ancient connections
  Christian Church, 132
  Constantine's
  destruction of
  religious texts, 134
  Constantine's divine
  status, 133
  Council of Arles, 133
  Diocletian Persecution,
  133
  Donatists, 133
  first ecumenical
  council, 133
  Nicene Creed, 134
  suppressing other
  religions, 134
  coded messages in
  scriptures, 137-139
  Essenes, 136-137
  Gnostics, 135-136
  litmus test, 132
  motive similarities, 140
  Sumerian creation myth,
  140
ancient utopia of Atlantis.
  See New Atlantis
Anderson, Dr. James, 190
Andrew, Abraham Piatt, 108
Angel of Death (Dr. Josef
  Mengele), 259
anti-Masonic movements
  Britain's Unlawful
  Societies Act, 185
  Islamic, 187
  Italy, 185
  Japan, 186
  Jewish members, 186
  Morgan Affair, 183-184
  Nazi Germany, 186
  political opposition, 184

religious objections, 186
Spain, 185
Anti-Masonic Party, 184
anti-Semitic campaigns, 186
Anunnaki, 140
Arcanum Arcanorum, 208, 227
Arians, 134
Ark of the Covenant, 148
"Assassinations Foretold in Moby Dick!" website, 139
Assassins
  Alamut stronghold, 152
  alliance with Knights Templar, 153
  destruction, 153
  founding, 151-152
  membership, 153
  objectives, 152
  terror tactics, 152
Association of Helpers, 60-61
Atlantic Charter, 245
AVG (American Volunteer Group), 246

B

Babel, Jean-Jacques, 6
Bacon, Sir Francis
  background, 199-200
  Freemason connections, 201
  The New Atlantis, 200
  Rosicrucian connections, 201
  utopian elements, 202
Bailey, Alice Ann, 123-125
Baker, James A. III, 53
banking history. *See also* Federal Reserve

American Revolution, 111
central banks
  decentralization, 113
  First Bank of the United States, 111
  function, 110-111
  Second Bank of the United States, 113
Federal Reserve Act of 1913, 114
one-man banking trust, 113
baraccas, 213
Barnet, Richard, 17
Barron, Clarence W., 231
Barruel, Abbé Austin, 166
Baruch, Bernard, 20, 65
Batten, Samuel Zane, 103
Battle of Waterloo, 100
Belcher, Jonathan, 203
Berlin Airlift, 26
Bernanke, Ben, 38
Bernhard, Prince, 33-35
Between Two Ages: America's Role in the Technetronic Era, 44
Bible Code, The, 137
Bible coded messages, 137-138
Bilderberg Group, 10
  agenda, 38-39
  first conference initiator, 32
  founding fathers, 34
    Bernhard, Prince, 33-35
    Healey, Denis, 32-33
    Retinger, 33
  unofficial CFR comparison, 36
  meetings, 31

membership
  American, 36
  corporate, 38
  influential members, 38
  Trilateral Commission members, 36
  motives, 40
  organizational structure, 36
  origins of name, 31
  purpose, 32
  Rockefeller connections, 36
  secrecy, 40-41
  Trilateral Commission connections, 45-46
  U.S. involvement, 35
Black, Edwin
  American corporations' involvement in Holocaust, 258-260
  Neo-Nazis, 260
Black Tuesday, 238
Blair, Prime Minister Tony, 39
Blavatsky, Helena Petrovna, 124
Bohemian Grove, 188
Bolshevik Revolution of 1917, 229
Bolsheviks, 229
Bonaparte, Charles-Louis-Napoléon, 216
Bonesmen. *See* Skull and Bones
Book of Constitutions, 190
Bowie, Robert R., 46
Braun, Eva, 255
Brit HaBirionim, 252

British societies
Chatham House
ancestry, 67
founding, 20
headquarters, 65
influence, 66-67
Institute of
International Affairs,
21
membership, 65
rules, 66
secrecy, 66
Royal Institute of
International Affairs,
21, 63
Unlawful Societies Act,
185
Brooke, Tal, 160
Brown, Dan, 146
Brzezinski, Zbigniew, 23,
44-45
buon cugino, 213
bureaucratic collectivism,
3-4
Burnett, Erin, 23
Bush, George H. W., 8
1992 election, 278
ambassador positions,
275
background, 275
CIA director, 275
coalition against Iraq, 274
first NWO speech,
276-277
following Reagan, 276
new world order
definition, 279
oil wars with Iraq, 283
Operation Desert Shield,
276
Persian Gulf War, 277
Reagan's vice president,
275

response to Iraq's invasion
of Kuwait, 274
second NWO speech, 278
Skull and Bones member,
275
unfinished business in
Iraq, 278
Bush, George W.
oil wars with Iraq, 283
Skull and Bones
connection, 90
Bush, Prescott, 86, 275
Byron, Lord, 216

C

Cabalist texts, 138-139
Cairo Conference, 264
Cannon, Lou, 53
Carbonari, 212
3WW, 218-222
addressing one another,
213
ancestry, 214
contributions to
communism, 233
Ferdinand, 216
flag, 215
founding, 214
Freemason connections,
213
hierarchical degrees, 213
lodges, 213
Mazzini, Giuseppe,
217-218
members, 216
Neapolitan revolution,
215
patron saint, 215
politics, 215

revolutionary offshoots,
217
symbols, 213
views on God, 213
vows, 215
Carr, William Guy, 162-163,
221-222
CCC (Civilian Conservation
Corps), 239
Cecil, Robert, 63
central banks
decentralization, 113
First Bank of the United
States, 111
function, 110-111
Second Bank of the
United States, 113
CFR (Council on Foreign
Relations), 9
agenda, 28
Cold War, 24-25
Colonel House
background, 19
Institute of
International Affairs,
21
meeting with British
scholars, 20
progressive reforms, 19
Wilson, 19-20
description, 17
Dulles brothers, 25
formation, 20-21
global government
motives, 28
influences on Eisenhower,
25
The Inquiry, 18
"International
Institutions and Global
Governance: World
Order in the 21st
Century" program, 27

Korean War, 269
Marshall Plan, 24
membership, 17, 22-23
NATO, 25
normalization with
    Communist China, 27
Sino-American relations,
    27
Treaty of Versailles, 18
U.S. nuclear policies, 25
Vietnam War, 270
War and Peace Studies
    Project, 243
wars, 26
World War II, 24
Charles F. Kettering
    Foundation, 45
Chatham House, 10
    ancestry, 67
    founding, 20
    headquarters, 65
    influence, 66-67
    Institute of International
        Affairs, 21
    membership, 65
    rules, 66
    secrecy, 66
Cheney, Dick, 23
Chinese intervention in
    Korean War, 267
Chomsky, Noam, 52
Christian Church, 132
    coded messages in
        scriptures, 137-139
    Constantine
        background, 135
        Council of Arles, 133
        destruction of religious
            texts, 134
        divine status, 133
        first ecumenical
            council, 133
        suppressing other
            religions, 134

Crusades
    15th and 16th century
        conflicts, 145
    Eastern expansion, 145
    Knights Templar,
        147-155
    Magdalene theory,
        146-147
    objective, 144
    search for truths of
        Christianity, 145
    Western expansion,
        145
Diocletian Persecution,
    133
Donatists, 133
Illuminati
    ban, 167
    connection with
        Freemasons, 165-166
    fear, 168
    founding, 164-165
    influences, 168
    Lucifer connection,
        163
    membership, 166
    modern survival
        theories, 160-163
    opposition, 167
    power, 168
    Weishaupt's exile, 167
Knights Hospitaller, 148,
    155
Nicene Creed, 134
Sovereign Military Order
    of Malta, 155-156
Churchill, Winston, 8,
    243-244
Cicero, Chic, 175
Civilian Conservation Corps
    (CCC), 239
Clinton, Bill, 38
coalitions, 274

coded messages in
    scriptures, 137-139
Cold War, 24-25
Coleman, John, 60
collectivist state, 241
College of William and
    Mary's Flat Hat Club, 83
colonial Freemasons
    American Revolution,
        203-205
    earliest proof, 202
    first accepted mason, 203
    first lodge meeting in
        Western Hemisphere,
        203
    first native-born North
        American mason, 203
    Great Seal of the United
        States, 206-207
Colt, Samuel, 96
communism
    Bolshevik Revolution, 229
    communal ownership, 227
    Communist Manifesto, 226
    contributing secret
        societies, 233
    facism similarities, 253
    factory system, 228
    global scope, 230
    history
        alternative version,
            230-232
        mainstream version,
            227-230
    inner circles, 227
    International
        Workingmen's
        Association (IWA), 234
    Jewish American
        financiers theory, 231
    New Economic Policy,
        229

one-world government,
226
Plekhanov's political
evolution idea, 228
proletariat revolution,
228-229
Russian Civil War, 229
Third International, 229
Wall Street financing for
revolutions, 230-232
World War II, 229
Communist Manifesto, 226
connections
ancient
Christian Church,
132-134
coded messages in
scriptures, 137-139
Essenes, 136-137
Gnostics, 135-136
litmus test, 132
motive similarities, 140
Sumerian creation
myth, 140
Assassins, 153
Bilderberg Group and
Trilateral Commission,
45-46
CFR members, 23
communism, 253
Freemasons
Illuminati, 192-193
Knights Templar, 192
Mormonism, 184
Illuminati
Freemasons, 165-166
Lucifer, 163
Skull and Bones, 88
Knights Templar
modern American secret
societies, 154-155
Morgans and Skull and
Bones, 101

OTS and Operation
Gladio, 178
Rockefeller, David Sr., 36
Rosicrucians, 179-180
Round Table movement
and Chatham House, 65
Skull and Bones
members, 89
conspiracy theorists
government, 5
nationalities, 5
New Age/specific
religious motives, 11
shadows of Socrates, 4
United Nations war
objective, 70
wars, 6
conspiratorial view of
history, 73
Conspirators' Hierarchy, 60
Constantine
background, 135
Council of Arles, 133
destruction of religious
texts, 134
divine status, 133
First Council of Nicaea,
133
suppressing other
religions, 134
containment, 24, 270
contentious issues, 78
corporations
Bilderberg Group
membership, 38
CFR membership, 22
corporatism, 254
Council of Arles, 133
Council on Foreign
Relations. *See* CFR
Covenant of the League of
Nations, 21
the Craft, 185

criticism
FDR's New Deal, 240
Trilateral Commission,
51-52
crooking, 85-86
*Crossfire: The Plot That Killed
Kennedy*, 6
Crusades
15th and 16th century
conflicts, 145
Knights Templar
alliance with the
Assassins, 153
arrests, 150
becoming Knights
Hospitallers, 155
chastity vows, 149
decline, 150-151
founding, 147
members, 147
military vows, 149
official mission, 147
papal blessing, 149
ranks, 149
recruiting members,
149
search for religious
relics, 148
settling in America,
154-155
survivors, 154
wealth, 149-150
Magdalene theory,
146-147
objectives, 144-145
Western expansion of
Christianity, 145
currency, 111
Currency Act of 1764, 111
Curtis, Lionel, 62-63

D

Da Vinci Code, The, 146
Daddy Warbucks, 110
Daraul, Arkon, 233
Davis, John W., 23
Davison, Henry P., 108
Declaration of Independence
  signers, 203
deliberative assemblies,
  75-76
Di Mambro, Joseph, 179
dialectic, 277
Die Spinne (the spider), 258
Dillon, C. Douglas, 23
Diocletian Persecution, 133
Donatists, 133
DRK (People's Democratic
  Republic of Korea), 265
Drosnin, Michael, 137
Dulles, Allen Welsh, 23, 25
Dulles, John Foster, 25
Dumbarton Oaks
  Conference, 72

E

ECOSOC (Economic and
  Social Council), 77
ecumenical, 134
Eisenhower, Dwight D.
  CFR influences, 25
  farewell speech, 94
  military-industrial-
    congressional complex,
    94-95
the elect, 61
End Time theology, 125-126
Engels, Friedrich, 226
enlightenment, 174

Enuma Elish, 140
Epperson, Ralph, 109
esoteric, 123
esperanto, 64
Essenes, 136-137
eugenics, 259
European Common Market,
  38
European Recovery Plan, 24
European Union, 38
evolution of NWO, 7-9
Export Control Act, 246

F

Fabian Society, 33-34
facism
  communism similarities,
    253
  description of globalism,
    253
  fasces symbol, 253
  Jewish-backed, 252
  overview, 253
  source of NWO, 254
factory system, 228
false-flag operations, 280
*Fama Fraternatis of the
  Meritorious Order of the Rosy
  Cross*, 172
Fatimid dynasty, 151
FDIC (Federal Deposit
  Insurance Corporation),
  239
FDR (Franklin Delano
  Roosevelt), 237
  1932 election, 239
  1936 election, 241
  court-packing scheme,
    241-242
  funeral procession, 237

New Deal, 239-240
World War II
  alliance with Britain,
    245
  armed neutrality, 243
  CFR War and Peace
    Studies Project, 243
  Lend-Lease Act, 244
  motives for war, 248
  neutrality acts, 242
  Pearl Harbor attack,
    245-247
  supporting Churchill,
    243-244
  war appropriations
    increases, 244
Federal Reserve, 12, 110-114
  founding
    Panic of 1907, 109-110
    reform agenda, 109
    seven founders, 108
  function, 115
  governing body, 116
  Great Depression, 115
  Jekyll Island secret
    meeting, 107
    agenda, 109
    members, 108
    Panic of 1907, 109-110
  New York City bank
    stockholders, 118
  power, 118
  structure, 117
Federal Reserve Act of 1913,
  114
Ferdinand, 216
Ferguson, Charles W., 190
*Fifty Million Brothers: A
  Panorama of American
  Lodges and Clubs*, 190
financial panic, 109

financiers
CFR, 23
wars
Morgans, 101-102
Rockefellers, 102-104
Rothschilds, 99-101
First Bank of the United
States, 111
First Council of Nicaea, 133
Fischer, David Hackett, 14
Flat Hat Club, 83
Fludd, Robert, 173
Flying Tigers, 246
Ford, Gerald, 38
Ford, Henry's anti-Semitic
theories, 259
Ford Foundation, 45
Foreign Affairs, 18
forestas, 213
Forsyth, Frederick, 257
founding
Assassins, 151-152
Bilderberg Group, 34
Bernhard, Prince,
33-35
Healey, Denis, 32-33
Retinger, 33
Carbonari, 214
CFR, 20-21
Federal Reserve
Jekyll Island secret
meeting, 107
Panic of 1907, 109-110
reform agenda, 109
seven, 108
Freemasons, 188
Hermetic Order of the
Golden Dawn, 175
Illuminati, 164-165
Knights Hospitaller, 155
Knights Templar, 147
New Atlantis, 200

Open Source Order of
the Golden Dawn, 175
OTS, 178
Republic of Korea, 265
Rosicrucians, 172-173
Round Table movement,
60
Royal Institute of
International Affairs,
21, 63
Societas Rosicruciana, 176
Theosophical Society, 124
Trilateral Commission,
44
Bilderberg Group
connections, 45-46
Brzezinski, 44-45
founding fathers,
46-47
members, 46-47
United Nations, 69
World Wildlife Fund, 34
Fourth Reich, 252
American corporations
complicity in
Holocaust, 259-260
involvement in
Holocaust, 258
relations with
ex-Nazis, 260
corporate rulers, 254
facism
communism
similarities, 253
description of
globalism, 253
fasces symbol, 253
Jewish-backed, 252
overview, 253
source of NWO, 254
Neo-Nazis, 260

Nuremberg Tribunal, 257
postwar Nazi safe havens,
257-258
Franco-Prussian War of
1870, 96
Franklin, George S., 46
fraternities, 83
Freemasons
18th century schism, 190
20th century, 191
accepted masons, 189
American colonies, 190
anti-Masonic movements
banning by totalitarian
regimes, 185
Britain, 185
Islamic, 187
Italy, 185
Japan, 186
Jewish members, 186
Morgan Affair, 183-184
Nazi Germany, 186
political opposition,
184
religious objections,
186
Spanish, 185
Arcanum Arcanorum, 208
Book of Constitutions, 190
colonial
American Revolution,
203-205
earliest traces in
America, 202
first accepted mason,
203
first lodge meeting in
Western Hemisphere,
203
first native-born North
American mason, 203

Great Seal of the
United States,
206-207
connections
Carbonari, 213
Illuminati, 165-166
Mormonism, 184
New Atlantis, 201
conspiracy theories
Illuminati connections,
192-193
Knights Templar
connections, 192
Operation Gladio,
193-194
plots, 187
secret inner circle, 187,
192
the Craft, 185
fear, 185
French Revolution,
207-208
Illuminized, 192-193
French Revolution, 208
Skull and Bones
connection, 89
influence on Cecil
Rhodes, 59
operative masons, 189
origins, 188
power, 194
revolutionary activity, 191
Rosicrucian similarities,
13, 173
Satanic accusations, 222
scope, 188
Societas Rosicruciana, 176
speculative masons, 189
spiritual regeneration, 136
symbols, 190
transition from craft
guild to gentlemen's
clubs, 189
United Grand Lodge, 190

French and Indian War,
203-205
French Revolution, 207-208
furtive fallacy, 14

G

Galbraith, John Kenneth, 98
Garibaldi, Giuseppe, 216
GATT (General Agreement
on Tariffs and Trade), 8
Geithner, Timothy, 38
German
Freemason suppression,
186
General Motors
expansion, 259
Geronimo's skull, 85
Gilded Age, 101
global governance, 27-28
globalization, 15
Gnostics, 135-136
GOdF (Grand Orient de
France), 207
Goebbels, Josef, 186
Golden Dawn, 175
Goldwater, Barry
Trilateral Commission
criticism, 51-52
With No Apologies, 28
Golovinski, Matvei
Vasilyevich, 162
gradualism, 79
Gray, Harold, 110
Great Depression in
America, 115, 238-239
Great Persecution, 133
Great Seal of the United
States, 206-207
Greenspan, Alan, 23, 46

H

Haig, Alexander, 53
Hall, Manly Palmer, 136,
199
Harriman, W. Averill, 23
headquarters
Assassins, 152
United Nations, 75
Healey, Denis, 32-34
Hegel, Georg Wilhelm
Friedrich, 193, 277
Hegelian process, 277
Hermes Trismegistus, 176
Hermetic Order of the
Golden Dawn, 175
Historians' Fallacies, 14
History of Secret Societies, 233
Hitler, Adolf, 8, 186
escape, 256
fall of the Third Reich,
254-255
legacy, 257
remains, 256
suicide, 255
Holy Lance, 148
Home Owners Loan
Corporation, 239
Hoover, Herbert, 238
Hopkinson, Francis, 207
Hornblower, Marshall, 46
House, Edward M.
background, 19
The Inquiry, 18
Institute of International
Affairs, 21
meeting with British
scholars, 20
progressive reforms, 19
Wilson
adviser, 19
Fourteen Points, 20

House of Lords, 39
Hussein, Saddam
  Bush's unfinished
    business, 278
  cease-fire, 277
  coalition against, 274
  invasion of Kuwait,
    274-276

I

I Paid Hitler, 275
IBM's Nazism support, 259
ICC (International Criminal
  Court), 77
ICJ (International Court of
  Justice), 77
Il Risorgimento, 218
Illuminati
  ban, 167
  connections
    Freemasons, 165-166,
      192-193
    Lucifer, 163
    Skull and Bones, 88
  fear, 168
  founding, 12, 164-165
  Illuminized Freemasons,
    192-193
    French Revolution, 208
    Skull and Bones
      connection, 89
  influences, 168
  membership, 166
  modern survival theories
    Brooke, Tal, 160
    French and Bolshevick
      revolutions, 161
    three world wars,
      162-163
    Zionism, 162

opposition, 167
power, 168
Rosicrucianism
  similarities, 13
Weishaupt's exile, 167
Illuminized Freemasons,
  192-193
  French Revolution, 208
  Skull and Bones
    connection, 89
imperial cults, 126-127
Inchon Landing, 267
industrialist fortunes based
  on wars, 96
Initiatic Tradition, 175
inner circle
  communism, 227
  Freemasons, 192
  Round Tables, 60-61
The Inquiry, 18
Institute of International
  Affairs, 21
Interchurch World
  Movement (IWM), 103
International Court of
  Justice (ICJ), 77
International Criminal
  Court (ICC), 77
International Institute for
  Strategic Studies, 32
"International Institutions
  and Global Governance:
  World Order in the 21st
  Century" program, 27
International Organization
  Conference, 74-75
International Workingmen's
  Association (IWA), 234
Iraq
  Bush's unfinished
    business, 278
  cease-fire, 277
  coalition against, 274-276

invasion of Kuwait, 274
oil wars, 283
Islamic anti-Masonic
  movements, 187
Italian Freemason
  suppression, 185
Italian secret society. *See*
  Carbonari
Italian unification. *See*
  Mazzini, Giuseppe
Ivy League, 82
IWA (International
  Workingmen's
  Association), 234
IWM (Interchurch World
  Movement), 103

J

Jackson, Charles Douglas, 35
Japanese
  embargo, 246
  Freemason suppression,
    186
Jewish
  American financiers of
    Bolshevism theory, 231
  backed Fourth Reich, 252
  Freemason membership,
    186
join or die slogan, 284
Jouret, Luc, 178
Judeo-Masonic conspiracy
  theories, 186
Judge, William Quan, 124
Jumonville, Joseph Coulon
  de, 204

K

Kahn, Otto, 23
Kennan, George, 24
Keynes, John Maynard, 9
Keynesian economics, 9
King Richard the Lionheart, 153
Kissinger, Henry
    normalization with Communist China, 27
    nuclear policies, 25
Knickerbocker run, 109-110
Knight Rose Croix, 177
Knights Hospitaller, 148, 155
    absorption of Knights Templar, 155
    becoming Sovereign Military Order of Malta, 155
    founding, 155
    taking over Knights Templar role, 148
Knights Templar
    alliance with the Assassins, 153
    arrests, 150
    becoming Knights Hospitallers, 155
    Cabalist texts, 139
    chastity vows, 149
    creation, 147
    decline, 150-151
    Freemason connections, 192
    members, 147-149
    military vows, 149
    official mission, 147
    papal blessing, 149
    search for religious relics, 148

settling in America, 154-155
survivors, 154
wealth, 149-150
Kohnstamm, Max, 46
Korean trusteeship, 73
Korean War, 265-269
    CFR, 26
    Chinese intervention, 267
    conspiracy theorists' version, 269
    DRK creation, 265
    fall of Seoul, 268
    Inchon Landing, 267
    independence from Japan, 264
    lack of congressional declaration of war, 263-264
    MacArthur's defiance, 268
    North Korean invasion of South Korea, 266
    partition arrangement, 265
    ROK creation, 265
    trusteeship, 265
    UN
        intervention for unification, 265
        Security Council resolution for military action against North Korea, 266
    U.S. support for South Korean military, 266
Kremlin, 227
Krupp, Alfred, 96
Kuwait invasion, 274
Kyoto Trilateral Commission meetings, 47-48

L

Lafayette, Marquis de, 216
League of Nations, 69
Lend-Lease Act of 1941, 242-244
Lenin, Vladimir, 227
Les Neuf Soeurs, 208
Lewin, Leonard C., 98
Lippmann, Walter, 23, 64-65
litmus test, 132
Little Orphan Annie comic strip, 110
Loeb, Nina J., 20
Logan Act, 54
Long Telegram, 24
Lucifer, 163

M

MacLeish, Archibald, 71
MAD (mutual assured destruction), 25
Magdalene, Mary, 146-147
Maier, Michael, 173
Manning, Paul, 257
Marrs, Jim
    American corporate relations with ex-Nazis, 260
    Anunnaki, 140
    background, 6
    Knickerbocker run, 109
    Reagan's administration and secret societies, 53
    Rule by Secrecy, 39, 187
    Sovereign Military Order of Malta members, 156
Marshall Plan, 24

Martin Bormann: Nazi in Exile, 257
Marx, Karl
  Communist Manifesto, 226
  IWA leader, 234
mass murder-suicides, 179
Mathers, Samuel Liddell MacGregor, 175
Mazzini, Giuseppe, 216
  3WW, 218
    Pike, Albert, 218-219
    Pike-Mazzini letter, 219-222
  background, 217
  Il Risorgimento, 218
  Young European movement, 217
McCain, John, 23
McGhee, George, 38
McKay, Brendan, 139
meetings
  Bilderbeg Group, 31
  Federal Reserve, 107-110
  Round Table movement, 62-63
  Trilateral Commission
    1975 Kyoto, 47-48
    1976 Kyoto, 48
    first, 43-47
Mein Kampf, 186
membership
  AMORC, 174
  Assassins, 153
  Bilderberg Group
    American, 36
    corporate, 38
    influential members, 38
    Trilateral Commission members, 36
    U.S., 35
  Carbonari, 216
  CFR, 17, 22

connections, 23
corporations, 22
Dulles brothers, 25
financiers, 23
individuals, 22
influential members, 22
types, 22
Chatham House, 65-67
communism, 227
Federal Reserve, 108, 116
fraternities/sororities, 83
Freemasons
  accepted masons, 189
  Catholics, 186
  first accepted member in America, 203
  first native-born North American mason, 203
  Jewish, 186
  operative masons, 189
  scope, 188
  speculative masons, 189
Illuminati, 166
Knights Templar, 147-149
Round Table movement, 63
Skull and Bones, 83
  Bush, George H. W., 275
  Bush, George W., 90
  criteria, 90
  influential jobs, 83
  initiation ceremony, 86-87
  Meyer, Cord Jr., 88
  prominent members, 89-90
  women, 84
Societas Rosicruciana, 176

Trilateral Commission
  Bilderberg Group membership, 36
  founding, 46-47
  Logan Act, 54
  present day, 48
  United Nations, 74
memento mori, 84
Memoirs Illustrating the History of Jacobinsim, 166
Mendelssohn, Moses, 139
Mengele, Dr. Josef, 259
Mensheviks, 229
Meyer, Cord Jr., 88
Mezes, Sidney Edward, 18
military-industrial-congressional complex, 94
  creation of wealth, 96
  creators, 95
  Eisenhower, 94-95
  Franco-Prussian War of 1870, 96
  power and class, 96
  Report from Iron Mountain, The, 97-99
  World War I outbreak, 97
millenarianism, 125-126
Miller, David Cade, 183
Miller, Edith Starr, 211
Mills, C. Wright, 96
Milner, Alfred, 62
Minh, Ho Chi, 26
money, 7
Moos, Malcom, 95
Morals and Dogma of the Ancient and Accepted Scottish Rite of Freemasonry, 219
More, Thomas, 228
Morgan, William, 183-184
Morgans, 102
  Affair, 183-184
  John Pierpont, 23, 101, 113

Juliet Pierpont, 101
Junius Spencer, 101
New York City Federal
Reserve Bank, 118
philanthropy, 104
Skull and Bones
connection, 101
Union arms deal, 102
motives. *See* agendas
Moyers, Bill, 23
Murat, Joachim-Napoléon,
214
mutual assured destruction
(MAD), 25

N

nation-state, 284
national banks, 112
National Recovery Act
(NRA), 239
nationalities, 5
nationhood, 284
NATO (North Atlantic
Treaty Organization), 8,
25, 268
Nazi Nexus, 258
Nazis
Nuremberg Tribunal, 257
postwar
American corporate
relations, 260
safe havens, 257-258
Neapolitan revolution of
1820, 215
Neo-Nazis, 260
neo-theosophy, 123-125
Neutrality Act of 1939, 243
New Age Movement
Bailey, Alice Ann,
123-125

religious motives, 11
socialism connection,
121-123
New Atlantis
Bacon, Sir Francis
background, 199
Freemason
connections, 201
Rosicrucian
connections, 201
New Atlantis, The, 200
utopian elements, 202
founder, 200
New Atlantis, The, 200
New Deal
court-packing scheme,
241-242
criticism, 240
programs, 239-240
New Republic, The, 64
New World Order. *See*
NWO
New World Order, The, 103,
122-123
New York City Federal
Reserve Bank stockholders,
118
NGOs (nongovernmental
organizations), 11
Nicene Creed, 134
Nixon, Richard, 82
Nizaris, 151
Nobel, Alfred, 96
normalization with
Communist China, 27
North Atlantic Treaty
Organization (NATO), 8,
25, 268
North Korean government,
265
Norton, Charles D., 108
Novum Organum, 200
Novus Ordo Seclorum, 205

NRA (National Recovery
Act), 239
*Nuclear Weapons and Foreign
Policy*, 25
Nuremberg Tribunal, 257
NWO (New World
Order), 3
defined, 3-4
evolution, 7-9

O

objectives. *See* agendas
Occult Theocrasy, 211
ODESSA (Organisation
der ehemaligen
SS-Angehörigen), 257
Odessa File, The, 257
oil wars with Iraq, 283
Olcott, Henry Steel, 124
oligarchs, 12
defined, 12
Morgans, 102
Affair, 183-184
John Pierpont, 23, 101,
113
Juliet Pierpont, 101
Junius Spencer, 101
New York City Federal
Reserve Bank, 118
philanthropy, 104
Skull and Bones
connection, 101
Union arms deal, 102
New York City
Federal Reserve Bank
stockholders, 118
philanthropy, 104
Rockefellers, 103-104
David Sr., 36, 44, 104
Foundation's eugenics,
259

John Davison, 23, 102
John Davison III, 104
John Davison Jr., 103
Laurence Spelman, 104
Nelson, 104
New York City Federal
  Reserve Bank, 118
philanthropy, 104
second-generation, 103
third-generation, 104
Winthrop, 104
Rothschilds, 99-101
  de facto nobility status,
  100
  family expansion, 99
  Mayer Amschel, 99
  Nathan Mayer, 100
  Nathan Mayer II, 100
  philanthropy, 104
  trans-European
  financial/mercantile
  network, 100
Open Conspiracy, The, 122
Open Source Order of the
  Golden Dawn, 175
Operation Desert Shield,
  276
Operation Gladio
  Freemason connections,
  193-194
  Rosicrucian connections,
  178
Operation Paperclip, 258
operative masons, 189
Opus Dei, 146
order, 149
Organization of Former
  Members of the SS
  (ODESSA), 257
Orwell, George, 273
OTS (Order of the Solar
  Temple)
  connections, 179-180
  founding, 178

murders/suicides, 179
  Operation Gladio
  connection, 178
Own, Henry D., 46
Oxford system, 59

P

P2 (Propaganda Masonica
  Due), 193
Panic of 1907, 109-110
papal bulls, 151
partitioning countries, 265
Pawns in the Game, 162
Pax Americana, 281
Payens, Hugues de, 147
PCE (Parti Communautaire
  Européen), 178
Peabody, George, 101
Pearl Harbor attack, 245-247
  Japanese embargo, 246
  U.S. knowledge, 247
People's Democratic
  Republic of Korea (DRK),
  265
Perfectabilists. *See* Illuminati
Persian Gulf War, 277
philanthropy, 104
*Philip Dru: Administrator, a
  Story of Tomorrow*, 19
Pike, Albert
  background, 218-219
  Civil War, 219
  Freemasons, 219
  Pike-Mazzini letter
  details, 219-220
  legitimacy, 221-222
  website, 221
  Supreme Councils of the
  Scottish Rite, 219
Plantard, Pierre, 146

Plekhanov, Georgi, 228
Poe, Edgar Allan, 7
population control, 103
Potsdam Conference, 265
power, 7
  class, 96
  Federal Reserve, 118
  Freemasons, 194
  Illuminati, 168
Power Elite, The, 96
Preamble to the United
  Nations Charter, 71
Priory of Sion, 146
proletariat revolution,
  228-229
*Proofs of a Conspiracy
  against all the Religions and
  Governments of Europe,
  carried on in the secret
  meetings of Freemasons,
  Illuminati, and Reading
  Societies*, 160
Propaganda Masonica Due
  (P2), 193
*Protocols of the Elders of Zion,
  The*, 162
PSYOPS (psychological
  warfare), 35
PSYWAR (psychological
  warfare), 35
Purloined Letter, The, 7
PWA (Public Works
  Administration), 239

Q-R

Quigly, Carroll, 160

*Radicalism of the American
  Revolution*, 203
Reagan, Ronald, 53-54

Red Fog over America, 162
Regan, Donald, 53
Reischauer, Edwin, 46
religions
  Assassins
    Alamut stronghold, 152
    alliance with Knights
      Templar, 153
    destruction, 153
    founding, 151-152
    membership, 153
    objectives, 152
    terror tactics, 152
  Christian Church, 132
    coded messages in
      scriptures, 137-139
    Constatine's
      destruction of
      religious texts, 134
    Constatine's divine
      status, 133
    Council of Arles, 133
    Crusades. *See* Crusades
    Diocletian Persecution,
      133
    Donatists, 133
    first ecumenical
      council, 133
    Nicene Creed, 134
    suppressing other
      religions, 134
  End Time theology,
    125-126
  Essenes, 136-137
  Freemason objections,
    186
  Gnostics, 135-136
  Illuminati. *See* Illuminati
  imperial cults, 126
  Knights Hospitaller
    absorption of Knights
      Templar, 155

becoming Sovereign
  Military Order of
  Malta, 155
founding, 155
taking over Knights
  Templar role, 148
motives, 11
neo-theosophy, 123-125
New Age movement
  Bailey, Alice Ann,
    123-125
  socialism connection,
    121-123
  Stalin's Soviet Union,
    123
relic searches, 148
Sovereign Military Order
  of Malta, 155-156
Sufi, 172
terrorism, 284
theosophy, 124
Remington, Eliphalet, 96
*Report from Iron Mountain,
  The,* 97-99
Republic of Korea (ROK),
  265
Retinger, Józef, 32-34
Reves, Emery, 275
Revisionist Maximalism, 252
Rhee, President Syngman,
  265
Rhodes, Cecil, 10
  background, 58
  diamond empire, 57-59
  influences, 58-59
  "The Rhodes Colossus"
    cartoon, 58
  Round Table's founding,
    60-61
*The Rise of the Fourth Reich:
  The Secret Societies That
  Threaten to Take Over
  America,* 6

Robbins, Alexandra, 84
Robison, John, 159
Rockefellers, 103-104
  David Sr., 104
    Bilderberg Group, 36
    founding the Trilateral
      Commission, 44
  Foundation's eugenics, 259
  John Davison, 23, 102
  John Davison III, 104
  John Davison Jr., 103
  Laurence Spelman, 104
  Nelson, 104
  New York City Federal
    Reserve Bank, 118
  philanthropy, 104
  second-generation, 103
  third-generation, 104
  Winthrop, 104
ROK (Republic of Korea),
  265
Roosevelt, President
  Franklin Delano. *See* FDR
Rose Cross, 173
Rosenkreuz, Christian, 172
Rosicrucians
  16th and 17th centuries,
    173
  18th century, 173
  20th century objectives,
    180
  AMORC, 174-175
  connections, 179-180
  conspiracy role, 177
  decline, 174
  Freemasonry similarities,
    13, 173
  Hermes Trismegistus, 176
  Hermetic Order of the
    Golden Dawn, 175
  Illuminism similarities,
    13
  lodge furniture, 174

New Atlantis
  connections, 201
Open Source Order of
  the Golden Dawn, 175
Operation Gladio, 178
origin, 172-173
OTS, 178-179
rebirth, 174
Rose Cross, 173
Societas Rosicruciana,
  176-177
truth-seeking, 180
Rothschilds, 99-101
  de facto nobility status,
    100
  family expansion, 99
  Mayer Amschel, 99
  Nathan Mayer, 100
  Nathan Mayer II, 100
  philanthropy, 104
  trans-European financial/
    mercantile network, 100
*The Round Table Journal:
A Quarterly Review of the
Politics of the British Empire*,
62
Round Table movement
  agenda, 62
  British conferences, 63
  Chatham House
    connections, 65
  Curtis, Lionel, 62
  evolution, 10
  first meeting, 62
  founding, 60
  growth, 61
  inner/outer circles, 60-61
  Lippmann, Walter, 64-65
  membership, 63
  Milner, Alfred, 62
  Rhodes, Cecil
    background, 58
    diamond empire, 57-59

influences, 58-59
"The Rhodes
  Colossus" cartoon, 58
Round Table's
  founding, 60-61
*The Round Table Journal:
A Quarterly Review of
the Politics of the British
Empire*, 62
Royal Institute of
  International Affairs
  split, 63
Royal Institute of
  International Affairs, 10.
  See also Chatham House
  formation, 21
  founding, 63
Rule by Secrecy, 6, 39, 187
Ruskin, John, 58
Russell, William H., 88
Russian communism
  Bolshevik Revolution, 229
  Civil War, 229
  Communist Manifesto, 226
  history
    alternative version,
      230-232
    communal ownership,
      227
    factory system, 228
    mainstream version,
      227-230
  inner circles, 227
  Jewish American
    financiers theory, 231
  New Economic Policy,
    229
  one-world government,
    226
  Plekhanov's political
    evolution idea, 228
  proletariat revolution,
    228-229

Third International, 229
Wall Street financing for
  revolutions, 230-232
World War II, 229

S

SALT I (Strategic Arms
  Limitation Treaty), 46
Sambourne, Edward Linley,
  58
Schiff, Jacob, 23, 231
Scottish Rite of Modern
  Freemasonry, 177
SCP (Spiritual Counterfeits
  Project), 160
Scranton, William, 47
scripture coded messages,
  137-139
SEC (Securities and
  Exchange Commission),
  239
Second Bank of the United
  States, 113
secrecy
  Bilderberg Group, 40-41
  Chatham House, 66
  Federal Reserve Jekyll
    Island meeting, 107-110
  Skull and Bones, 90-91
Secret of Secrets (Arcanum
  Arcanorum), 227
*The Secret Teaching of All
Ages: An Encyclopedic
Outline of Masonic,
Hermetic, Qabbalistic, and
Rosicrucian Symbolical
Philosophy*, 199
secretary-general of United
  Nations, 78

Secrets of the Tomb: Skull and Bones, the Ivy League, and the Hidden Paths of Power, 84
Selective Training and Service Act of 1940, 245
senior societies, 91
September 11 attacks
    casualties, 279
    conspiracy theories, 281-282
    overview, 279
    U.S. government, 280-281
Shadow Cabinet, 33
Shah, Idries, 233
Sheinkman, Jack, 39
Sino-American relations, 27
Skene, John, 203
Skorzeny, Otto, 258
Skull and Bones, 83
    322 in emblem, 84
    crooking, 85-86
    death fascination, 85
    history
        conspiratorial story, 88-89
        standard story, 87-88
    Illuminati roots, 88-89
    membership, 83
        Bush, George H. W., 275
        Bush, George W., 90
        criteria, 90
        influential jobs, 83
        initiation ceremony, 86-87
        Meyer, Cord Jr., 88
        prominent members, 89-90
        women, 84
    memento mori, 84
    Morgans connection, 101
    overview, 11

secrecy, 90-91
    the Tomb, 83
Smith, Gerard C., 46
Smith, Walter Bedell, 35
socialism, 122
    Stalin's Soviet Union, 123
    Wells, H. G.
        background, 121
        New World Order, The, 123
        Open Conspiracy, The, 122
Societas Rosicruciana, 176-177
Society of the Elect, 10, 60-61
Socrates' shadows, 4-6
sororities, 83
SOS (Synagogue of Satan), 163
"The Sources of Soviet Conduct," 24
South Korean government, 265
Sovereign Military Order of Malta, 155-156
sovereignty fetish, 73-74
Spanish Freemason suppression, 185
Spear of Longinus, 148
Special Study Group, 97
speculative masons, 189
the spider, 258
Spiritual Counterfeits Project (SCP), 160
spiritual regeneration, 136
St. Theobald, 215
Stalin, Joseph, 227
Strategic Arms Limitation Treaty (SALT I), 46
Strong, Benjamin, 108

Sufi, 172
suicides, 179
Sumer, 138
Sumerian creation myth, 140
symbols
    Carbonari, 213
    fasces, 253
    Freemasons, 190
    Rose Cross, 173
Synagogue of Satan (SOS), 163
synarchy, 124

T

Taft, Alphonso, 88
Taxil hoax, 222
Tennessee Valley Authority (TVA), 239
Theodor, Karl, 167
Theosophical Society, 124
theosophy, 124
think tanks, 10
Third International, 229
Third Reich
    American corporations
        complicity, 259-260
        involvement, 258
    fall, 254-255
    Hitler
        escape, 256
        legacy, 257
        remains, 256
        suicide, 255
three world wars theory. *See* 3WW
Thyssen, Fritz, 275
traditores, 133
Treaty of Versailles, 18, 21
Trialogue, 48

Triangle Papers, 50
Trilateral Commission, 43
  1975 Kyoto meeting,
  47-48
  1976 Kyoto meeting, 48
  agenda, 51
  Bilderberg Group
  membership, 36
  criticism, 51-52
  first meeting, 43, 47
  founding, 44
    Bilderberg Group
    connections, 45-46
    Brzezinski, 44-45
    members, 46-47
  membership
    Logan Act, 54
    present day, 48
  overview, 10
  Reagan, Ronald, 53-54
  Triangle Papers, 50
  website, 47
Trismegistus, Hermes, 176
Trotsky, Leon, 4
Truman, President Harry S.
  containment, 269
  Korean Conflict
    Cairo Conference, 264
    Chinese intervention,
    267
    DRK creation, 265
    fall of Seoul, 268
    Inchon Landing, 267
    lack of congressional
    declaration of war,
    263-264
    MacArthur's defiance,
    268
    North Korean invasion
    of South Korea, 266
    partition arrangement,
    265
    ROK creation, 265

trusteeship, 265
UN intervention for
  unification, 265
UN Security Council
  resolution for
  military action
  against North Korea,
  266
U.S. support for South
  Korean military, 266
Tucker, James P. Jr., 36
TVA (Tennessee Valley
Authority), 239
Two-Ocean Navy Act, 245

U

undeclared U.S. wars, 264
United Grand Lodge, 190
United Nations
  avoidance of war
  objective, 70
  charter creation, 74-75
  Dumbarton Oaks
  Conference, 72
  foundation, 11, 69
  as gradualist
  implementation of
  one-world government,
  78-79
  headquarters, 75
  Korean Conflict
  intervention for
  unification, 265
  Security Council
  resolution for
  military action
  against North Korea,
  266
  trusteeship, 73
membership, 74

new world order label, 8
one-world government
  view, 71-72
overcoming sovereignty
  fetish, 73-74
perpetuating war view of
  conspiracy theorists, 70
Preamble to the Charter,
  71
system, 75-79
  Economic and Social
  Council, 77
  General Assembly, 75
  International Court of
  Justice, 77
  International Criminal
  Court, 77
  Secretariat, 77
  secretary-general, 78
  Security Council, 76
  United Nations Day, 74
  Yalta Conference, 73
United Nations Day, 74
universities
  fraternities/sororities, 83
  secret societies, 82
  senior societies, 91
Unlawful Societies Act, 185
U.S. *See* America
Utopia, 228

V

validity, 14
  furtive fallacy, 14
  globalization, 15
Van Buren's skull, 85
Vanderlip, Frank A., 108
venditas, 213
Vespucci, Amerigo, 155
Vietnam War, 26, 269-270

Volcker, Paul, 38, 47
von Verschuer, Otmar
   Freiherr, 259

W

Waldseemüller, Martin, 155
Warburg, Paul, 20, 65, 108
Ward, Rear Admiral
   Chester, 28
wars
   American Revolution
      economy, 111
      Freemason
         involvement, 203-205
   CFR
      Cold War, 24-25
      Korean, 26
      Marshall Plan, 24
      NATO, 25
      Vietnam, 26
      World War II, 24
   conspiracy theorists, 6
   financiers/fomenters
      Morgans, 101-102
      Rockefellers, 102-104
      Rothschilds, 99-101
   French and Indian,
      203-205
   French Revolution,
      207-208
   Korean
      CFR, 26
      Chinese intervention,
         267
      conspiracy theorists'
         version, 269
      DRK creation, 265
      fall of Seoul, 268
      Inchon Landing, 267

independence from
   Japan, 264
lack of congressional
   declaration of war,
   263-264
MacArthur's defiance,
   268
North Korean invasion
   of South Korea, 266
partition arrangement,
   265
ROK creation, 265
trusteeship, 265
UN intervention for
   unification, 265
UN Security Council
   resolution for
   military action
   against North Korea,
   266
U.S. support for South
   Korean military, 266
military-industrial-
   congressional complex
   creation of wealth, 96
   Eisenhower, 94-95
   Franco-Prussian War
      of 1870, 96
   power and class, 96
   Report from Iron
      Mountain, The, 97-99
   World War I outbreak,
      97
oil wars with Iraq, 283
Persian Gulf War, 277
Vietnam, 269-270
World War I, 163
World War II. See World
   War II
Washington, George, 204
wealth
   creation, 96
   Knights Templar, 149-150

websites
   AMORC, 171
   "Assassinations Foretold
      in Moby Dick!," 139
   Pike-Mazzini letter, 221
   Trilateral Commission,
      47
Webster, Nesta Helen, 161
Webster, Sam, 175
Weed, Thurlow, 184
Weinberger, Caspar, 53
Weishaupt, Adam
   Cabalist connection, 139
   exile, 167
   founding the Illuminati,
      164
   Freemason induction, 165
Weishaupt, Bavarian Adam,
   12
Wells, H. G.
   background, 121
   New World Order, The,
      123
   Open Conspiracy, The, 122
Westcott, William Wynn,
   175
Williams, Ralph E., 95
Wilson, President
   Woodrow, 8
   Colonel House
      adviser, 19
   background, 19
   Institute of
      International Affairs,
      21
   meeting with British
      scholars, 20
   progressive reforms, 19
   Fourteen Points, 20
   presidency, 18
   Treaty of Versailles, 18
With No Apologies, 28
Wood, Gordon, 203

Woodman, William Robert, 175
work in secret societies, 213
Works Progress Administration (WPA), 240
World War I, 163
World War II
    American corporations
        complicity in
            Holocaust, 259-260
        involvement in
            Holocaust, 258
    CFR, 24
    communism, 229
    FDR
        alliance with Britain, 245
        armed neutrality, 243
        CFR War and Peace Studies Project, 243
        Lend-Lease Act, 244
        motives for war, 248
        neutrality acts, 242
        Pearl Harbor attack, 245-247
        supporting Churchill, 243-244
        war appropriations increases, 244
    Third Reich
        fall, 254-255
        Hitler's escape, 256
        Hitler's legacy, 257
        Hitler's remains, 256
        Hitler's suicide, 255
    United Nations
        avoidance of war objective, 70
        charter creation, 74-75

Dumbarton Oaks Conference, 72
Economic and Social Council, 77
foundation, 69
General Assembly, 75
as gradualist implementation of one-world government, 78-79
headquarters, 75
initial membership, 74
International Court of Justice, 77
International Criminal Court, 77
Korean trusteeship, 73
one-world government view, 71-72
overcoming sovereignty fetish, 73-74
perpetuating war view of conspiracy theorists, 70
Preamble to the Charter, 71
Secretariat, 77
secretary-general, 78
Security Council, 76
System, 75, 79
United Nations Day, 74
Yalta Conference, 73
World Wildlife Fund, 34
WPA (Works Progress Administration), 240

X-Y-Z

Yalta Conference, 73
Young European movement, 217

Zionism, 162